DAY BY ORDINARY DAY WITH MATTHEW

DAY BY ORDINARY DAY WITH
MATTHEW

*Daily Reflections for Ordinary Time
Weeks 10-21*

VOLUME 2

MARK G. BOYER

ALBA·HOUSE   NEW·YORK

SOCIETY OF ST. PAUL, 2187 VICTORY BLVD., STATEN ISLAND, NEW YORK 10314

ST PAULS

Quotations from the New Testament are taken from *The Alba House New Testament*, translated by Mark A. Wauck, copyright © 1997 by the Society of St. Paul, Staten Island, NY. All rights reserved.

Library of Congress Cataloging-in-Publication Data

Boyer, Mark G.
   Day by ordinary day with Matthew: daily reflections for ordinary time / Mark G. Boyer.
      p.   cm.
   Contents: v. 2. Weeks 10-21.
   ISBN 0-8189-0784-3
   1. Church year meditations. 2. Bible. N.T. Matthew— Meditations. 3. Catholic Church — Prayer-books and meditations — English. I. Title.
   BX2170.C55B72   1997
   242'.3 — dc20   96-44890
                                        CIP

Produced and designed in the United States of America by the Fathers and Brothers of the Society of St. Paul, 2187 Victory Boulevard, Staten Island, New York 10314, as part of their communications apostolate.

ISBN: 0-8189-0784-3

Printing Information:

Current Printing - first digit   1   2   3   4   5   6   7   8   9   10

Year of Current Printing - first year shown

1997   1998   1999   2000   2001   2002   2003   2004   2005

Dedicated to the staff of *The Mirror,*
newspaper of the Diocese of Springfield-Cape Girardeau:
Karla Essner,
Leon Gibbar,
Leslie Hunter Eidson,
Marilyn Vydra,
and Joan Ward.

TABLE OF CONTENTS

INTRODUCTION

Today, in Catholic circles there is a strong emphasis on the studying and the praying of the Gospels. In part, this has been brought on by the introduction of the three-year Sunday cycle of Gospel readings and the one-year weekday cycle of Gospel readings in 1974. When a person takes a course, attends a workshop, or participates in a Bible study group, the study of the Gospels is usually divorced from the praying of the Gospels. Likewise, when one takes a course, attends a workshop, or participates in a prayer group, the praying of the Gospels is divorced from the study of the Gospels.

This book attempts to bring such a divorce to an end.

This book joins the studying and the praying of the Gospels into a marriage of biblical spirituality that has become the foundation for the Church's proclamation and preaching of the good news during the thirty-three to thirty-four weeks of the liturgical year referred to as Ordinary Time.

According to the *General Norms for the Liturgical Year and the Calendar*, issued by the Congregation of Rites in 1969 and revised in 1975, Ordinary Time consists of those thirty-three or thirty-four weeks — distinct from Advent, Christmas, Lent and Easter — "that do not celebrate a specific aspect of the mystery of Christ. Rather... they are devoted to the mystery of Christ in all its aspects" (#43).

Ordinary Time, the longest of all the liturgical seasons, is separated into two parts. The first part usually begins on the Monday after the Sunday Feast of the Baptism of the Lord. In some years, when the Feast of the Baptism of the Lord is celebrated on the Monday following the Solemnity of the Epiphany, Ordinary Time begins on the following Tuesday; the first part ends on the Tuesday before Ash Wednesday.

The second part begins on the Monday after Pentecost Sunday and ends on the evening of the Saturday before the first Sunday of Advent. A Table of Movable Solemnities, Feasts and Sundays, which is found at the end of this Introduction, will assist the reader in determining the beginnings and endings of the Season of Ordinary Time.

According to the 1981 Introduction to the *Lectionary for Mass*, issued by the Sacred Congregation for the Sacraments and Divine Worship, "The Sundays in Ordinary Time do not have a distinctive character. Thus the texts of... the Gospel readings are arranged in an order of semi-continuous reading" (#67).

Except for the Second Sunday of Ordinary Time, when all three cycles of Gospel selections are from the Gospel According to John, the thirty-three or thirty-four Sundays in Cycle A consist of semi-continuous selections from the Gospel According to Matthew, in Cycle B from the Gospel According to Mark (except for the seventeenth through the twenty-first Sundays and the thirty-fourth Sunday or Solemnity of Christ the King, when selections from the Gospel According to John are read), and in Cycle C from the Gospel According to Luke.

The Introduction to the *Lectionary for Mass* states, "This distribution.... provides a certain coordination between the meaning of each Gospel and the progress of the liturgical year. Thus after Epiphany the readings are on the beginning of the Lord's preaching and they fit well with Christ's baptism and the first events in which he manifests himself. The liturgical year leads quite naturally to a termination in the eschatological theme proper to the last Sundays, since the chapters of the Synoptics that precede the account of the passion treat this eschatological theme rather extensively" (#105).

During some years, particular Solemnities and Feasts which fall on Sundays take precedence over the Sunday in Ordinary Time. These include the Solemnities of the Holy Trinity, the Body and Blood of Christ, the Birth of John the Baptist, Peter and Paul, the Assumption, and All Saints, as well as the Feasts of the Presentation, the Transfiguration, the Triumph of the Cross, the Dedication of St. John Lateran, and All Souls Day. The Gospel readings for these days are found in the Appendix.

The *Lectionary for Mass* also explains that "the weekday Order of Readings is governed by... application of the principles of harmony and of semi-continuous reading" (#69). The semi-continuous reading of the Synoptic Gospels is "arranged in such a way that as the Lord's life and preaching unfold the teaching proper to each of these Gospels is presented" (#105).

During the weekdays of Ordinary Time, the Gospels are arranged so that the Gospel According to Mark is read from the first through the ninth weeks, the Gospel According to Matthew from the tenth through the twenty-first weeks, and the Gospel according to Luke from the twenty-second through the thirty-fourth weeks. The Introduction of the *Lectionary for Mass* explains this schema: "Mark 1-12 are read in their entirety, with the exception only of the two passages of Mark 6 that are read on weekdays on other seasons. From Matthew and Luke the readings comprise all the matters not contained in Mark. From all three Synoptics or from two of them, as the case may be, all those passages are read that either are distinctively presented in each Gospel or are needed for a proper understanding of its progression. Jesus' eschatological discourse as contained in its entirety in Luke is read at the end of the liturgical year" (#109).

The three volumes of this series correspond to the weekday divisions indicated above. Volume I, *Day by Ordinary Day With Mark*, contains the second through the ninth Sundays of Ordinary Time: Cycles A, B, and C and the first through the ninth weeks of Ordinary Time, Monday through Saturday. Volume II, *Day by Ordinary Day With Matthew*, contains the tenth through the twenty-first Sundays of Ordinary Time: Cycles A, B, and C and the tenth through the twenty-first weeks of Ordinary Time, Monday through Saturday. Volume III, *Day by Ordinary Day with Luke*, contains the twenty-second through the thirty-fourth Sundays of Ordinary Time: Cycles A, B, and C and the twenty-second through the thirty-fourth weeks of Ordinary Time, Monday through Saturday.

Each book in this series is designed to be used by individuals for private study of the Gospels and for prayer and by homilists for study of the Gospels, prayer, and public preaching. A four-part exercise is offered for every day of the Season of Ordinary Time.

1. A few short verses of Scripture are taken from the Gospel reading provided in the *Lectionary for Mass* of each day.

2. A reflective study follows the Scripture selection. The reflection attempts to critique the Gospel selection in light of contemporary source, form, redaction, literary, and historical criticism. As it offers the individual and the homilist valuable background information concerning the Gospel selection, the reflection yields new perspectives on the Scriptures for personal study and homiletic exegesis in light of contemporary biblical scholarship.

3. The reflection is followed by a question for personal meditation. The question functions as a guide for personal appropriation of the message of the Scripture selection. The homilist can use the question as a basis for a homily or a homilette.

4. A prayer summarizes the original theme of the Scripture reading, which was studied and explored in the reflection and which served as the foundation for the meditation. The prayer concludes the daily exercise for the individual or it can be used as a fitting conclusion to the General Intercessions and the Liturgy of the Word during the celebration of the Eucharist.

Ordinary Time is the only liturgical season that leaves its mark on all four of the natural seasons of the year. Except for the Solemnity of Christ the King, the last Sunday of Ordinary Time, and a few other Solemnities and Feasts which may interrupt the Ordinary Time Sunday cycles, the color of the season is green. Green, a common color, represents stability, growth, and hope. The woolen green plaids of January and February Ordinary Time wrap people in the winter call of Jesus and the early days of his ministry. The light green of May and June Ordinary Time are the spring buds of response to Jesus' invitation to experience the kingdom of God. The dark green of July, August, and September Ordinary Time represent the summer growth in parables, which causes the reader to see the world with different eyes. Finally, the fading green of fall in October and November Ordinary Time serves as a reminder that the One who once died and was raised will come again.

It is the author's hope that through day by ordinary day study and prayer the reader will come to a deeper knowledge of and a closer relationship with the One around whom all the seasons turn — Jesus, the Christ and Lord.

Mark G. Boyer

TABLE OF MOVABLE SOLEMNITIES, FEASTS, AND SUNDAYS
Volume II

After Pentecost

Year	Sun. Cycle	OT begins on Mon.	in week #	Trinity Sunday	Body and Blood of Christ	June 24 29 replaces OT Sun. #	August 6 15 replaces OT Sun. #
1997	B	May 19	7	May 25	June 1	13	
1998	C	June 1	9	June 7	June 14		
1999	A	May 24	8	June 6	June 13		20
2000	B	June 12	10	June 18	June 25		18
2001	C	June 3	9	June 10	June 17	12	
2002	A	May 20	7	May 26	June 2		
2003	B	June 9	10	June 15	June 22	13	
2004	C	May 31	9	June 6	June 13		20
2005	A	May 16	7	May 22	May 26		

DAY BY ORDINARY DAY WITH MATTHEW

TAX COLLECTORS AND SINNERS

Matthew 9:9-13

Scripture: "Why does your teacher eat with tax collectors and sinners?" (Matthew 9:11)

Reflection: The call of Matthew, the tax collector, in Matthew's Gospel, is a slightly rewritten version of Mark's account of a tax collector named Levi (cf. Mark 2:14). A tax collector, such as Matthew (or Levi) was a Jew, who worked for the Romans — the governing occupational forces of the Jewish homeland.

A tax collector made his living by raising the amount of the Roman tax and pocketing the difference. In the eyes of his fellow Jews, he was a detestable person for two reasons: he had abandoned the practice of Judaism in order to work for the Romans (an apostate) and he represented the Roman government to his own people on their ancestral land, which was being ruled by the Roman occupation forces. Needless to add, then, a tax collector was hated by his fellow Jews.

Matthew, the author of this Gospel, portrays Jesus as calling this tax collector to follow him. The tax collector abandons his customs post and follows Jesus. The man who was once an apostate becomes a disciple of Jesus; he is converted.

Furthermore, Jesus joins Matthew and his friends — many tax collectors and sinners — at table. Eating with sinners is a sign of unity with them. In the mentality of the day, however, such table associations would render a person ritually impure. Here,

Jesus demonstrates his solidarity with those who were considered apostates. He calls them to discipleship, and they follow him.

Jesus makes it clear that he "did not come to call the righteous but sinners" (9:13). Righteousness, for Matthew, is a key theme. In the beginning of the Gospel, Joseph is held up as the example of authentic righteousness; Joseph does not adhere to the law, but takes pregnant Mary as his wife. He breaks the law in order to be righteous, correct in the ways of behavior, in the eyes of God.

Once again, Matthew is making the same statement. Some people, those who consider themselves righteous — those who are well and do not need a physician — have no need for Jesus. Sinners, like Matthew and his fellow tax collectors, do need Jesus to call them to conversion and a new way of life. They respond by abandoning their jobs. This, according to Matthew, is the behavior that God wants.

Meditation: Who do you think are the equivalent of tax collectors and sinners today?

Prayer: God of sinners, through Jesus you invite all people to leave behind their sinful ways and to follow you. Call us into the ranks of your disciples. Come and share our table. Heal us with the gift of your mercy. We ask this through our Lord Jesus Christ, your Son, who lives and reigns with you and the Holy Spirit, one God, for ever and ever. Amen.

TESTED

Mark 3:20-35

Scripture: "He is possessed by Beelzebul!" and "By the prince of demons he drives out demons." "He has an unclean spirit" (Mark 3:22, 30).

Reflection: The narrative concerning the charge by the scribes that Jesus is possessed and has an unclean spirit is sandwiched in between a narrative concerning the coming of Jesus' relatives, who believe that he is "out of his mind" (3:21). This technique of intercalating one story within another is a Marcan literary device.

To the first accusation that he is possessed by the prince of demons, Jesus responds with a parable. It is impossible for Satan to drive out Satan, because a kingdom divided against itself cannot stand. "No one can enter a strong man's house to plunder his possessions unless he first ties the strong man up. Then he can plunder his house" (3:27).

In effect, Jesus has already tied up the strong man — Satan. This was demonstrated at the time of his temptation in the desert, where he had been driven by the Spirit (cf. 1:12-13). For forty days he was tempted by Satan. He emerged victorious. He has plundered Satan's house through the power of the Holy Spirit. Jesus' victory over the prince of demons is through the work of the Holy Spirit. To attribute this power to Satan is to blaspheme

3

against the Holy Spirit and to be "guilty of an everlasting sin" (3:29).

In answering the second charge that he is possessed by an unclean spirit, Jesus declares that it is impossible. One cannot attribute the power of evil to the Holy Spirit.

"All the sins and blasphemies that people utter will be forgiven them" (3:28) except this one.

Meditation: In what ways have you been tempted and emerged victorious?

Prayer: God of all good things, after his baptism your Holy Spirit drove Jesus into the desert, where he was tempted and tested for forty days. Strengthen us with this same Spirit. Guide us in the ways of Jesus, who lives and reigns with you and the Holy Spirit, one God, for ever and ever. Amen.

LIFE AND FAITH

Luke 7:11-17

Scripture: [Jesus] went forward and touched the bier and the bearers stood still, and he said, "Young man, I say to you, arise!" Then the dead man sat up and began to speak, and Jesus gave him to his mother. (Luke 7:14-15).

Reflection: The narrative of the raising of the widow of Nain's son follows the healing of the centurion's slave and precedes the account of the questioning messengers sent by John the Baptist. The placement of the story is important to note as well as its Old Testament model.

After healing a Gentile's (centurion's) servant, who was dying, and thus evoking the centurion's faith, the likes of which could not be found in all of Israel, Jesus moves on to Nain. This time, it is not a servant but a son; he is not dying, but dead. The male centurion is now a female widow. With the death of her son, the widow is without a livelihood. She has no one to care for her. She, too, is as good as dead.

The model for this uniquely Lucan story is found in the first book of Kings (1 Kings 17:8-24). Elijah the prophet goes to the widow of Zarephath and resides with her and her son. When the son becomes ill and stops breathing, Elijah carries him to the upper room where he is living, and, after laying the boy on his own bed, he stretches himself out on the boy three times. With prayer the boy is revived. This act demonstrates to the widow

5

that Elijah is a man of God. She, then, comes to believe in the word of God, which Elijah speaks.

The emphasis of Luke's narrative, then, is not on the raising of the widow's son, but on the life which is restored to the widow and on the faith which is evoked from the crowd.

In telling this story, Luke is declaring that Jesus is a new Elijah, a great prophet who has arisen among the people. And, as a great prophet, Jesus speaks the word of God. People, therefore, according to Luke, should believe in him.

This story also functions as a pivot point between the healing of the centurion's servant and the questioning messengers sent by John the Baptist. When the messengers ask Jesus if he is the one they were expecting or if they are to look for another, he declares, "Go and tell John what you saw and heard: the blind can see again, the lame walk, lepers are made clean, the deaf hear, the dead are raised to life, the poor have the good news proclaimed to them" (Luke 7:22).

In some way, there is still a third function of this narrative. It serves as a summary and a prelude to the rest of Luke's Gospel. Jesus is the only son of a widowed mother (Mary), who dies, and is raised to life. Many people experience this great prophet arisen in their midst and come to believe in him.

Meditation: In what ways are you a widow, who needs to be restored to life?

Prayer: God of widows, you sent your prophet Elijah to the widow of Zarephath, and there you provided her with an unlimited supply of flour and oil. Through Elijah's prayer, you restored the breath of life to the widow's son, when he had died. Jesus, your Son, and the greatest of prophets, restored the life of the widow of Nain by raising her only son from the dead. Look upon us in our widowhood, and restore us to life as you restored the broken body of your Christ, who lives and reigns with you and the Holy Spirit, one God, for ever and ever. Amen.

WHAT GOD WANTS

Matthew 5:1-12

Scripture: "Blessed are those who hunger and thirst to do God's will, for they shall have their fill. Blessed are those persecuted for doing God's will, for the kingdom of heaven is theirs" (Matthew 5:6, 10).

Reflection: The first of five sermons in Matthew's Gospel is commonly referred to as the Sermon on the Mount. The author is no doubt drawing a parallel between Jesus and Moses, who is attributed with authorship of the Torah or Law, the first five books of the Bible (Genesis, Exodus, Leviticus, Numbers, and Deuteronomy). Jesus goes up to a mountain to deliver this first sermon (which consists of three chapters of monologue), just as Moses went up a mountain to receive the Law from God. The echo of Jesus as a new Moses is previously presented to the reader in the infancy account of the flight to Egypt, the death of the innocents, and the return from Egypt (Matthew 2:13-23).

Matthew begins this first sermon with nine beatitudes in contrast to Luke's four with their corresponding woes. A beatitude is a declaration of what is happening and what will happen. Each beatitude begins with the word "blessed," meaning that one shares in a characteristic of God. In its root sense, blessed means happy.

If analyzed carefully, the reader discovers that each beatitude has an inherent contradiction; happiness is contrasted to the state of the person described. Those persons who hunger and thirst for righteousness are declared to be happy now. One who is thirsty and hungry is usually not happy!

7

Matthew declares that those who are persecuted for doing God's will are happy now. People who are being persecuted are usually not happy!

Matthew is employing hyperbolic language in order to get his point across. In the case of the two beatitudes, which have been offered as examples, Matthew employs the dual metaphors of hunger and thirst to desire for righteousness, a particular Matthean theme throughout the Gospel. For Matthew, righteousness consists of correct moral behavior. The righteous person is one who has interiorized the teaching of Jesus and behaves accordingly. A righteous individual behaves a specific way because it is the right way to act. Joseph, in the infancy portion of Matthew's Gospel, is held up as an example of righteousness. He took pregnant Mary as his wife when he should have had her stoned; he behaved in a way that God wanted.

What Matthew is saying is that the person who desires what is right, like one hungers for food and thirsts for water, is happy and is behaving as God wants. Likewise, the person who endures persecution for the sake of what is right is happy; he or she is also doing what God wants.

In the future, their hunger and thirst for righteousness will be satisfied. A person who hungers and thirsts for it will end up looking like God. Likewise, the person persecuted for the sake of it, already possesses the kingdom of heaven.

Throughout the remainder of this first sermon, and indeed throughout the entire Gospel, Matthew declares that righteousness is what God wants. Correct conduct in conformity with God's will is a specifically Matthean theme.

Meditation: In what ways are you righteous?

Prayer: God of righteousness, you declare blessed those who hunger and thirst for your ways. Through the working of your Holy Spirit, form us in the ways of your kingdom. In times of persecution, make us realize that we already share in the kingdom, where you live and reign with your Son, our Lord and teacher, and your Holy Spirit, one God for ever and ever. Amen.

SALT AND LIGHT

Matthew 5:13-16

Scripture: "If salt loses its taste, with what can it be salted? … Let your light so shine before others, that they will see your good works and glorify your Father in heaven" (Matthew 5:13, 16).

Reflection: Immediately following the third-person beatitudes in Matthew are two second-person metaphors in the first sermon given by Jesus. The "you" of the metaphors is addressed to the crowds and the disciples (the reader); they are invited to understand who they are in comparison to salt and light, while keeping in mind the beatitudes which precede this section.

Salt is seasoning for food; once added, it cannot be removed. It leaves a definite taste in whatever it touches. Furthermore, it functions as a preservative; when used on meats and in canning vegetables, it keeps these fresh. Beatitude persons are the salt of the earth; they flavor whatever they contact. Such individuals know and understand the truth found in each inherent contradictory beatitude.

Those who aren't salt are useless, no longer good for anything. They can no longer season or preserve. They are flavorless.

Human-made light eliminates darkness. A lamp, once it is lighted, is placed on a lampstand, much like ceiling lights today. In this way everyone in the house can see. When many lamps are lighted or electric bulbs turned on, a city cannot be hidden

— especially if it is located on a mountain. Likewise, a beatitude person is the light of the world. The way he or she lives cannot help but be noticed. Failure to do good deeds makes this person as useless as a lamp put under a bushel basket!

In verse 16 of this section of his Gospel, Matthew tells the reader that salt and light are the "good deeds" of the beatitudes, which precede this section. One's good works glorify the Father. These "good deeds" demonstrate a person's righteousness; that is, such a person does good deeds and behaves in the way that God wants. From Matthew's perspective, a follower of Jesus is one who lights the way for others.

Meditation: In what ways are you salt and light?

Prayer: God of salt and light, you season your people with your grace and you guide them in the ways of your Son, Jesus. Make us salty with good deeds. Make us lights of the world so that others may see our good deeds and glorify you, heavenly Father, together with our Lord Jesus Christ and the Holy Spirit, who live and reign as one God, for ever and ever. Amen.

FULFILLMENT

Matthew 5:17-19

Scripture: "Do not think that I have come to do away with the Torah or the prophets. I have come not to abolish but to fulfill" (Matthew 5:17).

Reflection: This selection from the first sermon of Jesus follows the dual metaphors of salt and light and precedes the teaching about anger. Person also shifts from third in the beatitudes to second in the dual metaphors to first in this passage.

In Matthew's view, the Law (the Torah) and the prophets will continue to be observed in his community, which is composed of Jewish-Christians, who are in the process of defining who they are without a Temple (destroyed in 70 AD). What is necessary, according to Matthew, is keeping and teaching the commandments.

Matthew is trying to take the ancient Law and make sense of it in a new situation after the resurrection of Jesus, the Messiah, and the destruction of the Temple. He does not want to abolish the Law; this would not appeal to his community nor accord with the will of God. Yet, on the other hand, he does not advocate such strict adherence to the letter of the Law that the spirit of love behind it is killed.

To arrive at this dimension, Matthew talks about righteousness. Righteousness means to be set aright with God, to be put in the right position. The righteous person is authentic — in line with the intent of the law, the spirit behind the letter. Authenticity dictates that one does things or behaves in a particular way because this is the loving thing to do; this is the way these things should be done or this behavior should be observed.

With this understanding, Matthew gives no further guidelines. To do so would be to create a new law. Matthew wants his community to take the intention of the law and to live (teach, do) it. The challenge he issues to his community is this: "Unless your righteousness greatly exceeds that of the scribes and Pharisees (who represent legal adherents), you will never get into the kingdom of heaven" (5:20).

Meditation: In what ways are you righteous/authentic?

Prayer: God of the kingdom, in times past your people struggled to remain faithful to you by adhering to your Law. Your Son, Jesus, did not abolish the Law or the prophets, but he fulfilled them. Make of us who follow him today righteous and authentic disciples. Through your Holy Spirit teach us your ways and help us to put them into practice. We ask this through Christ our Lord. Amen.

ANGER

Matthew 5:20-26

Scripture: "You have heard that it was said to your ancestors, 'You shall not murder; and that whoever commits
murder shall be liable to judgment.' But I say to you, anyone who is angry with his (or her) brother (or sister) shall
be liable to judgment" (Matthew 5:21-22).

Reflection: The first sermon of Jesus in Matthew's Gospel continues with his teaching about anger. A pattern of "You have heard
that it was said..." followed by "But I say to you..." is employed
by Matthew in this and in the next five teachings about adultery,
divorce, oaths, retaliation, and love of enemies.

The Law declared murder to be wrong because the taking
of a human life, like its giving, belonged to God alone. Murder
was final. A life once taken could never be restored. It defini-
tively separated a person from the community of Israel. So, from
the beginning, the Law drew a line and prohibited the deliberate taking of a human life outside the parameters of justice and
the courts of law.

Jesus in Matthew's Gospel declares equivalent to what is
generally considered to be murder anything (anger, contempt,
insults) that irreparably separates one person from another and
from the community. In other words, anything that so divides
people that they are left without hope of reconciliation is tanta-
mount to murder.

Furthermore, any division in the community reflects a corresponding rift between the entire community and God.

For Matthew, a person's primary relationship is with the whole community. If an individual is not reconciled with the brothers and sisters of the community, then he or she is not reconciled to God. For Matthew, there exists no exclusively private relationship with God.

"Therefore, if you bring your gift to the altar and there recall that your brother (or sister) has anything against you, leave your gift at the altar, go first and be reconciled with your brother (or sister), then come and offer your gift" (5:23-24). In Matthew's Gospel, Jesus' reinterpretation of the law — of what is authentic, what is deemed righteous behavior — goes to the heart, not of the words but of the intention of the person performing the action. There are many ways for one to do away with a member of the community.

Meditation: In which ways have you recently "murdered" a brother or sister of your community?

Prayer: God of reconciliation, through Moses you taught your people not to kill their own kind. Through Jesus, the Christ, you have taught us to do nothing that will cause any division or separation in your Church. Purify our hearts that we may bring the gifts of righteousness to your altar. Make of us a new people who constantly seek reconciliation through your Son, our Lord Jesus Christ, who lives and reigns with you and the Holy Spirit, one God, for ever and ever. Amen.

ADULTERY

Matthew 5:27-32

Scripture: "Anyone who looks at a woman with lust for her has already committed adultery with her in his heart.... Anyone who divorces his wife (unless the marriage is unlawful) makes her an adulteress, and anyone who marries after putting her away commits adultery" (Matthew 5:28, 32).

Reflection: Everywhere in the Gospels we see Jesus strike unusually hard blows at hypocrisy, the problem of those who are clean on the outside but corrupt within. In his teaching about adultery and divorce in Matthew's Gospel, Jesus uses hyperbolic language to go straight to the core of a matter which he wanted to be taken very seriously — the sanctity of the relationships between men and women in the covenant of marriage.

He says in today's Gospel, "Anyone who looks at a woman with lust for her has committed adultery with her in his thoughts." Desires of the heart when sanctioned by the will are as moral or immoral as actual deeds done in favor of or in contravention of the Law.

In another setting at a later date he would continue the discussion. "No evil comes to you from the outside, but from within," he told them. "Your mouth speaks from the overflow of your heart! Where your treasure is, there your heart will likewise be."

Nothing, of course, could have angered the Pharisees more.

They knew "in their heart of hearts" that what he said was true. Moses had allowed the granting of a decree of divorce — not to women, who at that time and in that culture were considered little more than the property of men with no legal rights in such a matter — because of "the hardness of your hearts" (Matthew 19:8).

Knowing their attitude, and that of his own disciples as well, he asked them, "Why do you murmur about this in your hearts?" They found it hard to muster the courage to speak their minds openly, though Peter did eventually manage to say, "If that's the case between a man and his wife, it's better not to marry" (19:10).

This discussion gave Jesus the opportunity to explain the Creator's plan for marriage "from the beginning." "Have you not read that from the beginning the Creator 'made them male and female' and said, 'For this reason a man shall leave his father and mother and be joined to his wife, and the two shall become one flesh'? So they are no longer two, but one flesh. Therefore, what God has joined, let no man separate."

Women are equal partners with men in the lifelong covenant of marriage. Divorce is not an option; men can no longer dismiss the wives to whom their lives have become united in marriage. Paul would give further advice in his letter to the Ephesians in this regard. This teaching explains why so many women were attracted to Christianity in its early days. Christianity raised women to a status equal in dignity, honor and rights to that of men. This was a radical move in a culture which considered women to be little more than possessions to be bought and sold.

Meditation: In which ways do you not treat all people equally?

Prayer: God of all, like a potter you formed man and woman from the clay of the earth and breathed into them the breath of your Spirit. You clothed them with equal dignity. Remove all prejudice from our midst. Enable us to honor every man and woman as you intended from the first day of creation. We ask this through our Lord Jesus Christ, your Son, who lives and reigns with you and the Holy Spirit, one God, for ever and ever. Amen.

OATHS

Matthew 5:33-37

Scripture: "Do not swear at all.... Let your 'Yes' mean 'Yes,' and your 'No' mean 'No'" (Matthew 5:34, 37).

Reflection: The purpose of an oath is to guarantee the truthfulness of what a person is about to say by calling upon God to be the person's witness.

A person takes an oath because of human weakness; that is, human beings have a tendency to lie. Matthew is interested in demonstrating that the human ability to lie cannot be counterbalanced by taking an oath. An oath does not guarantee truthfulness. How many instances can we point to where an individual has perjured himself by lying under oath?

Matthew's theme of righteousness, which has been prevalent in this first sermon of Jesus, prohibits calling upon God as witness for an individual's truthfulness. In this passage, Jesus directs his followers not to use oaths or swear at all. A relationship of truthfulness between two people cannot be guaranteed by God. A third, outside party is not needed for the community which observes righteousness. Therefore, the righteous person is always honest. If we mean "Yes," that is what we must say. When we mean "No," that is the response we must make.

If righteousness cannot be the guide for truthfulness between two people, then according to Matthew, nothing else can. No one is able to make a single hair white or black on his or her head by taking an oath. According to Jesus, oaths are not necessary in a community which practices righteousness.

Meditation: In which ways do you find that you take oaths in order to guarantee your truthfulness?

Prayer: God of truth, you uphold the honesty and righteousness of your people. Teach us to always speak the truth. Let our "Yes" mean "Yes" and our "No" mean "No" so that we may avoid what is evil and come to share your life in perfect Trinity — Father, Son, and Holy Spirit, one God, for ever and ever. Amen.

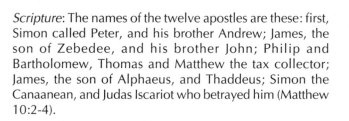

CALL AND MISSION
Matthew 9:36-10:8

Scripture: The names of the twelve apostles are these: first, Simon called Peter, and his brother Andrew; James, the son of Zebedee, and his brother John; Philip and Bartholomew, Thomas and Matthew the tax collector; James, the son of Alphaeus, and Thaddeus; Simon the Canaanean, and Judas Iscariot who betrayed him (Matthew 10:2-4).

Reflection: After a reference to the crowds, who are like "sheep without a shepherd" (9:36), a reference to the abundance of the harvest but the paucity of laborers (9:37-38), and the list of the twelve apostles, Matthew begins the second of the five sermons of Jesus. This discourse is commonly referred to as the Missionary Sermon, since it details the mission of the disciples — reflecting more of the missionary activity of the early Church at the time of its composition, of course.

Matthew records no story of Jesus' choosing twelve men. In fact, he makes no clear distinction between disciples, apostles, and the Twelve. He uses disciples and the Twelve interchangeably throughout the Gospel, while introducing apostle and using it only in the beginning of this discourse because the word means "One who is sent" and fits nicely in the context of the missionary sermon. Also, the number twelve recalls the twelve tribes of Israel.

It is important to note that the disciples are sent "to the lost sheep of the house of Israel" (10:6). Not only does this echo the preceding reference to the crowd as "sheep without a shepherd" (9:36), buy it sparks a remembrance of the image of the people of Israel, who are the sheep of God's flock.

The Matthean portrayal of Jesus reflects a very early and maybe historically accurate understanding that Jesus was sent only to the Jews whom he refers to as "the lost sheep of the house of Israel" (15:24).

This original Jewish-Christian refusal of the mission to the Gentiles is balanced in Matthew's Gospel with the story about the visitation of the magi Gentiles. In Mark's Gospel the mission to the Gentiles is dealt with through geography; some of Jesus' works are performed in Gentile territory.

While Matthew reflects the early Jewish-Christian understanding of the mission of Jesus, he also reflects the mission to the Gentiles. The disciples are to "make disciples of all nations" (28:19) and proclaim that "the kingdom of heaven is at hand" (10:7), that is, God is present and at work in the world now.

"The harvest is abundant but the laborers are few" (9:37). In Matthew, Jesus explicitly invites Israel to come into the kingdom. The early Church, through its missionary endeavors, invites all people into the kingdom. Matthew's missioners have received their own call and mission from Jesus. Early Christians received their own call and mission from Jesus. Today, Christians continue to receive a call and a mission from Jesus. They are to pass this on without cost.

Meditation: In what ways are you a missionary?

Prayer: Missionary God, in times past you sent your prophets with the good news of your kingdom. Jesus, the greatest of the prophets, proclaimed that your kingdom was at hand. Raise up men and women who are willing to proclaim this good news, for the harvest of your kingdom is abundant, but laborers are few. We ask this through Christ our Lord. Amen.

HIDDEN KINGDOM

Mark 4:26-34

Scripture: "The kingdom of God is like this; it is as if a man were to scatter seed upon the earth and would sleep and rise night and day and the seed would sprout and grow, while he is unaware. Of its own accord the earth bears fruit, first the shoot, then the head of grain, then the full grain in the head. When the grain is ripe, he sends for the sickle, for the time to harvest has come" (Mark 4:26-29).

Reflection: This uniquely Marcan parable can be divided into four stages. (1) A man scatters seed. (2) The seed sprouts and grows. (3) The land yields fruit in a definite order. (4) The grain is harvested.

The emphasis of the parable, however, is found in the second and third stages. The word preached by Jesus is effective; it brings about the intended results both during the day and during the night. No one knows how it does this until it is accomplished.

Mark is declaring that the kingdom of God is hidden. This hidden quality of the kingdom is being contrasted to an expected and visible kingdom of power. God, according to Jesus, does not bring about his kingdom in a powerful way. He does it without anyone knowing, just as seed grows and reaches maturity without anyone being aware. What is hidden will be known only at the end of the world, when the harvest is gathered in.

A further inversion of usual thought occurs in the parable

of the mustard seed, which follows the parable of the seed growing of itself. In this parable, the greatness of the kingdom of God
is contrasted to the smallness of a mustard seed. Such small beginnings of God's kingdom yield great results, however. Using
hyperbolic language, Mark declares that the mustard seed grows
into the largest of plants so that birds can make nests in its
branches. In other words, when the kingdom is finished growing
it becomes large enough for all people. God establishes his kingdom in these hidden and small ways.

Meditation: To what would you compare the kingdom of God
today?

Prayer: Sower God, through your prophets you planted the seed
of your word in your people. Through the teaching of Jesus, you
have planted your hidden word in us. When we look for the greatness of your works, point us in the direction of smallness. When
we seek the visible manifestation of your kingdom, enable us to
realize its hiddenness. Through your Holy Spirit working within
us, bring us to the fullness of the kingdom, where you live in
perfect Trinity as Father, Son, and Holy Spirit, one God, for ever
and ever. Amen.

GOD'S FIRST MOVE

Luke 7:36-8:3

Scripture: "Two people were in debt to a certain money-lender; one owed five hundred days' wages and the other owed fifty. Since they were unable to repay the debt, he forgave it for both. Which of them will love him more?" (Luke 7:41-42).

Reflection: The scene for this riddle is the house of Simon the Pharisee. Jesus is dining there when a sinful woman (prostitute) from the city enters the house, stands behind Jesus at his feet weeping and bathing his feet with her tears, wiping them with her hair, kissing them, and anointing them with ointment from an alabaster flask. From all outward appearances, this woman is flirting with Jesus.

This woman is contrasted to Simon the Pharisee, who suspects Jesus to be a prophet but who did not give Jesus any water with which to wash his feet, who did not kiss him, who did not anoint his head with oil — the customary ways of greeting a guest.

Simon the Pharisee is self-righteous. First, he is a Pharisee, one who scrupulously and supposedly observes all the prescriptions of the law.

Second, he knows that the person with the larger debt will love the creditor more, if the debt is canceled. Since Simon considers himself to have no debt, he has nothing for which to demonstrate the need for forgiveness. He is "the one to whom little is forgiven" and, therefore, he "loves little" (7:47).

Third, Simon is a legal purist; he knows that if the prostitute touches him, he will be defiled. He uses his own criterion for judging Jesus: "If this man were a prophet, he would know who and

23

what sort of woman this is who is touching him, that she is a sinner" (7:39).

The prostitute, on the other hand, recognizes her sinfulness. By her outlandish behavior she demonstrates that she has been forgiven. Simon thought that Jesus might be a prophet. The woman declares him to be the prophet. Her many sins are forgiven and she shows great love. Her love is the consequence of her forgiveness.

Furthermore, in demonstrating her acceptance of forgiveness, the woman also demonstrates her faith in Jesus, something Simon never does. The woman's great debt has been lifted; she loves greatly. Simon's small debt has not been lifted; he loves little.

In narrating this story, Luke is demonstrating that God makes the first move in the lives of people. God offers forgiveness to all people, if they are willing to repent. Once God's forgiveness is accepted, then a person's behavior reveals this acceptance. By washing, drying, kissing, and anointing Jesus' feet, the woman demonstrates her acceptance of God's offer of forgiveness. By not demonstrating his acceptance of God's offer of forgiveness, Simon, in effect, refuses it.

Both the woman and Simon are invited by Jesus to share the Father's forgiving love. Jesus opens the kingdom of God to all people — even to those who, like Simon, would rather close it off. In Luke, Jesus demonstrates to Simon and to the reader that he is a prophet — not on Simon's terms, which means he would have to condemn the woman — but on his own terms, whereby he sees through Simon and exhorts his host to imitate the woman in accepting God's offer of forgiveness.

Meditation: In what ways do you find that you are like the woman? In what ways do you find that you are like Simon the Pharisee?

Prayer: God of forgiveness, throughout the ages you have never ceased to call your people back to you when they strayed. Through the power of your Holy Spirit, make us aware of our sin. Move us to accept your constant offer of forgiveness. Enable us to love each other as you are joined in love with your Son, our Lord Jesus Christ, and your Holy Spirit, one God, for ever and ever. Amen.

RETALIATION

Matthew 5:38-42

Scripture: "But I tell you not to resist the evildoer" (Matthew 5:39).

Reflection: This teaching concerning retaliation continues the pattern of "You have heard it was said… but I say to you" in the first sermon of Jesus in the Gospel of Matthew. In the Old Testament book of Leviticus, the law concerning retaliation states, "Whoever takes the life of any human being shall be put to death; whoever takes the life of an animal shall make restitution of another animal. A life for a life! Anyone who inflicts injury on his neighbor shall receive the same in return. Limb for limb, eye for eye, tooth for tooth! The same injury that a man gives another shall be inflicted on him in return" (Leviticus 24:17-20).

While it seems harsh today, this law concerning retaliation represents a moderation in the law in the culture of the time. It moderated vengeance so that the punishment did not exceed the injury done. When injured, a person could respond only proportionately.

According to Jesus in this Gospel passage, however, the righteous person may not respond proportionately: "When someone strikes you on (your) right cheek, turn the other one to him as well. If anyone wants to go to law with you and take your tunic, give him your cloak as well. Should anyone force you to go one mile, go with him two. Give to the one who asks of you, and do not turn away from one who wishes to borrow from you" (5:39-42).

These are, of course, excessive hyperbolic statements. Matthew is using them to make a point: the righteous person may not only not respond proportionately to injury, but he or she may not even respond to evil at all. Authenticity, righteousness, forces the reader to see that the old law of retaliation is excessive. In declaring its excess, however, Matthew typically does not specify what kind of response demonstrates righteousness. To do so would be to establish a new law, and this would undermine Matthew's whole theological perspective of righteousness or authenticity.

Meditation: In which recent conflict situation have you not responded with a retaliatory attitude or action? What were the results?

Prayer: God of moderation, when your people needed your moral guidance, you gave them the Law and the prophets. Through the teaching of Jesus, your Son, you have refined the old Law and called us to be righteous. Instill in us a spirit of authenticity. Remove all retaliation from our hearts. Help us to seek true reconciliation. We ask this through Christ our Lord. Amen.

LOVE OF ENEMIES
Matthew 5:43-48

Scripture: "Love your enemies, and pray for those who persecute you, so that you may be children of your Father in heaven, for he causes his sun to rise on the bad and the good, and causes rain to fall on the just and the unjust" (Matthew 5:44-45).

Reflection: The teaching concerning the love of one's enemies is the last of the six "You have heard it was said… but I say to you" statements of Jesus in Matthew's record of his first sermon. The point of this teaching is perfection: "Be perfect, as your heavenly Father is perfect" (5:48).

What does it mean to be perfect? In the Gospel according to Matthew, Jesus' understanding of perfection does not mean being without fault or defect. Perfect means being righteous, authentic, like God.

God does not separate people. God permits the sun to rise on the bad and the good. God causes the rain to fall on the just and the unjust. If a person is to be perfect, he or she must be like God, who does not segregate or separate or divide people between good and bad; God loves all people.

The righteous person, therefore, loves his or her enemies and prays for his or her persecutors. In so doing, this individual imitates God. There is nothing laudatory about loving those who love you. Sinners, tax collectors, Jewish apostatizers, loved each other. There is nothing laudatory in greeting those you love. Pagans and non-believers do as much.

What distinguishes authentic disciples of Jesus from others is their unwillingness to be a source of division. To engage in separatist behavior is wrong and unbecoming a child of God.

If the perfect God makes no distinctions, then imperfect disciples who want to be like God can do no less — they must judge no one and love everyone as their heavenly Father has taught them.

In this teaching, Matthew is holding the community to a new standard. The old values, which were based on prohibitions against killing, adultery, divorce, oaths, retaliation, and hatred of the enemy, no longer suffice to define relationships under the new law. These teachings, according to Matthew, no longer bind the community together. These old ways of bonding must give way to the law of love, righteousness, and authenticity — the new binding force of the community.

Throughout this section of his Gospel (5:21-48), Matthew has been searching for a way to maintain the underpinnings of community by upholding righteousness, authenticity, integrity and subverting isolation or individuality. He has been careful not to specify which behavior is appropriate and which is not; to do so would put him right back into the moral/legal mindset which he is trying to avoid.

The conclusion of this section of the Gospel brings the reader back to the beginning of the first sermon. The person who is righteous and authentic is happy. He or she is beatitudinal.

Meditation: In what ways do you demonstrate the Matthean understanding of perfection?

Prayer: God of perfection, you do not separate your people, but you love all men and women unconditionally. You cause the sun to rise on both the good and the bad. You send the rain to fall on both the just and the unjust. Instill in us a love for all people. May we tear down the walls which divide. Help us to bring the human family together in peace and in love, so that we may be perfect as you are perfect in Trinity — Father, Son, and Holy Spirit, one God, for ever and ever. Amen.

ALMSGIVING, PRAYING, FASTING

Matthew 6:1-6, 16-18

Scripture: "When you give alms, do not let your left hand know what your right hand is doing, so that your almsgiving may be in secret.... When you pray, go to your inner room, and when you have closed the door, pray to your Father who is hidden.... When you fast, anoint your head and wash your face, so others won't see that you are fasting.... Your Father who is hidden will see and reward you" (Matthew 6:3-4, 6, 17-18).

Reflection: In this section of the first sermon of Jesus, Matthew presents three teachings about almsgiving, prayer, and fasting. The Lord's Prayer, a subsection of the teaching about prayer is edited out and presented as an independent selection on Thursday of Week Eleven.

Almsgiving, prayer, and fasting are three distinctive acts of Jewish piety in Matthew's community. The problem that Matthew is tackling in this teaching is the difficulty of expressing righteousness before people. In other words, Matthew is attempting to deal with the attitude the community displays publicly of its piety.

Almsgiving, the first of the standard threefold virtues of Jewish righteousness, is how wealth is shared with others.

In the culture of the time, goods were limited; it was believed that there was only a certain amount of wealth in the world.

The way for another person to get some of the wealth was for another person to give it to him or her.

According to Matthew, there are two ways to practice almsgiving: publicly and privately. Those who do so publicly, hypocrites (Matthew's favorite word for scribes and Pharisees), by blowing trumpets (a call to the poor to come forward to receive alms), receive their reward publicly in terms of the praise of others.

Those who give alms privately — so privately that, hyperbolically, the left hand does not know what the right hand is doing — will be rewarded privately. Thus, Matthew upholds almsgiving as a righteous act for his community, but makes the action a secret one. A person's motivation for almsgiving is not public recognition but righteousness — it is done because it is the right thing to do; this is the behavior that God wants.

Prayer, done publicly in Judaism three times a day, is considered as almsgiving to God. Prayer represents a person's dependence on God for everything. God claims all of creation as God's own; prayer recognizes God's claim. Anything people have is a gift from God.

There are likewise two ways to pray, according to Matthew: publicly and privately. Those who pray publicly, the hypocrites, "love to stand and pray in the synagogues and on street corners so that others see them" (6:5). Their motivation for prayer is public notice. When others notice them, they have received their reward.

Those who pray privately go to their inner room, close their doors, and pray in secret. Their motivation for prayer is righteousness. They pray because it is the right action to do; this is the behavior God wants.

Fasting is another type of almsgiving. A person fasts not for his or her own sake, but for others. One does without some food so that others can have some food.

There are two ways to fast: publicly and privately. Those who fast publicly, hypocrites, mark their appearance with gloom.

They receive their reward when they are noticed by others.

Those who fast privately do not reveal any indication of their fasting. They wash their faces and comb their hair.

Their fasting is hidden; it is done because this is the behavior that God wants. God wants fasting which springs from righteousness.

In presenting almsgiving, prayer, and fasting in this hidden manner, Matthew is upholding the practice, but reinterpreting the motivation. All three of these acts demonstrate absolute dependence on God. All three of these acts demonstrate absolute dependence on others to share the gifts of God.

By turning these righteous deeds into secret acts, Matthew eliminates the motivation of being publicly seen.

What deeds are done in secret will be rewarded in secret by God, when God decides (for Matthew, this occurs at the end of Chapter 25, vv. 31-46, during the judgment of the nations narrative). Until that time, whenever it is, the community does deeds of righteousness because this is the behavior which pleases God. One acts like God, who is hidden, by doing the good deeds of almsgiving, prayer and fasting privately.

Furthermore, such secret deeds eliminate judgment. If almsgiving, prayer, and fasting cannot be seen, then no one can judge who is engaged in these deeds and who is not. People cannot be known by their fruits, Matthew is saying. The righteous do not display their fruits.

Meditation: In what ways do you imitate the Matthean understanding of almsgiving, prayer, and fasting?

Prayer: God of all righteousness, you have always urged your people to engage in almsgiving, prayer and fasting in order to demonstrate their dependence on you. Call us to authentic almsgiving that we might share your gifts with all people. Through your Holy Spirit move us to genuine prayer that we might know your secret and do it. Guide us to fast so that those who have nothing may be able to share in all your gifts. May we not perform these righteous deeds in order that people may see them, but because this behavior is pleasing in your sight. We ask this through Christ our Lord. Amen.

THE LORD'S PRAYER

Matthew 6:7-15

Scripture: "In praying, do not babble on like the Gentiles...
Your Father knows what you need before you ask him"
(Matthew 6:7-8).

Reflection: In Matthew's Gospel, the Lord's Prayer is a subsection of the teaching about prayer. In order to understand it, one must examine it in its Matthean context.

The issue in the entire teaching about prayer is the excessive display involved in public prayer. The usual posture for prayer for the Jews is standing; for intense prayer one places one's head between one's knees. Such positions in the synagogues and on street corners indicate that a person is praying.

Using excessive hyperbolic language, as is characteristic of Matthew, he declares that authentic prayer should take place in the "inner room," where the door is closed, where one prays in secret. A better translation of "inner room" is "closet or storeroom." By hiding in one's closet to pray, one imitates God, who is secret and hidden.

Furthermore, authentic prayer does not involve a lot of words. Pagans usually recited long lists of divine names in the hope that they would get a response from some god. Their prayer was designed to force or coerce their gods to act.

Jesus insists in this passage that this is not authentic prayer. Authentic prayer does not consist of a multitude of words nor does it attempt to force God into acting, since God already knows what the pray-er needs before he or she asks.

The typical way a Christian prays is related by Matthew in the Lord's Prayer. It is a liturgical version, which was probably being used in his community. The prayer also appears in Luke's Gospel (11:2-4) in a different context and in a different form.

The prayer is addressed to "Our Father in heaven," which indicates that it was being prayed by Matthew's community, and it is typical of other invocations used in many Jewish prayers.

The "hallowed be your name" can be understood as reverence for the divine. In this Matthean context, it is the reverence showed by righteous people at prayer.

Authentic pray-ers petition God to bring about the fullness of his kingdom and that his will, which is already done in heaven, may be done on earth. Righteousness involves behaving as God wills.

"Give us today our daily bread," is another petition for the fulfillment of the kingdom. Christians await the completion of the kingdom on a daily basis. "Bread" refers to a feast, another important metaphor used for the fullness of heaven.

Matthew is particularly interested in the last petition of the Lord's Prayer — "forgive us our debts, as we forgive our debtors; and do not subject us to the final test, but deliver us from the evil one" (6:12-13). "The final test" is a reference to the end of the world. Those who are righteous (as is seen in the judgment of the nations narrative, 25:31-46) are spared this final test.

"Debtors" refers to that which is owed to God because of sin. For Matthew, forgiveness is reciprocal and not conditional: "If you forgive others their transgressions, your heavenly Father will forgive you, too. But if you do not forgive others, neither will your Father forgive your transgressions" (6:14-15). Matthew is concerned with not breaking the bond of his community. He sees great virtue in keeping the community together. By mutual forgiveness between people and God and people and people this can be accomplished.

Thus, Matthew reaches a balance between private and public prayer. Private prayer is valuable as long as it is done with the right intention — to be like the Father, who is hidden — and not for the wrong intention — to be seen by others. Public prayer, according to Matthew, is to be short and to the point. It is valuable because it bonds the community, whose members are ready and willing to forgive as they are forgiven.

Meditation: In what ways does your private and public prayer reflect the Matthean balance?

Prayer: Our Father in heaven, hallowed be your name, your kingdom come, your will be done, on earth as it is in heaven. Give us today our daily bread; and forgive us our debts, as we forgive our debtors; and do not subject us to the final test, but deliver us from the evil one. Amen.

TREASURE

Matthew 6:19-23

Scripture: "Where your treasure is, there, too, will your heart be" (Matthew 6:21).

Reflection: The three sections of Jesus' first sermon which follow the teaching about almsgiving, prayer, and fasting in Matthew's Gospel function as a commentary on the first part of this discourse. The commentary consists of three verses about treasure in heaven: two verses about the lamp of the body being the eye, and one verse about God and money. In each of these sections a contrast is made.

In the first section, treasure in heaven is contrasted to treasures on earth. Earthly goods of cloth are destroyed by moths; food decays; thieves break into homes and steal. In the end, this treasure proves to be useless. Heavenly treasure, on the other hand, righteousness, cannot be destroyed, does not decay, and cannot be stolen. The person who gives alms, prays, and fasts — as Matthew has taught — stores up heavenly treasure. In order to determine where a person's heart (authenticity) is located, he or she needs only look at his or her treasure and its location.

In the second section, light is contrasted with darkness. A person sees with his or her eyes. The lamp of the body, the source of light for a person, is the eye. If one can see clearly, that is, learn from the teaching concerning almsgiving, prayer, and fasting, that person has a good eye. However, if one does not see, does not learn from what Jesus has taught, then that person will be in great darkness. People have been enlightened about the transitory nature of material treasure; they need to take a good look and see where their treasure is.

In the third section, two masters — God and mammon — are contrasted. Jesus declares emphatically in this passage from the Gospel of Matthew that a person cannot serve both God and wealth (or property or cash). One either hates one and loves the other, or is devoted to one and despises the other. A choice has to be made concerning which treasure one wants to possess. By practicing authentic almsgiving, prayer, and fasting, one serves God. By not being authentic, one serves cash. The two are not compatible.

It is obvious which choice Matthew would prefer that his readers make. In the section on dependence on God, which follows the three sections mentioned above, Matthew gives his readers reasons for choosing treasure in heaven and warns them against making human needs a master.

Meditation: Are your treasure and your heart in the same place? Give examples to illustrate your answer.

Prayer: God our master, in your kingdom neither moth or decay destroys nor thieves break in and steal your treasure. In your kingdom all is filled with light. Through the teaching of Jesus guide us to store up heavenly treasure. Help us to love and serve you, who live and reign with our Lord Jesus Christ and the Holy Spirit, one God for ever and ever. Amen.

PRIORITIES

Matthew 6:24-34

Scripture: "Don't go on worrying, saying, 'What will we eat?' or 'What will we drink?' or 'What will we put on?' All these things the Gentiles seek. Your heavenly Father knows you need them! But first seek the kingdom and will of God and all those things will be given to you besides" (Matthew 6:31-33).

Reflection: According to Jesus, it is important for us to question our priorities, if we are to determine upon which path — mammon or God — we are traveling. Matthew poses a series of questions which leads the reader to uncover his or her real priorities. Of course, the answers to the questions also form Matthew's argument of why one should choose the kingdom of God and God's righteousness (his will) above all else.

"Is not life more than food and the body more than clothing?" (6:25) is the first question. The obvious answer is that life *is* more important than food — although we cannot have life without food — and the body *is* more important than what we wear — although clothes protect the body.

In order to emphasize the obvious, Matthew employs the image of the birds in the sky. Birds have no concern about planting, raising, and harvesting a crop. They trust (insofar as it is possible to attribute trust to birds) that God will feed them and our own observation proves that God does indeed provide for them.

39

In comparison, human beings are more important than birds. Therefore, they should trust that God will take care of their needs for food and drink as well.

"Why are you anxious about clothing?" (6:28) is the next question, which, in fact, is the second part of this first one. The example given is that of the wild flowers, which do not spin in order to array themselves in attractive finery. Yet, the wild flowers are decked out in greater splendor even than king Solomon. If such beauty is the clothing of the grass of the field, which is here today and gathered and used as fuel tomorrow, one can only believe that God will provide the necessity of clothing, since people are more important than the wild flowers in the field.

Sandwiched in between the questions about food and clothing is one about worrying in general: "Which of you can add a single moment to your life-span by worrying?" (6:27). This question is answered later in this section of the Gospel. "So don't go on worrying about tomorrow; tomorrow will take care of itself. One day's evil is enough for a day" (6:34). In other words, no one can add a second to his or her life by worrying. In fact, worry may subtract time from one's life!

These questions lead to a typical Matthean comparison. Pagans, non-believers, the Gentiles, seek food, drink and clothes; these are their top priorities. Authentic followers of Jesus, those who are righteous, seek the kingdom of God first. They trust that all their needs will be met by God. They depend on God for their life.

People who have their priorities straight behave differently from the pagans. They submit to God's kingdom, to God's way. Their moral conduct is in conformity with God's will. What they discover as a result of this is that all their needs are met. Matthew is not saying that people do not need to eat or to drink or that they do not need to wear clothes. He simply questions how important these "things" (which pagans seek) are in comparison to the kingdom of God and his righteousness (which Christians seek).

Meditation: Do you think that you are perceived to be a person who is more concerned about food, drink and clothes or one who is focused on the kingdom of God and his righteousness? Give examples to support your answer.

Prayer: Heavenly Father, you feed the birds of the sky and you clothe the grass of the field with wild flowers. Nothing in your creation escapes your loving care; all is held intimately in your hand. Through the message of Jesus, teach us to trust you to fulfill our needs. Move us to seek first your kingdom. Enable us to live your way of righteousness. Then, free from daily worry, bring us at last to the fullness of life, which you share with your Son, our Lord Jesus Christ, and your Holy Spirit, one God, for ever and ever. Amen.

PROCLAIM!

Matthew 10:26-33

Scripture: "Nothing is concealed that will not be revealed, nor hidden that will not be known. What I tell you in the darkness, speak in the light; what you hear whispered, proclaim on the rooftops" (Matthew 10:26-27).

Reflection: This section of Matthew's Gospel is taken from the second sermon which Jesus gives. It is commonly referred to as the missionary discourse. After naming the twelve disciples, Jesus commissions them, tells them what will happen to them because they are his followers, and urges them to have courage when they are persecuted.

In this "have courage when you are persecuted" section of the sermon, Matthew echoes and reinforces themes stated earlier and later in the Gospel. The kingdom of God is hidden — like the leaven which a woman hides in three measures of flour (13:33) but which eventually makes its presence known when the dough rises. Through the missionary work of Jesus' disciples, this hidden kingdom will be revealed through the effects of their preaching.

The kingdom of God is hidden — like the treasure buried in a field (13:44). Through the missionary work of Jesus' disciples, this hidden treasure will be found and made known.

Followers of Jesus are "the light of the world" (5:14).

Therefore, they are to speak in the light what they hear in

43

the darkness. Likewise, what they hear whispered, they are to proclaim from the rooftops — for they are like the wise man who built his house on rock (7:24). When persecution comes, they stand firm.

According to Matthew, the followers of Jesus are always taken care of by the Father. Using hyperbolic statements in order to stress this point, Matthew compares the love that God has for people to that of God's love for useless sparrows. If God cares for the sparrows, which are sold for a small coin, then how much more does God care for people. In fact, God cares so much that he has counted all the hairs on everyone's head!

Because of God's care, the followers of Jesus are not to be afraid. If they acknowledge Jesus before others, that is, if they stand firm in their mission to proclaim God's kingdom, then on the judgment day (25:31-46) the king (Jesus) will acknowledge (recognize) them. However, if one denies Jesus before others, that is, fails to recognize him in the least of his brothers and sisters, then Jesus will deny knowing this disciple on judgment day.

Meditation: In what ways do you demonstrate discipleship?

Prayer: Father, your loving care stretches from one end of the universe to the other. Not even the sparrows are without your care. In your great love, you count the hairs of our heads in order to demonstrate how much you are concerned with us. Give us courage to speak your truth. Enable us to reveal your kingdom to all we meet. We ask this through our Lord Jesus Christ, your Son, who lives and reigns with you and the Holy Spirit, one God, for ever and ever. Amen.

QUIET!

Mark 4:35-41

Scripture: Jesus woke up, rebuked the wind, and said to the sea, "Quiet! Be still!" The wind ceased and there was a great calm (Mark 4:39).

Reflection: Mark's narrative of the calming of a storm at sea demands that the reader have a basic working knowledge of the Old Testament. This section of Mark's Gospel is filled with images which tease new meanings out of old events.

The time of the day is evening. Darkness envelops the disciples, who have observed Jesus' miracles, healings, and exorcisms and listened to his parables. They do not understand. The disciples are in the same state as the world in the opening scene of the book of Genesis.

Furthermore, a violent squall comes up and waves break over the boat as the disciples and Jesus cross the sea. The disturbance functions both as an image of the turbulence of the disciples and as a reference to the chaos which existed before God spoke his first word of creation.

Jesus commands that the wind cease and that the sea be still. Not only does Jesus bring order out of this physical chaos, but he also brings order out of the chaos of the lives of those who are willing to hear and follow him. The disciples, representing all Christians, continue to struggle with faith. It is difficult for people to give up control of their lives and trust that Jesus will calm and quiet them.

One experience of trust, however, is sufficient to lead a person to trust again. Like the disciples, once one has dared to let Jesus calm the disturbances of life, he or she is filled with great awe. The question which the disciples ask is one asked by every follower of Jesus: "Who is he, that both wind and sea obey him?"

The answer to the question sends one back to the book of Genesis, where the mighty wind of the Spirit sweeps over the primordial waters, where God calms the demonic chaos, where life emerges for the first time on the earth. Jesus is the one whom the wind and sea obey. Through this narrative, Mark is declaring that Jesus is God.

Meditation: In which recent turbulent time of your life did you turn to Jesus and experience his quiet and calm?

Prayer: God of the sea, out of the primordial waters you fashioned the earth and all of the life upon it. When the storms of life engulf us and threaten to drown us, awaken in us the faith of Jesus. Bring his quiet, calm, and peace to our lives. We ask this through our Lord Jesus Christ, your Son, who lives and reigns with you and the Holy Spirit, one God, for ever and ever. Amen.

IDENTITY

Luke 9:18-24

Scripture: And it happened that while he was praying in solitude, the disciples were with him and he asked them, "Who do the crowds say I am?" (Luke 9:18)

Reflection: The question of Jesus' identity, borrowed from Mark and reworked by Luke, follows the mission of the Twelve, Herod's opinion about Jesus, and the feeding of the five thousand. This section is followed by a discourse on the conditions of discipleship and the Transfiguration narrative. One of the threads which Luke weaves throughout this section of his Gospel in order to hold it together is that of the identity of Jesus. The question of identity is first raised by Herod: "Who is this, then, whom I hear so much about?" (9:9) It is a stroke of Lucan irony that Herod poses the question. Later in the Gospel, Herod interviews Jesus, after which Herod and Pilate become friends (23:6-12).

The first answer to Herod's question that Luke gives is found in the narrative of the feeding of the five thousand. Just as God fed his people with manna in the wilderness, so Jesus feeds his people in a deserted place. In Jesus, God's power is present — a power which meets the needs of God's people.

The second answer to Herod's question is given by Peter: "The Messiah of God" (9:20). Messiah means "anointed," and sends the reader back to Jesus' first discourse in Luke where, after reading from the prophet Isaiah, "The Spirit of the Lord is upon me, because he has anointed me," Jesus declares that "today this Scripture passage is fulfilled in your hearing" (4:18, 21). Jesus brings salvation for all people.

It is to be noted that Peter's answer to the question comes after a period of prayer. The major, revelatory events of the life of Jesus in the Gospel of Luke always occur after prayer.

The third answer is given by Jesus: "The Son of Man" (9:22). In Mark's Gospel this title indicates the imminent "suffering and death" aspects of Jesus' life. Since Luke has borrowed this section from Mark, he retains the title and uses it as Mark did.

The fourth answer is also given by Jesus; he is the one to be followed daily. "If anyone wishes to come after me, he (or she) must deny himself (or herself) and take up his (or her) cross daily and follow me" (9:23). Jesus is the master, the teacher, who is to be followed to death.

The fifth answer is given by God in the Transfiguration account: "This is my Son, my Chosen One; listen to him" (9:35). This voice from heaven is an echo of the voice heard when Jesus was baptized: "You are my beloved Son: in you I am well pleased" (3:22).

These five answers to Herod's question surround the answers that the crowds give. Some think that Jesus is John the Baptist. This is incorrect, of course, since John was put in prison by Herod before Jesus' baptism (3:19-20), and Jesus has already declared that "among those born of women, none is greater than John; yet whoever is least in the kingdom of God is greater then he" (7:28).

Others think that Jesus is Elijah. It was a popularly held belief that Elijah would return before the day of the Lord. Luke understands John the Baptist to have fulfilled this role: "He will go before him in the spirit and power of Elijah" (1:17).

Still others think that Jesus is one of the ancient prophets who has arisen. Again, Jesus has already focused attention on John the Baptist as a prophet (7:26). Furthermore, Luke declares Jesus to be the fulfillment of the words of the prophets in Jesus' opening sermon (4:21).

The person who can correctly identify Jesus is a disciple. This person knows that following Jesus daily demands a willingness to take up the cross and follow him.

Meditation: In what ways can you answer Jesus' question, "Who do you say that I am?" What is the meaning of each of your answers?

Prayer: God of Jesus, in the past through the words of your prophets you promised one who would save your people. John the Baptist was the herald of the good news of Jesus, your Chosen One. May we always deny ourselves and take up our crosses and follow him that we may share forever in your triune life — Father, Son and Holy Spirit, one God, for ever and ever. Amen.

JUDGING OTHERS

Matthew 7:1-5

Scripture: "Don't judge, so that you won't be judged. For as you judge, so will you be judged" (Matthew 7:1).

Reflection: In the beginning of this last section of Matthew's first sermon of Jesus, the tone changes. The language is direct. Here Jesus warns the community about a number of issues, the first of which concerns judgment of others.

Matthew's theology is that the way people deal with each other in the community corresponds with how God deals with people. There is a difference between recognizing the faults of another and judging that person. Using hyperbolic language to get the point across, Matthew asks, "Why do you notice the speck in your brother's (or sister's) eye, yet don't notice the log in your own eye?" (7:3). Those who are judgmental usually do not see their own faults.

Before pointing out the fault of another, we should first examine ourselves carefully to determine if we possess the same fault, according to Matthew. Contemporary psychology would concur that we tend to readily dislike in another what we dislike in ourselves. Once the fault is recognized (that is, once we remove the log from our own eye), then we can point out the faults of another in a spirit of charity (that is, remove the speck from a brother's or sister's eye).

It should not be missed that Matthew refers to one's own

fault as a "log," while he calls the fault of another a "speck." This is the attitude which is needed if one member of the community is to correct another member. The person doing the correcting must always realize how much greater his or her faults are in comparison to the person he or she is correcting.

This attitude eliminates or at least reduces our judgments of one another; it gets rid of arrogance; it keeps us from forgetting our own sinfulness. This attitude puts us all on the same level; we all have blind spots. The righteous person readily recognizes this and judges no one. In this way, the measure used is measured back to him or her.

Just as one person helps another in the community to extract the speck from his or her eye, so God helps us all to remove the logs from our own eyes. If God does not judge (but, rather, helps), then we should not judge (but, like God, should help others).

Meditation: In what ways do you find that you judge others' specks instead of recognizing your own logs? Make a list of the logs which blind you.

Prayer: God of mercy, you do not judge. You call all people to the way of righteousness. When we see a speck in another's eye, turn us around to see the log that blinds us. Through the working of your Spirit, guide us to cease our judgment of others and to measure out mercy as you measure it out to us. We ask this through our Lord Jesus Christ, your Son, who lives and reigns with you and the Holy Spirit, one God, for ever and ever. Amen.

THE GOLDEN RULE

Matthew 7:6, 12-14

Scripture: "Whatever you want others to do for you, do so for them as well" (Matthew 7:12).

Reflection: For Matthew, the law and the prophets are summed up in what has come to be known as the "Golden Rule" "Do unto others what you would have them do unto you" (Matthew 7:12). To reduce the entirety of the law and the prophets to this one proverb is quite a feat, until one recalls Matthew's basic theme of righteousness.

Righteousness in Matthew's Gospel consists of correct behavior, doing the will of God because it is the right way to act and it is the way that God wants a person to act. If we are righteous, then we will first of all reflect upon what we would like others to do for us. Armed with this knowledge, we will then treat others accordingly.

Yet, there is still another dimension to the "Golden Rule." If a righteous person considers the other person first, by treating the other as he or she would like to be treated, that individual may spark in the other a desire to become righteous too.

Matthew compares righteousness to material things which are considered to be of great value, like a precious pearl (7:6). He says that it is the narrow gate that leads to life (7:14). Those who are not righteous are "dogs" and "swine" (7:6); they have no difficulty entering through the wide gate that leads to destruction (7:12), whereas those who do the will of God (are righteous) pass easily through the narrow gate and find themselves on the path that leads to life.

Meditation: In what recent situation did you treat another person in exactly the way you wanted that person to treat you?

Prayer: Holy God, you have endowed all people with equal human dignity. Through the teaching of Jesus, may we realize our own redeemed status and treat others as brothers and sisters. Open for us the narrow gate that we may enter through it and be led to the life you share with our Lord Jesus Christ, your Son, who lives and reigns with you and the Holy Spirit, one God, for ever and ever. Amen.

FALSE PROPHETS

Matthew 7:15-20

Scripture: "By their fruits you will know them" (Matthew 7:20).

Reflection: This second-to-last section of Jesus' first sermon deals with the issue of false prophets. In the Old Testament a prophet was a person who spoke in the name of God. Christian prophets, who proclaimed the gospel, were a part of Matthew's community. Reference is made to these prophets two other times in Matthew's Gospel (10:41 and 23:34). It is easy to conclude that these prophets were an influential group within that community.

The community's question being dealt with here concerns the criteria for distinguishing true Christian prophets from false ones. Using an old and well-known proverb, Jesus warns his listeners against those who pretend to be authentic prophets but are, in reality, only wolves in sheep's clothing (7:15). However, this proverb does not supply the necessary criteria in order to know the difference between true and false prophets.

Jesus' Jewish background leads him to propose criteria based on examples from the Old Testament. He knows that in the past there were both true and false prophets. How were they distinguished? The criterion used was the quality of their deeds — their fruits.

The righteous person is able to recognize an authentic prophet just as he or she knows the difference between trees. Lapsing into an "orchard" metaphor, he then uses what was common experience to help his listeners distinguish between true and false prophets.

A person does not pick grapes from thorn bushes nor figs from thistles. One looks for grapes on grape vines and figs on fig trees. The tree (or person) itself (himself, herself) is the first criterion. In other words, one must consider the source — the one who claims to speak the word of God.

The second criterion is: "By their fruits you will know them" (7:16). "Every good tree bears good fruit, and a rotten tree bears bad fruit" (7:17). This is obviously an exaggeration used to make a point. Trees either bear fruit or they do not; there is no such thing as "bad fruit" — unless it has been left on the tree too long and rots! The analogy here is stretched in order to make a point. The deeds of a person reveal that individual's authenticity. If one claims to speak the word of God, then the way that person behaves (righteousness) shows whether he or she is a true prophet. "A good tree cannot bear bad fruit, nor can a rotten tree bear good fruit" (7:18). An authentic, righteous person does not engage in the wrong type of behavior; the unauthentic, unrighteous person does not engage in the right type of behavior.

Of course, following his earlier advice not to judge so as not to be judged, Matthew warns his community not to be too hasty to root out the "bad fruit." On the day of judgment, "every tree that does not bear good fruit will be cut down and thrown into the fire" (7:19). Until that day, however, Matthew's community will be wise to examine carefully the deeds of those who claim to be prophets before following after them. If their words and deeds are one, then they are probably authentic; if there is no unity between what they preach and how they act, then they are probably false.

Meditation: Name two or three persons who are considered to be modern prophets. In which ways do they measure up to Matthew's criteria?

Prayer: God of the prophets, in times past you called men and women to speak your word to your people. Through their words and deeds they delivered your commandments and taught your people how to live. Jesus, your Son, the greatest of the prophets, delivered your message of love for all people. Raise up more prophets today. Send them forth filled with your Spirit and on fire with your word. Open our minds and hearts to listen attentively to what they say. Move us to recognize in them the signs of your love for us. We ask this through Christ our Lord. Amen.

HOUSE BUILDING
Matthew 7:21-29

Scripture: "Many will say to me on that day, 'Lord, Lord, didn't we prophesy in your name and drive out demons in your name? Didn't we do mighty deeds in your name?' Then I will declare to them, 'I never knew you. Depart from me, you evildoers'" (Matthew 7:22-23).

Reflection: The discussion concerning who is or who is not a true disciple and the two foundations upon which one can build his or her life brings to a close the first sermon of Jesus.

Matthew continues the discussion concerning false prophets by addressing true discipleship. He draws a line which distinguishes those who claim to be and look like disciples from those who truly are authentic disciples.

Simply knowing that Jesus is Lord is not a mark of authentic discipleship. "Not everyone who says to me, 'Lord, Lord,' will enter the kingdom of heaven"(7:21). Anyone can call Jesus "Lord."

Likewise, prophesying in Jesus' name, exorcising demons, and doing mighty deeds in Jesus' name are not necessarily marks of authentic discipleship. Those who are able to do these things may look like they are disciples, but in reality they may be "evildoers," they may be morally corrupt. Their behavior may not be righteous.

Authentic discipleship is characterized by doing the will of the Father in heaven. After hearing Jesus' words, the authentic follower (the righteous one) acts on them. He or she is as shrewd as the man who builds his house on rock.

Unauthentic followers of Jesus hear his words but do not practice them. They cannot figure out what they should do and are like those foolish individuals who build their homes on sand.

It is important to note that throughout this discourse Matthew never explains in detail what a righteous person does or doesn't do; to do so would be to put Matthew into the very trap of the law out of which he was trying to get his community. Rather, he paints the ideal follower as one who does the will of the Father. It is up to the shrewd person (the one who builds on rock) to figure out the details.

In this passage from Matthew's Gospel, Jesus is addressing those who already believe. The question he is answering is this: What does one do with what one has heard? The answer is: Put it into practice. How? By taking Jesus' interpretation of the Law (Torah) and doing something with it; that is, by building your life (house) on the solid rock of this teaching: hearing and doing.

The concluding images of building a house on rock and on sand in a way summarize the whole first sermon of Jesus. Matthew has been trying to move the reader from the act of hearing to the act of doing. He believes that the words of Jesus are the only true interpretation of the Law. They are an explanation of God's building plans, as it were. The righteous (authentic) follower is responsible for taking these words and constructing a life based or founded on them. To specify what the house should look like when done, would be to create a new floor plan or law, — something which Matthew wants to completely avoid.

Meditation: In which ways is your house built on solid rock? In which ways is your house built on sand?

Prayer: God our rock, through your servant Moses you gave us your law. In Jesus, your Son, you fulfilled that law and taught us to follow him. Make of us authentic disciples. Open our ears to hear the voice of Jesus, and through your Holy Spirit move us to put into practice what we hear. We ask this through our Lord Jesus Christ, who lives and reigns with you and the Holy Spirit, one God, for ever and ever. Amen.

NO SEGREGATION

Matthew 8:1-4

Scripture: "Be made clean." And at once his leprosy was cleansed (Matthew 8:3).

Reflection: The healing of a single leper is the first of the nine miracle stories which Matthew narrates after Jesus' first sermon. The account of the healing of the leper is borrowed from Mark, one of Matthew's sources for his own Gospel.

The account is fashioned after two Old Testament stories, both of which detail the healing of a leper. First, in the book of Numbers, after Aaron and Miriam speak against Moses, God afflicts Miriam with leprosy. Moses, however, intercedes with God, and Miriam is returned to health (cf. Numbers 12:9-15).

Second, in the second book of Kings, Naaman, a Syrian army commander, seeks out the prophet Elisha, whom he hopes will cure his leprosy. Elisha instructs Naaman to plunge himself into the Jordan River seven times. Naaman doubts, but later does it, and is cured of leprosy.

Leprosy was a generic name for a whole variety of skin diseases which were believed to be contagious. The leper was ostracized, placed outside the camp, forced to live outside the city, pushed out of his or her religious community. Such a person was thought to be unworthy of God, because leprosy represented God's punishment for some sin.

Matthew's portrayal of Jesus in this narrative makes three

important points for his community. First, Jesus is the agent of healing for the leper. When the echoes of the two Old Testament stories of the healings of lepers are "heard," it is easy to see that Matthew is proclaiming that Jesus is God; Jesus is now (at the time of Matthew's writing) doing what God did in the past — he is healing the afflicted.

Second, Matthew sees Jesus in this cure making a strong statement against segregation. He reaches out and touches the leper. He sends him to the temple priests, who were responsible for re-incorporating a leper into the mainstream of society. For Jesus, no one is to be ostracized from society. Everyone belongs to the community — a highly esteemed value for Matthew.

Third, Matthew is emphasizing the value of trust. Moses trusted that God would restore Miriam. Naaman trusted the directions of Elisha. Those who need healing must trust God. God is worthy of all trust, Matthew declares as he portrays the leper doing homage to Jesus.

The modern analogy to leprosy is undoubtedly AIDS. People withs AIDS are often ostracized and punished by society because of this disease. Many think them unworthy of God. In addressing the problem of leprosy, Matthew also addresses the problem of AIDS. Likewise, he demonstrates the appropriate Christian response to both.

Meditation: In which ways do you segregate or separate people? How can you begin to "heal" this divisive behavior?

Prayer: Lord God, you stretched out your hand and touched the leprosy of Miriam and brought about reconciliation between her, Aaron and Moses. Through your prophet, Elisha, you touched Naaman the Syrian and restored him to health. Finally, in Jesus you have touched all that needs healing in humanity. Free us from our fear that we may be willing to let Jesus' hand rest upon us. Fill us with trust that we may be willing to tear down the walls of separation that divide your people. We ask this through Christ our Lord. Amen.

MORE FAITH

Matthew 8:5-17

Scripture: "Amen, I say to you, nowhere have I found such faith in Israel. I tell you, many will come from east and west and will recline at table with Abraham, Isaac, and Jacob in the kingdom of heaven, but the children of the kingdom will be driven out into the outer darkness, where there will be wailing and gnashing of teeth" (Matthew 8:11-12).

Reflection: The account of the healing of a centurion's servant is found in both Matthew and Luke. Scholars conclude that it comes from source Q (an abbreviated form of the German word "Quelle," which means "source").

Scholars believe that Matthew's Gospel was composed from three sources: Mark, Q, and Special Matthew. Almost all of Mark's Gospel is contained in Matthew. Also, in Matthew and Luke there is material which is similar, but is not found in Mark; this is the hypothetical source referred to as Q. Finally, there is material in Matthew's Gospel which is found nowhere else in any other gospel; these verses are referred to as Special Matthew.

It is to be noted that the narrative concerning the healing of a centurion's servant is also found in John. However, this is not due to a similar written tradition, as in Matthew and Luke (Q), but to a common oral tradition.

The centurion is a Roman soldier who commands a hun-

dred men. He represents the Roman occupation forces in the
Jewish homeland. He is a pagan and a Gentile. Therefore, he is
the most unlikely candidate to be the object of a healing. It is for
this very reason that Matthew chooses to narrate the story.

As in many of the "healing accounts," there is little or no
mention of the process of healing. The author is not interested in
the healing. He is interested in who requests healing and who is
healed. The centurion requests healing for his servant. His request
is one of faith: "Just say the word and my servant will be healed"
(8:8), he tells Jesus.

The centurion, who should not be a believer, is still a man
of faith; he knows that if Jesus' word is obeyed, his servant will
recover.

The object of healing is the servant, another Gentile. In a
way, this is Matthew's way of doubly making his point. Jesus is
the savior of all people — Jews and Gentiles alike. There is a
certain irony in the statement that the Gentiles profess "more"
faith than anyone in Israel!

Matthew is warning his community against exclusivism and
against presumption. In order to keep his church from thinking
that only Jewish-Christians can inherit the kingdom, Matthew
reminds them that "many will come from the east and the west,
and will recline at table with Abraham, Isaac, and Jacob in the
kingdom of heaven" (8:11). This means that Gentiles will join
the Jewish patriarchs in the kingdom. God's kingdom is open to
all people; there can be no exclusivism.

Furthermore, no one can presume that he or she will get
into the kingdom. "The children of the kingdom will be driven
out into the outer darkness, where there will be wailing and
gnashing of teeth" (8:12), Jesus says. "The children of the kingdom" refers to Matthew's Jewish-Christian community; they must
be careful unless they wake up to discover that they have been
disinherited. The result will be condemnation.

This is Matthew's first use of the phrase "wailing and gnashing of teeth," which will be employed throughout the rest of the
Gospel to describe the final condemnation of those who do not

believe, those who exclude others from the kingdom, and those who presume that they are guaranteed a place in the kingdom.

By including this story in his Gospel, Matthew is placing further emphasis on the importance of the early Church's mission to the Gentiles. Matthew had already prepared the reader for this narrative by relating the visit of the magi in the early part of the Gospel. They were the first to visit and pay homage to the newborn king of the Jews; they were Gentiles.

Meditation: Which groups of people do you judge to be outside the kingdom? Is it possible that they may have a stronger faith than you have?

Prayer: God of all people, you offer your gift of grace to men and women of every time and place. Through the working of your Holy Spirit, bring the human race to unity. Remove all that divides us, and bring us to a deep faith through the teaching of your Son, our Lord Jesus Christ, who lives and reigns with you and the Holy Spirit, one God, for ever and ever. Amen.

NOT-SPECIFIED REWARDS

Matthew 10:37-42

Scripture: "Whoever receives a prophet because he is a prophet will receive a prophet's reward, and whoever receives a righteous man because he is a righteous man will receive a righteous man's reward" (Matthew 10:41).

Reflection: The conditions of discipleship and the rewards which will be given to authentic disciples form the two concluding sections of Jesus' second sermon in the Gospel According to Matthew — commonly referred to as the missionary discourse.

First, Matthew lays out the conditions of discipleship. An authentic follower of Jesus loves no one more than the Master. The authentic disciple puts Jesus ahead of father, mother, son, and daughter. He or she is willing to take up the cross, just as Jesus did, and be put to death for his or her faith.

This is the first time that Matthew mentions the cross in his Gospel. Members of his community were probably being put to death on crosses — a popular form of Roman capital punishment. He is exhorting them to behave as Jesus did. If they are crucified, they are conformed to the image of Jesus.

Typical of Matthew is the reversal involved in discipleship. "Whoever finds his life will lose it, and whoever loses his life for my sake will find it" (10:39).

Matthew is warning his community that those who deny their faith in Jesus in order to save their lives will end up destroyed. On the other hand, whoever endures persecution and death bravely for Jesus' sake will discover real life — everlasting life — in the kingdom.

Second, Matthew equates Jesus and the members of the community. This equation is begun in the missionary discourse, but it is seen most clearly in the last judgment scene (25:31-46). Whenever one member of the community receives another member of the community, the one doing the receiving also welcomes Jesus and God, who sent Jesus. The visible community is the new body of Christ, to borrow a Pauline metaphor.

Also, since prophets were still in Matthew's community — probably proclaiming the Gospel — anyone who welcomes a prophet for no other reason than that he or she is a prophet will be rewarded in the same way as the prophet. Of course, Matthew never specifies of what this reward will consist, because he doesn't know, leaving that to God.

Matthew inserts one of his favorite themes — righteousness — into this section. Anyone who receives a righteous person because such a one is righteous will receive the same reward as the righteous one. Again, Matthew does not specify of what the reward will consist. However, since righteousness is demanded of all followers of Jesus, Matthew is upholding the importance of behaving as God wills.

Little ones — either children or the least of society — further fill out Matthew's equation of the community and Jesus. Those who reach out to the forgotten, the outcast, and the poor will be rewarded at the last judgment.

Those who function as missionaries in the community put everything — including their very lives — on the line for Jesus. The other members of the community must respond by receiving these missionaries — no matter if they be prophets, righteous people, or little ones — for in doing so they receive Jesus and God.

Meditation: Whom have you most recently received as a missionary? What was his or her message for you?

Prayer: God of missionaries, you call people to hear the teaching of Jesus, your Son, and to place their love of him above everyone else. Make us worthy of those you send us. Help us to identify the prophets in our midst. Make of us righteous people who will inherit the kingdom, where you live and reign with Jesus and the Holy Spirit, one God, for ever and ever. Amen.

WHO TOUCHED ME?

Mark 5:21-43

Scripture: Jesus said to (the woman afflicted with hemorrhages for twelve years), "Daughter, your faith has saved you. Go in peace and be cured of your affliction." ... Jesus took the child (of the synagogue official named Jairus) by the hand and said to her, "Little girl, I say to you arise!" (Mark 5:34, 41).

Reflection: Mark's account of the raising of the daughter of Jairus, one of the synagogue officials, is divided into two parts with the account of the healing of a woman with hemorrhages sandwiched in between. This technique, referred to as intercalating, is used extensively by Mark throughout his Gospel.

A number of points are presented for our consideration. First, the faith of Jairus and that of the unnamed woman with hemorrhages is contrasted to the lack of faith of the crowd and the disciples. Jairus requests that Jesus come and lay his hands on his daughter for the purpose of healing, a gesture used frequently by Mark. The woman with the hemorrhages for twelve years just wants to touch Jesus' clothing. In both cases physical contact with Jesus accompanied by faith effected a cure. The emphasis is not on the cure, however, but on the faith of these two people.

Second, in order to demonstrate how spiritually obtuse the disciples are, Mark adds a touch of ironic humor to the narrative of the woman with the hemorrhages. All hemmed in by a crowd, much like lines in an amusement park or in an airport, where lots of people touch each other, Jesus asks, "Who touched my cloak?" (5:30) The answer is impossible, except for Jesus, who is "aware… that power had gone out from him" (5:30). The disciples do not understand. Thus, the "unlikely but present faith" of a smart woman is set side-by-side with the "likely but not present" faith of Jesus' own disciples.

Third, the story of Jairus becomes even more complicated with the reported death of his daughter. He had sought a cure; now, he must seek her life. "Don't be afraid; just believe," Jesus tells him (5:36). Thus, the faith of Jairus is contrasted to the lack of faith of the people of his household, who were weeping and wailing loudly.

Fourth, the awakening of the little girl by Jesus faintly echoes the resuscitation of the son of the widow of Zarephath (1 Kings 17:17-24). When the life breath returns to the boy, his mother declares, "Now indeed I know that you are a man of God.… The word of the Lord comes truly from your mouth" (17:24). In relating this story, Mark is declaring Jesus to be a great prophet like Elijah, who will later appear in the transfiguration narrative.

Fifth, it is no accident that Peter, James, and John are taken into the house with Jesus and the little girl's parents in this narrative. These same three on the Mount of the Transfiguration will be taken into the cloud — an apocalyptic representation of God — prior to Jesus' passion, death and resurrection. In both instances the divinity of Jesus is manifested — in the raising of the dead and in the proclamation of his Sonship by the heavenly Father. This marks as well the turning point of Mark's Gospel.

Sixth, the Greek word used in Jesus' command to the little girl, "Arise" is the same verb usually used to refer to Jesus' resurrection from the dead. Mark has given us a preview of the end of the Gospel. The Father will say to his Son, "My beloved, arise," and he, too, like the little girl will rise from the dead.

Seventh, Mark has also given the reader a hint concerning the food necessary for life. Later in the Gospel, Mark will narrate the feeding of the five thousand (6:34-44) and the feeding of the four thousand (8:1-10) where Jesus gives the crowd "something to eat" (5:43).

Eighth, Mark has placed an emphasis on Jesus' power in these two stories. The reader must be cautious, because this type of healing power is not Mark's interest. In the second half of the Gospel, he will eschew this kind of power. For Mark, true power consists of powerlessness. Jesus suffers and dies. For this reason, the transfiguration, which is usually viewed as a demonstration of Jesus' power, is framed by the first and second prediction of Jesus' passion. For Mark, transfiguration means powerlessness, and it points the way to suffering and death.

Meditation: In which ways does your faith resemble that of Jairus and the woman with the hemorrhages? In which ways does it resemble that of the disciples and the crowd?

Prayer: God of life, faith is your gift to your people. Strengthen our trust in you. Reach out your healing hand and deliver us from all our afflictions. Make us realize your power in our suffering and death. Raise us up on the last day to the eternal life you share with your Son, our Lord Jesus Christ, and your Holy Spirit, one God, for ever and ever. Amen.

DON'T LOOK BACK

Luke 9:51-62

Scripture: "No one who puts his hand to the plow and looks behind is fit for the kingdom of God" (Luke 9:62).

Reflection: The last twelve verses of chapter nine of Luke's Gospel begin the ten-chapter (9:51-19:27) travel narrative of Jesus' journey to Jerusalem. His Galilean ministry is complete. The first prediction of his suffering, rejection, death, and resurrection was given before the account of the transfiguration, during which Moses and Elijah speak "of his exodus that he was going to accomplish in Jerusalem" (9:31) — that is, his suffering, death, resurrection, and ascension — and the second prediction of the passion — that "the Son of Man is to be handed over to men" (9:44). These three indications of what will happen in Jerusalem set the stage for the next ten chapters of the Gospel.

To be sure that the reader understands the point of the journey to Jerusalem, Luke introduces this travel narrative with the phrase, "Now it happened that as the days were drawing near for Jesus to be taken up, he resolutely made up his mind to journey to Jerusalem" (9:51). According to Luke, Jesus was determined to accomplish the suffering, death, resurrection, and ascension which awaited him in Jerusalem.

At the beginning of Jesus' Galilean ministry in Nazareth he was rejected by the people in the synagogue. "They rose up, drove him out of the town, and led him to the brow of the hill on which their town had been built, to hurl him down headlong" (4:29). Likewise, as Jesus begins his journey to Jerusalem, he is rejected by the Samaritans.

Shortly after his rejection in Nazareth, Jesus begins to call disciples. Using the same parallel arrangement, a literary device of which Luke is fond of using, three would-be disciples are presented along with Jesus' teaching concerning the demands of discipleship.

First, discipleship is not home-bound. For a person to say, "I will follow you wherever you go" (9:57), and want the security of a home, a place to live, and the comforts of an affluent life is not to accept the insecurities of discipleship. "Foxes have dens and birds of the sky have nests, but the Son of Man has nowhere to lay his head" (9:58). In other words, the animals have more security than disciples of Jesus, because the animals have a place to live. Disciples of Jesus claim no place a home.

Second, familial obligations, such as burying a dead relative, cannot come before the proclamation of the kingdom of God. Disciples of Jesus resolutely determine to follow Jesus all the way to Jerusalem, where the worst will happen.

Third, there can be no turning back for a disciple. Once one has accepted the call, there is no going back to say good-bye to family at home. Such looking back renders one unfit for the kingdom of God.

These three incidents are given by Luke to stress the unconditional and severe demands of being a follower of Jesus. If a person is going to follow Jesus, then he or she cannot turn back, change his or her mind, look for excuses to return home, seek security. What awaits a disciple of Jesus is what awaited Jesus in Jerusalem, viz. a cross. Luke wants his readers to make sure that they understand what believing in Jesus is all about.

Meditation: In which three ways do you characterize yourself as a disciple of Jesus?

Prayer: God of suffering, death, and resurrection, through Jesus you issued a call and demonstrated a way of life for all people. Guide us in our life's journey. Form us into disciples intent on proclaiming the kingdom, where you live and reign with Jesus, your Son, and the Holy Spirit, one God, for ever and ever. Amen.

SECURITY

Matthew 8:18-22

Scripture: "Foxes have dens and birds of the sky have nests, but the Son of Man has nowhere to lay his head" (Matthew 8:20).

Reflection: After narrating the cleansing of a leper, the healing of a centurion's servant, the cure of Peter's mother-in-law, and other miscellaneous healings, Matthew inserts two responses to two statements from "would-be" followers of Jesus before resuming his narrative with the calming of the storm at sea, the healing of the Gadarene demoniacs, and the healing of a paralytic. The two statements and responses are from Q (an abbreviation for "Quelle," the German word for "source"); both of these statements and their responses are found in Luke (9:57-62), who records a third statement and response, which Matthew has edited out.

It is important to note that it is a scribe who approaches Jesus and says, "Teacher, I will follow you wherever you go" (8:19). Scribes play a major role in all the Synoptic Gospels, but more so in Matthew's Gospel.

The Jewish scribe was the scholar and the intellectual. His knowledge was of the Law, which was considered the supreme wisdom and the only true learning. He held a respected position in the community. Like the Pharisees, and sometimes Pharisees themselves, they adhered to a strict interpretation of the law. In chapter 23 of Matthew's Gospel, Jesus issues a strong denunciation of the scribes.

Matthew is not narrating historical events; he is interested in his own community at the time he was writing. Since most of his readers were Jewish in background, they knew the position of leadership that the scribes had once held. In his own unique style, Matthew is warning them about being like the scribes.

This scribe addresses Jesus as "Teacher," a title which Jesus uses of himself in this Gospel. However, when someone else — an opponent — uses it in the Gospel, it designates one who does not really understand.

The scribe in this section knows Jesus to be a teacher, and he is willing to follow him wherever he goes. This is laudatory, but it is for the wrong reason. The scribe is well-disposed, but has not grasped the costs of discipleship, which for Matthew consists of righteousness: knowing, accepting and doing the will of God.

Jesus, therefore, challenges him with security. He is already secure in his strict interpretation and knowledge of the Law. Jesus pulls out the rug of any security and declares that an authentic follower is less secure than the foxes and the birds. These have dens and nests where they are secure, but Jesus, and consequently his followers, have no such security.

Those in authority, those with knowledge, those who are considered to be learned and wise, according to Matthew, are not necessarily the righteous, the authentic followers of Jesus.

"Therefore, do and observe whatever they tell you, but do not follow their example, for they talk but they do not act" (23:3). An authentic follower of Jesus finds security in doing the will of the Father, practicing righteousness.

Meditation: In which ways do you seek security in "right" answers instead of in righteousness — or "right" behavior?

Prayer: God our teacher, through Moses and the prophets you delivered your Law, the Torah, to your people. Through Jesus, your Son, you revealed your righteousness. Make of us authentic disciples. May we find our security in doing your will. We ask this through our Lord Jesus Christ, who lives and reigns with you and the Holy Spirit, one God, for ever and ever. Amen.

EARTHQUAKE

Matthew 8:23-27

Scripture: "What sort of man is this, that even the winds and sea obey him?" (Matthew 8:27).

Reflection: Matthew borrows Mark's account of the calming of a storm at sea and rewrites it to fit his own purpose (Mark 4:35-41; Matthew 8:23-27). In Mark's Gospel the account functions as a new Genesis creation story. The book of Genesis begins with God bringing order from the chaotic waters. When Jesus rebukes the winds and the sea and a great calm follows, Mark is "secretly" declaring Jesus to be God. He has implicitly answered the explicit question presented to the reader by the disciples, "Who then is this that even wind and sea obey him?" (Mark 4:41) Thus, for Mark, Jesus is the God who brings order out of chaos.

In his rewritten version of Mark's story, Matthew adds his own touches to the account. First, instead of Mark's "violent squall," Matthew uses "a violent storm," which, in Greek, is often used to refer to an earthquake. The Greek form of this word is commonly used in apocalyptic literature to indicate the shaking of the old world when God would bring forth his kingdom and "make all things new." It is used by all synoptics in reference to events preceding the coming of the Son of Man on the clouds of heaven (Matthew 24:7; Mark 13:8; and Luke 21:11). However, Matthew has introduced it in this narrative. He will reuse it in his account of the death and resurrection of Jesus

75

(27:51; 28:2). For Matthew, Jesus' calming of the earthquake at sea "predicts" the earthquake of his death and resurrection. In other words, God's kingdom is present now.

Second, Mark's disciples rebuke Jesus, who is asleep on a cushion in the stern of the boat: "Teacher, doesn't it matter to you that we are going to die?" (Mark 4:38). Matthew's disciples reverently plead with Jesus: "Lord, save us! We are going to die!" (Matthew 8:25). Mark's disciples never figure out who Jesus really is. Matthew's disciples have already identified Jesus, and they call on him for help.

Mark's story ends with the question, "Who then is this?" (4:41). Matthew's story ends with the question, "What sort of man is this?" (8:27).

Third, after he quiets the wind and calms the sea, Jesus asks the disciples in the Gospel of Mark, "Why are you so afraid? Do you not yet have faith?" (Mark 4:40). Before he rebukes the winds and the sea, the Matthean Jesus asks the disciples, "Why are you so afraid, O you of little faith?" (Matthew 8:26). For Matthew, the "O you of little faith" phrase is meant to echo the section of Jesus' first sermon which deals with dependence on God (Matthew 6:25-34). Matthew is stating that God always provides for the needs — food, drink, clothes — of his people, if they but trust him and cease their worry and fear. No matter how violent the storms of life may be, Jesus is there in the boat; he calms and strengthens those who authentically believe.

Meditation: In which most recent and violent storm (earthquake) of your life have you experienced the quieting and calming presence of Jesus?

Prayer: God of the sea, in the beginning when the wind of your spirit hovered over the waters of chaos, you brought forth order and life. Jesus, the author of the new creation, taught that fear flees before authentic faith. Give us this faith. When the storms of life threaten us, when the waves of doubt swamp us, remind us of the presence of the kingdom, where you live and reign with your Son, our Lord Jesus Christ, and your Holy Spirit, one God, for ever and ever. Amen.

CONQUEROR OF EVIL

Matthew 8:28-34

Scripture: The demons pleaded with him, "If you drive us out, send us into the herd of swine." And he said to them, "Be gone!" When they came out they entered the swine, and behold, the whole herd rushed down the steep slope into the sea where they drowned (Matthew 8:31-32).

Reflection: Matthew's account of the healing of the Gadarene demoniacs (8:28-34) is a rewritten, condensed, and edited version of Mark's healing of the Gerasene demoniac (5:1-20). In Mark's Gospel, this account is the longest and most detailed of the exorcism stories. Its geographical setting is in the territory of the Gerasenes, that is, in pagan (Gentile) territory. Only one man was possessed by an unclean spirit, which was identified as Legion — a reference to the Roman occupation forces. By sending the unclean spirit(s) into the pigs, Mark humorously calls the Romans pigs.

After the exorcism, the man sat clothed and in his right mind — the same position of the young man in the resurrection account (16:5). Finally, the exorcised man became a disciple and was sent off by Jesus to announce all that the Lord in his pity had done for him.

For Mark, then, this story has multiple functions: it places Jesus in Gentile territory and validates the early Church's mission to the Gentiles; it pokes fun at the Roman occupation forces; it points toward the resurrection; and it validates Gentile discipleship.

Since Matthew is not interested in these points, he is free to shorten the account and emphasize only those things which pertain to his Gospel. The geographical setting is Gadara, a Gentile territory. Matthew, fond of doubling Mark's single characters, changes the one man with an unclean spirit to two demoniacs.

Mark's ironic humor at the expense of the Roman occupation forces does not interest Matthew, so he eliminates all of these details. Since he has already established a mission to the Gentiles in the visit of the magi narrative (1:1-12) and in the healing of a centurion's servant story (8:5-13), there is no need to make exorcised demoniacs disciples of Jesus. Finally, the Marcan resurrection echo has been taken away entirely as well as the other graphic details concerning the possession and the cure.

While he has removed much of Mark's original story, Matthew has added some of his own elements as well. As already mentioned above, this author enjoys doubling characters. This is done with many of Mark's stories. The demons cry to Jesus, "Have you come here to torment us before the appointed time?" (8:29) In Jewish apocryphal literature, there is a notion that evil spirits were allowed by God to afflict human beings until the time of the final judgment. Matthew is using this notion in a different sense: his interest in the "appointed time" throughout the Gospel refers to his last judgment scene (25:31-46) as well as the apocalyptic events surrounding Jesus' death (27:51-53) and resurrection (28:2-4).

As in Mark, the swine in Matthew all rush down a steep bank into the sea where they drown. The reader must remember that in Judaism the tending of pigs was forbidden because they were considered unclean. Anyone who was considered a swineherd was also considered to be a Jewish apostate; such a person had "gone over to the Gentiles."

For Matthew, Jesus already defeated Satan, demons, and all that is evil. In the desert, Jesus, like Israel of old, was tempted for forty days and forty nights. He has conquered all that is evil. Satan and his demons drown themselves before him. His power as Son of God has eliminated evil and given it the same status as swine.

Meditation: In which ways have you experienced Jesus eliminating evil from your life?

Prayer: God of power and might, after forty years of testing in the desert, you led your chosen people into the promised land. After forty days and forty nights in the wilderness, you led your Son, Jesus, the conqueror of evil, to your people to teach them how to live. May we learn from his teachings and follow his ways. We ask this through Christ our Lord. Amen.

AUTHORITY TO FORGIVE

Matthew 9:1-8

Scripture: When the crowds saw this they were struck with awe and glorified God who had given such authority to human beings (Matthew 9:8).

Reflection: The narrative of the healing of a paralytic in Matthew (9:1-8) is a condensed version of Mark's account of a healing of a paralytic (2:1-12). Matthew has eliminated the account of removing the roof and lowering the man down on the mat. Matthew has also edited some of the material surrounding the issue of blasphemy; in his community everyone would have known that God alone had the power to forgive sins.

In Jewish understanding physical illness was a manifestation of sin. Someone, the person himself or his parents had sinned, and the paralysis was God's way of punishing that sin. Illness and sin are both dealt with in the narrative.

Matthew's thrust, however, is directed toward the community's role in the forgiveness of sins. In his unique declaration to Peter, Jesus states, "Whatever you bind on earth shall be bound in heaven; and whatever you loose on earth shall be loosed in heaven" (16:19). This same sentence is repeated in the story of a brother who sins (18:18). Matthew's community is claiming authority to forgive sin. This is indicated by the end of the healing of a paralytic section. In Mark, the crowd is astounded and glorify God, saying, "We have never seen anything like this"

(2:12). In Matthew, the crowds "were struck with awe and glorified God who had given such authority to human beings" (9:8).

In Matthew's church the forgiveness of sins has been entrusted to the community, human beings. When it acts, God acts. God mediates forgiveness through people. The community is the "body of Christ," if a Pauline metaphor can be used. "Where two or three are gathered in my name, there am I in the midst of them" (18:20), is a Matthean metaphor. This identification of God and Jesus with the community is brought to a peak in the judgment of the nations account.

The Son of Man declares, "Whatever you did for one of these least brothers (or sisters) of mine, you did for me.... What you did not do for one of these least ones, you did not do for me" (25:40, 45).

In the account of the healing of the paralytic, Matthew is telling the reader that not only God has the power to forgive sins, but people have the ability to forgive sins. God acts through people to bring his healing and forgiveness to the world. For one person to refuse to forgive another is to refuse to permit God to continue the forgiveness which he brought about through Jesus.

Meditation: In which recent way did you experience God's forgiveness as mediated through the Church and/or another person?

Prayer: God of healing, you sent Jesus, your Son, to reconcile the world. He taught us how to experience your forgiveness — by forgiving each other. Give us the faith we need to welcome back those who sin. Give us the courage we need to return when we stumble and fall. May we always glorify you, the one God — Father, Son, and Holy Spirit — who has given such authority to human beings, now and for ever and ever. Amen.

MERCY, NOT SACRIFICE

Matthew 9:9-13

Scripture: "Go and learn the meaning of the words, 'I de-sire mercy and not sacrifice'" (Matthew 9:13).

Reflection: The call of Matthew in Matthew's Gospel (9:9-13) is taken almost word for word from Mark's Gospel (2:13-17).

Two changes have been made by Matthew in the Marcan original.

First, Matthew has changed Mark's Levi to Matthew, because no Levi appears in the lists of the twelve companions of Jesus. For whatever reason, Matthew believed that he was correcting Mark's Gospel.

Second, Matthew adds the sentence, "Go and learn the meaning of the words, 'I desire mercy and not sacrifice'" (9:13), to Mark's account. These words, taken from the prophet Hosea (6:6), form a call to the Israelites to sincere conversion.

The Temple sacrifice of animals was held in high esteem. Still Hosea declares that mercy is superior to sacrifice. Jesus, in this passage from Matthew's Gospel, also takes the position that mercy is superior to sacrifice.

This becomes especially important to Matthew's community after the year 70 A.D. when the Temple was destroyed by the Romans. When Matthew wrote his Gospel, he gave the words of Hosea a new interpretation. They now apply to followers of Jesus. The mercy shown by one person to another is what God wants. If God would have sacrifices, he would not have permitted the Temple to have been destroyed.

If this is true, then the laws of ritual impurity are also of lesser importance than mercy. Jesus eats with tax collectors — specifically Matthew — and sinners. Tax collectors are Jewish apostates; they are Jews who work for the Romans. They sit at the customs post and collect the Roman tax. They make their own living by raising the tax and pocketing the difference. Anyone who sits down at table and eats with them is considered to be contaminated by them. Jesus eats with tax collectors and sinners. Therefore, according to the law, he is ritually impure.

But Matthew, a tax collector, is called by Jesus to follow him. Matthew leaves his post and follows. Matthew should not have responded this way. Jesus should not have sat down at table with him. In the kingdom of heaven, however, all is reversed. God is a God of mercy; as he shows mercy to people and calls them to be disciples of his Son, so he declares that people do the same for each other. Those who are righteous have no need for the divine physician; only sinners need to be healed.

Meditation: Who are the tax collectors and sinners of today whom Jesus calls to table fellowship?

Prayer: God of tax collectors and sinners, you call all people to follow the teaching of your Son, Jesus. Open our ears to hear your voice. Gather us around the table of your fellowship. Help us to trust your divine and eternal mercy. We ask this through our Lord Jesus Christ, who lives and reigns with you and the Holy Spirit, one God, for ever and ever. Amen.

FASTING

Matthew 9:14-17

Scripture: "The wedding guests cannot mourn as long as the bridegroom is with them" (Matthew 9:15).

Reflection: The narrative surrounding the question of fasting in Matthew has been borrowed from Mark (2:18-22). Other than a few minor editorial changes, Matthew preserves Mark's story intact.

For Matthew, the question of fasting echoes the teaching about fasting, which is found in the first sermon of Jesus (6:16-18). There fasting is upheld as one of three religious acts of Jewish piety: prayer, fasting, and almsgiving. A person's righteousness is expressed by fasting, which represents one's dependence upon God.

Furthermore, a person fasts in order that those who have nothing might have something; one does without some so that others can have some. Matthew cautions, however, that fasting is not done for the individual's benefit but for the sake of the preservation of the community.

The question of fasting for Matthew's community is a legitimate one. Using the bridal metaphor, Matthew explains that fasting is out of place during a marriage feast, a reference to the kingdom of heaven. In the prophets, God is considered the bridegroom and Israel is his bride. The fullness of the kingdom is depicted as a marriage banquet.

According to Matthew, the marriage feast reached its fullness in Jesus. He is the bridegroom and those who follow him are the bride. By stating this, Matthew subtly declares Jesus' divinity and re-emphasizes the proclamation of the kingdom.

In Matthew's community, fasting has not lost its importance. "The days will come when the bridegroom is taken away from them, and then they will fast" (9:15). Fasting, as a sign of mourning, is as inappropriate during the days of Jesus as patching an old cloak with a piece of unshrunken cloth or pouring new wine into old wineskins.

What is Matthew saying? He is declaring that fasting is still a legitimate practice, if it is done at the right times and for the right reasons. The disciples of John and the Pharisees were fasting out of mourning. While upholding the practice of fasting, Matthew wants his community to realize that Jesus initiated the kingdom (new wine) and that the reason to fast must be commensurate with this fact (new wineskin).

During the time of Matthew's church, when Jesus is no longer with them, fasting is appropriate as long as it looks forward to the culmination of the kingdom. Together, the members of the community join in fasting — not for an individual's own merit — because they are dependent on God and upon each other. Thus fasting draws them closer together as the bride awaiting the bridegroom's return.

Meditation: How often and why do you fast?

Prayer: God of the kingdom, you have chosen all people on the earth to be your own. Through Jesus, your servant and your Son, you proclaimed the presence of your kingdom. Form your people into a faithful bride. Make our fasting pleasing in your sight, as we wait in joyful hope for the coming of the bridegroom, Jesus Christ, who lives and reigns with you and the Holy Spirit, one God, for ever and ever. Amen.

CHILDLIKE WISDOM
Matthew 11:25-30

Scripture: "I praise you, Father, Lord of heaven and earth, because you hid these things from the wise and the learned and revealed them to the merest childlike" (Matthew 11:25).

Reflection: The section of Matthew's Gospel referred to as the praise of the Father (11:25-27) is taken from Q, and, therefore, has a parallel in Luke (10:21-22). The placement of the verse within the whole Gospel reveals the evangelist's understanding and use of the verses.

Matthew places these verses after Jesus reproaches the unrepentant towns of Chorazin, Bethsaida, and Capernaum. In the midst of unbelief, Matthew records a note of joy — typical of Matthean style.

The "wise and the learned" refer to the scribes and the Pharisees, who play prominent roles throughout the Gospel.

They reject Jesus' preaching and his deeds. Of course, Matthew is not interested in specific scribes and Pharisees whom he once may have known, but those of his community who continued to believe that the way to righteousness consisted of adhering strictly to the Law. Scribes and Pharisees represent those who burden others with the Law. "They tie up heavy burdens (hard to carry) and lay them on people's shoulders, but they won't lift a finger to move them" (23:4).

85

Authentic followers of Jesus are "childlike." A child represents powerlessness and dependence. Those who relinquish their power and independence trust in God alone. These receive the Son's revelation of the Father; all things are handed over to the righteous, the childlike.

Authentic followers of Jesus accept his yoke in contrast to that of the burden of the scribes and Pharisees. Jesus' yoke is easy and his burden is light; it consists of obedience to his word. Such obedience to Jesus' teaching is the way of righteousness for Matthew.

"Come to me, all you who are weary and burdened, and I will refresh you" (11:28), Jesus declares in the Gospel of Matthew. "Take my yoke upon you and learn from me, for I am gentle and humble of heart; and you will find rest for your souls. For my yoke is easy, and my burden light" (11:29-30). These uniquely Matthean verses echo the wisdom found in the book of Sirach.

"Come aside to me, you untutored, and take up lodging in the house of instruction.... Submit your neck to her yoke, that your mind may accept her teaching" (Sirach 51:23, 26).

According to Matthew, the authentic follower of Jesus is the wise person who builds a house on the rock (7:24) of the gentleness and humility of the teacher, Jesus.

Meditation: In which ways do you find that you obey the wisdom taught by Jesus?

Prayer: Praise to you, Father, Lord of heaven and earth. From the learned and the clever you hide your wisdom, but to the childlike you reveal everything. Make us obedient to the word of your Son. May our labor always be inspired by his teaching and our burden be doing your will. Give us rest as we come to know you and the Son you have sent, Jesus Christ, who is Lord for ever and ever. Amen.

HOMETOWN REJECTION

Mark 6:1-6

Scripture: "Where did this man get all this? What kind of wisdom has been given him that such mighty works should come from his hands! Isn't he the carpenter, the son of Mary, and the brother of James and Joses and Judas and Simon? And aren't his sisters right here among us?" (Mark 6:2-3)

Reflection: The first six verses of chapter six of Mark's Gospel narrate the rejection of Jesus at Nazareth, his native place. In the very place where he should have been accepted and understood, Jesus is rejected. The people take offence at him.

They question what he teaches and with what wisdom he teaches. The answer is not as important to an historical crowd in a synagogue on some specific Sabbath in Nazareth as it was to the community for whom Mark wrote his Gospel.

In Mark, Jesus teaches outside of the Jewish tradition, where truth is not supposed to be found. But what is discovered is that that is where truth exists. Jesus speaks in his own name; a teacher usually speaks in the name of his teachers. These facts in the Marcan community raise the question about authority. Where did Jesus get his authority to teach without having been taught, that is, without being grounded in tradition?

Mark answers this question by placing these words on Jesus' lips: "A prophet is not without honor except in his native place and among his own kin and in his own house" (6:4). In other words, just as in the past God spoke his word through the prophets, who were rejected by the people, so now he speaks his word through Jesus, the greatest of the prophets, who is rejected by his own people. Jesus' authority, like that of the prophets of old, comes from God.

The people see a carpenter; no other Gospel refers to Jesus as a carpenter. This is Mark's way of contrasting Jesus' authority with his lack of ancestry.

The people refer to Jesus as just another common, hometown boy with brothers and sisters in their midst. This is Mark's way of contrasting Jesus' uniqueness to that of the common crowd.

The lack of faith on the part of the crowd distresses Jesus. Mark is warning his readers not to look for great displays of power in order to believe. For Mark, faith comes through powerlessness. The prophet Jesus, who is without honor in his native place, will be put to death. Those who lay claim to discipleship must be willing to relinquish all power in order to profess faith.

Meditation: In which ways is Jesus rejected by his own people today?

Prayer: God of the prophets, you spoke your words through your messengers, the prophets, in times past. In our own day you have revealed yourself in the teaching of Jesus of Nazareth. Open our ears to hear his word. Make our hearts receptive to his call. Enable us to receive him in faith. We ask this though Christ our Lord. Amen.

THE KINGDOM IS AT HAND

Luke 10:1-12, 17-20

Scripture: "Say to them, 'The kingdom of God is at hand for you...' Know this: the kingdom of God is at hand" (Luke 10:9, 11).

Reflection: Once Jesus begins his journey to Jerusalem in Luke's Gospel and he begins to separate his would-be followers, he sends out seventy-two on a mission. This sending of seventy-two (some manuscripts read "seventy") is unique to Luke. While it is similar to the mission of the twelve (9:1-6), it displays Luke's missionary concern to carry the Gospel to the ends of the earth. This latter theme is fully developed in Luke's second volume, the Acts of the Apostles.

Luke's mention of seventy-two others echoes the selection of the seventy elders by Moses (Numbers 11:16-30). Two more elders were not at the gathering when God placed some of Moses' spirit upon the seventy, but these two others, Eldad and Medad, received the spirit anyway. Thus, seventy-two come to share "the burden of the people" (Numbers 11:17) with Moses.

In Luke, Jesus sends out seventy-two to proclaim that the kingdom of God is at hand. In Luke's understanding, the kingdom of God is present now. Therefore, there is an urgency about the mission. A single-mindedness is required of the seventy-two — symbolic of the early Christian missionaries; they cannot have any attachment to material possessions. Even customary greetings are eliminated in order to focus solely on the proclamation of the kingdom of God.

Nothing is to get in the way of the missionaries. If they are not enthusiastically received, then they are to shake the dust from their feet and move on — after having proclaimed the presence of the kingdom of God.

Luke wants his readers to understand that they are the new missionaries. They are responsible for continuing the work of proclaiming the kingdom: "The harvest is abundant but the laborers are few" (10:2). Luke promises them success. As the kingdom of God gradually grows, evil is defeated. "I have observed Satan fall like lightning from the sky" (10:18), Jesus declares to the seventy-two upon their return.

Just as Jesus was successful during his temptation (4:1-13) and overcame the devil, so the group of followers of Jesus, the Church, is successful in its proclamation of the kingdom of God.

Later in his Gospel, during the passion narrative, Luke brings forth his missionary concern again. Before Jesus goes to the Mount of Olives, he instructs his apostles to be prepared for the opposition that they would face when they proclaim the kingdom of God (Luke 22:35-38). While there is success in spreading the kingdom, missionaries encounter hostility, like Jesus. They are "like lambs among wolves" (10:3).

Meditation: In what ways are you a missionary who proclaims the kingdom of God?

Prayer: God of the kingdom, you have never ceased to call men and women to be messengers of your good news to your people. The harvest is abundant, but the laborers are few. We ask you to send out laborers for the harvest. Fill all people with your spirit of mission that your kingdom may continue to grow throughout the world. We ask this through our Lord Jesus Christ, your Son, who lives and reigns with you and the Holy Spirit, one God, for ever and ever. Amen.

LIFE-GIVING NEWNESS

Matthew 9:18-26

Scripture: An official came forward, knelt down before him, and said: "My daughter has just died. But come, lay your hand on her, and she will live." ... He came and took her by the hand, and the little girl got up (Matthew 9:18, 25).

Reflection: Matthew's narrative concerning a dead official's daughter and the cure of a woman suffering hemorrhages for twelve years (9:18-26) is a much shortened version of Mark's story about Jairus' daughter at the point of death and the detailed account of how the woman with the hemorrhages plotted the way she would touch Jesus' cloak and be healed (5:21-43).

Matthew has abbreviated Mark's account in order to serve his own purposes. Matthew is interested in showing that when a person professes faith, healing is the outcome. Mark is interested in Jesus' display of power — which he subverts in the second half of his Gospel. In order to accomplish his own purposes, Matthew makes a number of changes.

First, in Mark the daughter is near death. Matthew heightens the faith of the official by portraying his daughter as already dead. Thus, the official asks for a resuscitation.

Second, meanwhile the word of Jesus confronts the woman suffering hemorrhages for twelve years. The details concerning the rebuke of the disciples as well as the flow-of-power aspect of Mark's story have been omitted by Matthew. In Matthew, Jesus knows the woman; he declares that her faith has saved her.

Third, when in Matthew Jesus arrives at the official's house he does so without the inner group of disciples — Peter, James, and John — as in Mark. Other than Matthew's own unique description of flute players and a crowd making a commotion (9:23), there are no details. Matthew is not interested in a miracle for its own sake; he is interested in it for the sake of faith.

In Matthew, Jesus says nothing to the little girl. He merely takes her by the hand and she gets up. All of Mark's "messianic secret" has been deleted by Matthew. "News of this spread throughout all that land" (9:26). For Matthew, revelation is not secret; it is public.

In relating these healings, Matthew is interested in showing the life-giving newness which the word of Jesus brings. Those who hear and believe in his word are healed. Like the woman, who was ostracized from her religious community because of her ritually unclean flow of blood, and like the girl who was separated from the community by death, those who profess faith in Jesus are restored to the body of believers. In this narrative Matthew has emphasized the importance of preserving the community of believers.

One more uniquely Matthean addition to this narrative needs recognition. The woman with the hemorrhages touches the tassel on Jesus' cloak. A tassel or fringe was prescribed by the Mosaic law as a reminder for one to keep the commandments; it was also a sign of Jewish piety.

Why did Matthew add this detail when he omitted so many other details of Mark's story? Matthew is interested in showing the continuity between the old and the new (13:52). He wants to demonstrate a balance. By situating the old in a new perspective, Matthew attempts to offer a balanced approach to his community.

Matthew has accomplished this by taking Mark's old story and rewriting it in a new way. He has also recast the figure of

Jesus. In Matthew, Jesus does not abolish the law or the prophets, but he fulfills them (5:17). Those who hear the word of Jesus and act on it (profess faith) share in the new life that Jesus brings to an old community.

Meditation: In which ways have you experienced new life after hearing the word and acting on it? Or, in which ways has the word of Jesus awakened you from sleep?

Prayer: God of healing, you spoke your word through the Law and the prophets; now, you speak through your Son. When we fall asleep, awaken us to hear his teaching again. When we are in need of healing, turn us toward authentic faith. May we come to recognize your continuous revelation in our lives. We ask this through Christ, our Lord. Amen.

SHEPHERDLESS SHEEP

Matthew 9:32-38

Scripture: Jesus went around to all the towns and villages, teaching in their synagogues, proclaiming the good news of the kingdom, and healing every disease and illness (Matthew 9:35).

Reflection: The last four verses of chapter nine of Matthew's Gospel can be divided into three units. The first two units are closely connected and the third unit prepares for the mission of the twelve in chapter ten.

The first unit (9:35) consists of a Matthean summary statement of the activity surrounding Jesus' ministry of teaching, proclaiming the kingdom of God, and healing. An almost identical statement was used at the end of chapter 4 (v. 23) to conclude Matthew's introduction to Jesus' Galilean ministry before the delivery of Jesus' first sermon. In chapters 5-7 (the first sermon) Matthew portrays Jesus as the preacher of the word; in chapters 8-9 he presents Jesus as the doer of the word. In this way, Matthew presents Jesus as a model to be imitated by his community.

The second unit (9:36) is connected to the first insofar as it relates the pity that Jesus has for the crowds and how they "were troubled and helpless, like a sheep without a shepherd." Mark compares the crowd to sheep without a shepherd before he narrates the feeding of the five thousand (Mark 6:34). Matthew has probably borrowed this comparison from Mark but is using it to echo Old Testament images, a favorite Matthean technique.

In the book of Numbers, Moses asks God to set over the community a man who will act as their leader in order "that the Lord's community may not be like sheep without a shepherd" (27:17). Joshua is then appointed as Moses' successor. Matthew is declaring that Jesus is the new leader of the community, and it is no accident that his name in Hebrew is Joshua, which means "Yahweh helps" or "Yahweh saves" (cf. Matthew 1:21). In the first book of Kings, Micaiah refuses to make the same prophecy as the other prophets concerning the outcome of an attack against Ramoth-gilead. Micaiah declares, "I see all Israel scattered on the mountains, like sheep without a shepherd, and the Lord saying, 'These have no master! Let each of them go back home in peace'" (1 Kings 22:17). Ahab, the King of Israel, pays no attention to Micaiah, whom he has thrown in prison and fed rations of bread and water. Ahab is slain in the ensuing battle. Matthew is warning his community to listen to Jesus, a great prophet like Micaiah, lest they, like Ahab, mistakenly enter into the battle of life without having listened to the word of God and lose.

The third unit (9:37-38) is from Q (cf. Luke 10:2). Luke uses these verses to introduce the mission of the seventy-two. Matthew uses them to introduce the mission of the twelve.

In this passage Jesus instructs his disciples, "The harvest is plentiful but the laborers are few; so implore the lord of the harvest to send out laborers for his harvest" (9:37-38). If the "lord of the harvest," a metaphor for the "end of the age" (Matthew 13:40), is God, then this instruction presupposes that only God can take the initiative and send out laborers — teachers, preachers, and healers. However, in chapter ten, after naming the twelve, Jesus sends them out.

In Matthew's community, Jesus has become the lord of the harvest, whose return is expected. So, Matthew is instructing his community to teach, preach and heal as Jesus did. By making Jesus lord of the harvest, Matthew is also making a subtle statement concerning Jesus' divinity.

Meditation: Today, what groups of people are like sheep without a shepherd? How do you think you can encourage leaders who will teach, preach, and heal these groups?

Prayer: God our shepherd, we are the sheep of your pasture where you give us repose. Beside restful waters you lead us, and you guide us in the right paths. Through the teaching and preaching of Jesus, you have spread the table of your word before us, anointed us with your Spirit, and made the cup of our lives overflow. May your goodness and kindness follow us all the days of our lives. After the harvest bring us to dwell for years to come in your house, where you live and reign with Jesus, your Son, and the Holy Spirit, one God for ever and ever. Amen.

THE TWELVE

Matthew 10:1-7

Scripture: Now these are the names of the twelve apostles: first, Simon who is called Peter, and his brother Andrew; James the son of Zebedee and his brother John; Philip and Bartholomew, Thomas and Matthew the tax collector; James, the son of Alphaeus, and Thaddeus; Simon the Zealot, and Judas Iscariot who handed him over (Matthew 10:2-4).

Reflection: Both Mark (3:13-14) and Luke (6:12-16) portray Jesus as going up onto a mountain and choosing the Twelve.

Matthew has no such scene; he presumes that the group is already known to the reader of his Gospel. Therefore, he begins with a summons of the twelve disciples by Jesus.

Some distinction needs to be made between the "Twelve," "apostles," and "disciples." These were probably three separate groups which became closely associated through oral tradition and were finally synchronized in written tradition.

Luke (6:13) seems to distinguish between a larger group of "disciples" and "Twelve," who are named apostles. Mark (4:10, 34) also distinguishes between "disciples" and the "Twelve." Throughout Matthew's Gospel, there is an association of "disciples" and the "Twelve." Only in 10:2 does Matthew equate "Twelve" and "apostles." Since the word "apostle" means "one who is sent," and Matthew's next scene is the sending out of these "Twelve," he employs the term to fit his own situation.

The obvious significance of the "Twelve" for Matthew stems from the Old Testament twelve tribes of Israel. In scenes from the Infancy Narratives and in the five sermons that Jesus preaches, Matthew continuously echoes the story of Moses. Just as Moses led the twelve tribes from slavery to freedom, Jesus, the new Moses, continues the pilgrimage to freedom with the "Twelve." Jesus calls all people, especially Israel, into the kingdom.

While the list of Matthew's "Twelve" is close to Mark's "Twelve" and Luke's "Twelve," there is one important point that needs to be made. The Matthew who appears in the synoptics' lists is mentioned as the tax collector only by Matthew, the writer of the Gospel. Both Mark (2:14) and Luke (5:27) call the tax collector Levi, but neither mention him in their list of the "Twelve."

The "Twelve," according to Matthew, share the same authority as Jesus. They are able to exorcise and to cure. They, however, do not teach until after Jesus' resurrection (Matthew 28:20). Only after the resurrection are they fully instructed. Only after people have been fully instructed and baptized into the mission of Jesus are they commissioned to teach, according to Matthew.

After the "Twelve" are named, Jesus begins the second of his five sermons. This second one is commonly referred to as the missionary discourse. It deals with the missionary activity of the disciples (vs. 5-15) but then moves quickly into the missionary activity of the Church during the time between the resurrection and the second coming of Christ.

The first bit of instruction given by Jesus points the "Twelve" toward "the lost sheep of the house of Israel" (10:6). This theme is in keeping with Jesus' own mission: "I was sent only to the lost sheep of the house of Israel" (15:24). It represents a probable historical limitation that Jesus observed during his ministry.

Matthew, of course, is not interested in limiting missionary activity in this way, but he must be faithful to this historical detail in order to maintain credibility with his reader. He steers a middle course by expanding the mission to the Gentiles, a mission already in operation at the time that he was writing, by portraying the Gentile magi as worshiping the newborn king (2:1-12), as well as the healing of a centurion's servant (8:5-13) and the Gadarene demoniac (8:28-34). In other words, Matthew is attempting to justify the mission to the Gentiles, which was taking place in his community at the time he was writing, by portraying Jesus' ministering to the Gentiles.

The message with which the "Twelve" are entrusted — "The kingdom of heaven is at hand" (10:7) — is the same as that of John the Baptist (3:2) and Jesus (4:17). In Matthew, then, there is a continuity of the proclamation from one generation to the next. What was handed on to Jesus by the Baptizer, was, in turn, passed on to the "Twelve," and is now the responsibility of every authentic follower of Jesus — Jewish-Christian and Gentile-Christian alike.

Meditation: In which ways have you been commissioned as an apostle, "one who is sent"?

Prayer: God of apostles, throughout time you have called men and women to hear your word, and, then, you have sent them to others with your good news. Your Son, Jesus, chose twelve, instructed them, and sent them forth with his teaching. Through the waters of baptism you have called us. Help us to listen attentively to your word and to bring it faithfully to all to whom we are sent. We ask this through our Lord Jesus Christ, who lives and reigns with you and the Holy Spirit, one God, for ever and ever. Amen.

FREE GIFTS

Matthew 10:7-15

Scripture: "Freely you have received; freely you are to give" (Matthew 10:8).

Reflection: The second of Jesus' sermons in Matthew's Gospel consists of the missionary discourse, which includes the commissioning and instructing of the Twelve. What Jesus says to the Twelve is addressed to those who were proclaiming that the kingdom of heaven was at hand at the time that Matthew was writing his Gospel. What Jesus says to the Twelve is also addressed to every Christian, who, by the fact of baptism (cf. Matthew 28:16-20), is a missioner today. A follower of Jesus continues to do what Jesus did. He or she cures the sick, raises the dead, cleanses lepers, and drives out demons. These gifts, which have been freely conferred by God, are to be freely given away. Since it cost the disciples nothing to receive the gifts, they are to mirror their master and set no price on their use. "Freely you have received; freely you are to give" (10:8).

The worthiness of the host is judged by his or her acceptance of both the missionary and the message of the missioner. In other words, hospitality and faith are intimately connected. Therefore, Jesus instructs his followers-missioners to "look for a worthy person... and stay there until you leave.... Whoever will not receive you or listen to your words — when you leave that house or town, shake the dust from your feet" (10:11, 14). By shaking dust from their feet, the missionary disassociates himself or herself from unbelievers and declares that no hospitality or faith has been found there.

103

The instruction to wish peace to the house which is entered carries with it a corresponding promise that the greeting will manifest itself as effective. In this way, the missioner is like the Old Testament prophets, whose words were effective. If there is no worthy recipient in the house which is offered the gift of peace, then the offerer will receive it back and forsake that house. Peace, in other words, is the reward for hospitality and faith.

In the last verse (15) of this selection, Matthew returns to one his favorite themes — judgment: "Amen, I say to you, it will be more tolerable for the land of Sodom and Gomorrah on the day of judgment than for that town" (10:15) which does not receive or listen to the words of the missioner. For Matthew, judgment is hard on those who hear the good news of the kingdom but fail to act on it. Sodom and Gomorrah, the Old Testament book of Genesis' example of the epitome of sin, will get off easier on the day of judgment than those people who hear and do not practice the word of Jesus as it is proclaimed by his followers-missioners.

The supreme harshness of judgment for those who fail to act on what they have heard occurs when the nations are judged. To those who did nothing, Jesus will declare, "'I was hungry and you gave me no food, I was thirsty and you gave me no drink, a stranger and you gave me no welcome, naked and you gave me no clothing, ill and in prison, and you did not care for me....' These will go off to eternal punishment" (25:42-43, 46).

Meditation: Today, in which ways do you function as a missionary and cure the sick, raise the dead, cleanse lepers, and drive out demons?

Prayer: God of missioners, you have shared with us the message of your kingdom through the preaching and teaching of Jesus, your Son. Enable us to share with others the good news that you have given us. Through the working of your Holy Spirit, set us on fire with your peace that we may make your name known throughout the world by the way we live your word. We ask this through our Lord Jesus Christ, who lives and reigns with you and the Holy Spirit, one God, for ever and ever. Amen.

FAMILIAL BETRAYAL

Matthew 10:16-23

Scripture: "Brother will hand brother over to death, and the father his child; children will rise up against their parents and have them put to death" (Matthew 10:21).

Reflection: As Jesus continues his second sermon, commonly referred to as the missionary discourse, he speaks about persecution, which was taking place in Matthew's church at the time of the writing of this Gospel. As the church began to spread after the resurrection, those who professed belief in Jesus experienced hostility and rejection. Matthew characterizes their situation as being "like sheep in the midst of wolves" (10:16).

Persecution for the members of Matthew's community took various forms. Early believers were accused of being traitors to the state in the courts. Jewish-Christians were expelled from their own synagogues. Others were paraded before governors and kings and suffered such cruel deaths as being burned alive and used as lion fodder and dog food.

Belief in Jesus was a cause for division in families, a theme to which Jesus returns later in the sermon. Brothers and sisters betrayed each other to the authorities in order to save their own skins. Likewise, parents and children betrayed each other. Echoing the prophet Micah (7:6), Matthew is telling the members of his community that betrayal exists everywhere.

The betrayal theme will be fully explored in Matthew's account of the passion and death of Jesus, showing how Jesus himself was betrayed by everyone and experienced the ultimate tragedy. In the betrayal and tragic death of Jesus, Matthew declares, one must not lose sight of the resurrection. God does not wipe away human tragedy and death; God participates in it, ultimately overcoming it, and this gives it its redeeming quality.

Therefore, those who suffer persecution, betrayal and tragedy are being conformed to the likeness of Jesus, according to Matthew. When they are handed over, they are not to worry about what they are going to say or how they are going to defend themselves. The Spirit of the Father will speak through the persecuted members of the community.

"No disciple is above his teacher, no servant above his master. It is enough for the disciple to become like his teacher, and the servant to become like his master" (10:24-25).

If Jesus, who was betrayed and experienced tragedy, was accused of driving out demons by the prince of demons (9:34; 12:24), and he is the "master of the house" (10:25), then those who follow Jesus can expect nothing less than the same accusation, betrayal, and death. In a word, Matthew is exhorting the members of his community to remain faithful in the face of persecution to death. Just as God saved Jesus, he will also save those who are authentically faithful (cf. 10:22).

Meditation: In which ways do you experience persecution because you remain faithful to Jesus?

Prayer: Faithful God, throughout time you have kept the covenant you made with your chosen people. When the body of your Son, Jesus, hung betrayed and abandoned on the cross, you participated in this human tragedy and demonstrated your constant presence with your people. In the face of opposition and persecution send your Spirit to keep us faithful. Give us the words we are to speak, and conform us to the image of our master and teacher, Jesus Christ, who lives and reigns for ever and ever. Amen.

COURAGE!

Matthew 10:24-33

Scripture: "What I tell you in the darkness, speak in the light; what you hear whispered, proclaim on the house-tops" (Matthew 10:27).

Reflection: Immediately after discussing the persecutions afflicting his community, Matthew, through his second sermon of Jesus, exhorts his church to have courage. He tells the members of his community to not be afraid. The good news cannot be concealed or secreted by persecution.

Even death should not be feared, according to Jesus. The Father watches over his people. He is concerned about every detail of their lives — even the hairs on their heads. His concern and care for his people is compared to his concern and care for two sparrows, which are "sold for a small coin. Yet not one them falls to the ground without the Father's knowledge" (10:29). People "are worth more than many sparrows" (10:30).

With this assurance, followers of Jesus can confidently bear witness to Jesus before others; that is, they can reveal what is concealed and make known what is secret. If this is done, then Jesus will acknowledge them before the heavenly Father.

Matthew also issues a warning to those who apostatize, those who in fear deny that they are followers of Jesus when persecution comes. In this passage Jesus declares, "Whoever denies me before others, I will deny before my heavenly Father"

(10:33). Matthew is interested in preserving his community in the face of destructive persecution. Using this material from Q (cf. Luke 12:8-9), the evangelist fosters courage and calls forth authentic faith. Authentic followers of Jesus speak the truth which they have heard in the darkness about him in the light, and they proclaim on the housetops what they have heard whispered indoors. Because of their witness, they will be acknowledged by Jesus before the Father.

Meditation: In which ways have you recently witnessed to your faith?

Prayer: Heavenly Father, you care for everything that you have created, even the sparrows in the sky. You never abandon us, even when we abandon you. Through your Holy Spirit give us courage to reveal the truth and make known the secret of your love. Strengthen our wills so that we can speak in the light what we have heard in the darkness and proclaim on the housetops what we heard whispered indoors: You are God — Father, Son, and Holy Spirit — in perfect Trinity for ever and ever. Amen.

SEED OF TEACHING

Matthew 13:1-23

Scripture: "A sower went out to sow. And as he sowed, some seed fell on the path, and the birds came and ate it up. Other seed fell on rocky ground, where it didn't have much soil. It sprouted at once because the soil was not deep, but when the sun rose it got scorched, and since it had no roots it withered away. Still other seed fell among thorns, and the thorns grew up and choked it. But some seed fell on rich soil, and produced fruit, a hundred or sixty or thirty fold" (Matthew 13:3-8).

Reflection: The parable of the sower introduces the third of the five sermons of Jesus found in Matthew's Gospel. Matthew follows Mark's account of this parable, Jesus' purpose of telling parables, and his explanation of the parable of the sower (4:1-20). Matthew adds some of his own interests, such as an expansion of Mark's quotation from Isaiah (6:9; Matthew 13:14-15) and two verses concerning the privilege of discipleship (13:16-17).

Matthew has three principal concerns in narrating the parable of the sower, the purpose of parables, the privilege of discipleship, and the explanation of the parable and the sower.

First, the original Marcan parable enables Matthew to portray Jesus as a great teacher, who sits in a boat and teaches the crowds gathered along the shore. In this regard, Jesus is functioning as the sower in the parable that he tells; he is sowing his teaching in the crowd.

A large amount of the seed is wasted on the path, on rocky ground, and among thorns. But even with this waste, an exceptional harvest is produced — a hundred or sixty or thirty fold. In other words, despite lots of opposition and little response from most of his hearers, Jesus expresses confidence that the Father will bring his kingdom to abundant fruition through his teaching.

Second, the purpose of telling parables is not to portray the disciples as lacking in understanding, as Mark does. In Matthew the disciples are those who do understand and accept Jesus' teaching. They see with their eyes and they hear with their ears what "many prophets and righteous people longed to see... but did not see... and to hear ... but did not hear" (13:17).

Matthew's disciples stand in contrast to Isaiah's prophecy to Israel, who hears but does not understand and looks but never sees. For Matthew, the parables represent Israel's unbelief. Jesus, in Matthew's Gospel, teaches openly from the beginning of his ministry, but only his disciples understand. In Mark, Jesus speaks in mysterious parables from the beginning of his ministry, and the disciples never understand.

Third, Matthew's allegorical interpretation of the parable of the sower is focused on his community. It deals with the different ways that people receive the proclamation of the kingdom. Some hear but do not understand the message; some hear but do not endure because of tribulation and persecution; some hear but riches occupy their time; and some hear and bear fruit, that is, they hear and put into practice what they hear. In this homily-like explanation of the parable of the sower, Matthew encourages his community to continue to hear and to do God's will. This is the mark of authentic discipleship.

Meditation: When you hear the word of proclamation of the kingdom, are you like a path, rocky ground, thorns, or rich soil?

Prayer: Sower God, you delivered the seed of your word through your patriarchs and prophets of old. In these last days you have sown your word through the parables of Jesus, your Son. Open our ears that we may hear him; open our eyes that we may see him. Bring forth fruit of a hundred or sixty or thirty fold by working your will in our lives. We ask this through our Lord Jesus Christ, who lives and reigns with you and the Holy Spirit, one God, for ever and ever. Amen.

MISSION AND REPENTANCE

Mark 6:7-13

Scripture: He summoned the Twelve and began to send them out two by two and he gave them authority over unclean spirits. They drove out many demons and anointed many who were sick with oil and cured them (Mark 6:7, 13).

Reflection: The narrative of the mission of the Twelve is strategically placed in Mark's Gospel between Jesus' rejection at Nazareth and the death of John the Baptist.

Thus, Mark establishes a pattern of rejection, mission, and death, which will be used throughout the Gospel, especially in the second half (8:31-33; 9:30-32; 10:32-34).

The Twelve preach repentance, a favorite Marcan theme. "John (the Baptist) appeared... in the desert proclaiming a baptism of repentance for the forgiveness of sins" (1:4).

Jesus began his Galilean ministry by saying, "Repent, and believe in the good news" (1:15). For Mark repentance represents conversion. The Twelve do not preach the imminence of the kingdom of God because they are characterized throughout the Gospel as never understanding who Jesus is or what he is all about.

The instruction to the Twelve was most probably not a historical admonition to Jesus' original group of followers, but Mark's instruction to those who were continuing the mission of Jesus at the time that Mark was writing this Gospel (70 AD).

According to Mark, disciples of Jesus are dependent on others. They take "no food, no sack, no money in their belts" (6:8). Wherever they enter a house, they stay there until they leave the place (cf. 6:10). In this way followers of Jesus witness to their mission while at the same time demonstrating their dependence on God for food and shelter. Mark will emphasize this dependency aspect of discipleship when he narrates the feeding of the five thousand (6:34-44) and the feeding of the four thousand (8:1-9).

If missioners are not received, then they engage in a particularly interesting ritual — they shake the dust from their feet in testimony against those who do not receive them (cf. 6:11). After walking in foreign territory, Jews would often shake the dust of the heathens from their feet before re-entering Palestine. Thus, this ritual is a symbolic action indicating that those who do not receive Jesus' disciples are no more than heathen — pretty low on the totem pole!

In summarizing this section, Mark tells the reader that disciples share in the exorcising and healing ministry of Jesus. One of Mark's characterizations of Jesus in the early chapters of the Gospel is that of an exorcist, one who conquers evil. In this regard, Jesus is also a healer. The mention of oil used in healing refers to its medicinal characteristics.

By making this mention of it, Mark may be referring to its use in the early Church in what gradually evolved into the sacrament of the anointing of the sick.

Meditation: In which ways does your lifestyle preach repentance?

Prayer: Missionary God, from the beginning of time you have sent patriarchs and judges, prophets and kings, men and women to your people. In the fullness of time, you sent Jesus, your Son, to be the messenger of your good news. Send us out with his authority that we may preach repentance, overcome evil, and offer your healing hand to those who are sick. We ask this through our Lord Jesus Christ, who lives and reigns with you and the Holy Spirit, one God, for ever and ever. Amen.

NEIGHBORLY SAMARITAN

Luke 10:25-37

Scripture: "Which of these three (priest, Levite, Samaritan), do you think, was neighbor to the man who ran into the robbers?" (Luke 10:36)

Reflection: The parable of the good Samaritan is unique to Luke's Gospel. It is preceded by a dialogue between Jesus and a scholar of the law, that is, one who is an expert in the Mosaic law and all its details. The scholar of the law asks, "Teacher, what must I do to inherit eternal life?" (Luke 10:25). The scholar makes eternal life an issue of following the law.

Since it is a scholar of the law who is asking the question, Jesus turns the question back to him, "What is written in the law? How do you read it?" (10:26). If anyone knows the answer to the question, it should be the scholar.

The answer given by him is commendable. He joins together two separate Old Testament commandments. The first of these, commonly referred to as the great commandment or the *Shema*, declares, "The Lord is our God, the Lord alone! Therefore, you shall love the Lord, your God, with all your heart, and with all your soul, and with all your strength" (Deuteronomy 6:4-5; cf. 10:12).

The second commandment is found in the book of Leviticus: "You shall love your neighbor as your self" (19:18). While it is the scholar of the law who combines these two commandments

113

in Luke's Gospel, it is Jesus who unites them in Matthew's Gospel (cf. 22:37-39) and in Mark's Gospel (cf. 12:29-31).

The response of Jesus in Luke is important to notice. He tells the scholar, "You have answered correctly; do this and you will live" (10:28). However, this does not answer the original question concerning "eternal life"; it only answers the question about "life." The parable, one about "life," then follows. This introduction and transition to the parable is obviously Lucan.

The scholar of the law, having answered his own question, poses a second question to Jesus, "Who is my neighbor?" (10:29). In other words, the scholar wants a detailed answer to the general law about loving one's neighbor as one's self. The story follows. Robbers attack a Jew, who is making his way from Jerusalem to Jericho. "They stripped and beat him and went off leaving him half dead" (10:30). Two models of "neighbor" come down the road. The first is a priest, who sees his fellow Jew in the ditch but passes by on the opposite side. The second is a Levite, who does the same.

Jews, hearing or reading this parable, would have found the behavior of the priest and the Levite acceptable. If the man along the road were dead, and if either of these two models of "neighbor" would have touched him, they would have been ritually impure and unable to perform their religious duties. So, in this case, their behavior can be excused; the law permitted them to behave in this fashion.

Next, a Samaritan traveler comes upon the half-dead man. He "was moved with compassion at the sight. He came up to him, poured oil and wine over his wounds and bandaged them. Then he set him on his own mount, brought him to an inn and took care of him. The next day when he left he gave the innkeeper two silver coins and said, 'Look after him. If you spend more than what I have given you, I'll repay you on my way back'" (10:33-35).

There was a deep and long-standing hostility between Jews and Samaritans. This rivalry manifested itself in politics and religion. To say that Jews and Samaritans hated each other is to put the case mildly! This Samaritan, then, is out of character. He should have done what the priest and the Levite did — but for a different reason.

But he did not. The scholar of the law is put on the spot by Jesus. "Which of these three, do you think, was neighbor to the man who ran into the robbers?" (10:36). In other words, who is the model "neighbor"?

The scholar of the law, the one who knows the law and all of its details, is now stuck. He has only one possible answer to give, and it puts him in one huge bind. "The one who treated him with mercy," he says (10:37). He cannot even pronounce the word "Samaritan"!

Needless to say, making the Samaritan the hero and model of "neighbor" in this parable shocked the Jewish audience. All social, political, ethnic, and religious barriers are broken down. By serving as a friend to the Jew, the Samaritan emerges as the most unlikely model of "neighbor" in the Jewish world.

And if this is not enough, Jesus tells the scholar of the law to "Go and do likewise" (10:37). The scholar is instructed to go and act like the Samaritan. Finally, the initial question is answered.

"What must I do to inherit eternal life?" (10:25). "Go and do likewise" (10:37). For Luke, the way to "eternal life" is the way of "life" — compassion, mercy. Everyone is "neighbor" to everyone else. The law does not excuse anyone from treating another human being with compassion and mercy.

Meditation: How have you recently behaved like a Samaritan? like a priest or Levite? like a scholar of the Law?

Prayer: God of unlimited compassion, your mercy is offered to all your people. Break down the ethnic, racial, political, social, and religious barriers that divide people. Make us realize our equal human dignity in your sight. Move us to your kind of compassion that we might be neighbor to all we meet. We ask this through our Lord Jesus Christ, your Son, who lives and reigns with you and the Holy Spirit, one God, for ever and ever. Amen.

FAMILIAL DIVISION

Matthew 10:34-11:1

Scripture: "Whoever receives you receives me, and whoever receives me receives the One who sent me" (Matthew 10:40).

Reflection: In the last section of Jesus' second sermon in
Matthew's Gospel, often called the missionary discourse, three
themes are presented: division, the cross, and rewards.

First, Matthew re-emphasizes the idea that Jesus is a cause
of division. He presented this theme earlier in the same sermon
when discussing persecution, which is a result of following Jesus:
"Brother will hand brother over to death, and the father his child;
children will rise up against parents and have them put to death"
(10:21).

For Matthew, Jesus brings the sword (division) — not peace
— into a family. Authentically accepting discipleship and its
mission entail family separation. In Matthew's community, this
was taking place and causing a problem. In this section, then,
the author is attempting is explain the cause — Jesus — of the
divisiveness which was occurring in families in his community,
while at the same time holding the whole church together.

Second, Matthew is interested in promoting faithfulness to
discipleship, even if it does cause division. No one can be more
important than Jesus. "Whoever loves father or mother more than
me is not worthy of me, and whoever doesn't take up his cross

117

and follow me is not worthy of me" (10:37). To place Jesus first in one's life is to accept the cross — both explicitly in terms of Roman capital punishment and implicitly in terms of the division caused by authentic discipleship.

Those who deny their discipleship in order to save their life have already lost their life in the kingdom. While those who lose their life for the sake of Jesus, discipleship, and mission will find life in the kingdom.

Third, reward is not understood by Matthew to mean a specified gift in return for following Jesus. Matthew does not dare specify anything concerning reward, because he cannot, that is, he does not know what God will do, and because to do so would undermine his whole understanding of righteousness — one is righteous, behaves as God wills, because it is the correct thing to do; it is the behavior which God wills.

The "rewards" which Jesus mentions in the Gospel of Matthew are, therefore, unspecified. "Whoever receives a prophet because he is a prophet will receive a prophet's reward" (10:41).

In other words, whoever welcomes another person who speaks in the name of God — Christian prophets who proclaim the Gospel — will be rewarded in the same way as they are — whatever way that may be! Likewise, "whoever receives a righteous man because he is righteous will receive a righteous man's reward" (10:41). In other words, anyone who welcomes a person who is doing God's will, behaving correctly, will be rewarded just as this person will be rewarded — whatever that may be! In this section of his Gospel, Matthew gives the first hint of one of his theological understandings, that is, the community of believers form the new presence of Jesus. In Pauline terminology, this is the "body of Christ." In Matthew Jesus declares, "Whoever receives you receives me, and whoever receives me receives the One who sent me" (10:40).

The Christian missioner is Christ being brought to others, who, when they receive the Gospel of the missioner, receive Christ and the Father, who sent him.

Matthew's theological perspective is that Jesus is "Emmanuel," which means "God is with us" (1:23). He is with the Church "always, until the end of the age" (28:20). He identifies himself with the community: "Where two or three are gathered together in my name, there am I in the midst of them" (18:20).

This identity of Jesus with the community of believers reaches a climax for Matthew in the account of the judgment of the nations. In this passage Jesus declares, "Whatever you did for the least of these brothers (or sisters) of mine, you did for me" (25:40). Therefore, in the final words of the missionary sermon Jesus states, "Whoever gives even a cup of cold water to one of these little ones because he is a disciple — amen, I say to you, he will not lose his reward" (10:42). The "reward," as discovered in the judgment of the nations narrative, is the "kingdom prepared... from the foundation of the world" (25:34).

Using a formula similar to that which he employed to conclude the first sermon of Jesus (7:28-29), Matthew brings the second discourse of Jesus to a close by writing, "When Jesus finished instructing his twelve disciples, he went away from that place to teach and to preach in their cities" (11:1).

Meditation: In which ways has discipleship caused division in your life?

Prayer: God of division, your Son, Jesus the Christ, caused division among those who believed and those who did not believe in his good news. Enable us to always love him more than anyone else in our lives. Keep us faithful as disciples, and bring us to the kingdom where you live and reign with Jesus and the Holy Spirit, one God, for ever and ever. Amen.

REPENTANCE

Matthew 11:20-24

Scripture: "If the mighty works which took place in your midst had occurred in Tyre and Sidon, they would long ago have repented in sackcloth and ashes.... If the mighty deeds that happened in your midst had been done in Sodom, it would have remained until this day" (Matthew 11:21, 23).

Reflection: The reproaches given by Jesus to unrepentant towns in the Gospel of Matthew follow the account of the messengers sent by John the Baptist and Jesus' testimony to John, which are omitted in the semi-continuous daily reading from this Gospel. Matthew's source for the reproaches is Q; however, he expands Q in order to give the reproaches a parallel structure.

Chorazin, Bethsaida, and Capernaum, the unrepentant towns, are all located in Galilee. However, Matthew records no works of Jesus located in either Chorazin or Bethsaida. He is merely repeating an earlier oral tradition concerning the ministry of Jesus in these two towns.

In Capernaum, according to Matthew, Jesus heals a centurion's servant and Peter's mother-in-law (8:5-15), a paralytic (9:1-8), the official's daughter and the woman with a hemorrhage, two blind men, a mute person, and many others (9:18-35). Capernaum, it is to be noted, is where Jesus lives after John is arrested (4:12-13). Matthew refers to it as Jesus' "own town" (9:1).

The issue is the repentance that should have followed the witness of Jesus' "mighty deeds" (11:21, 23) — manifested in healings, miracles, preaching, teaching. Because Matthew portrays Jesus as a new Moses, Matthew's "mighty deeds" of Jesus echoes Moses' mighty deeds of God in the book of Exodus. "Forced by my mighty hand, he (Pharaoh) will send them (Israelites) away; compelled by my outstretched arm, he will drive them from his land" (Exodus 6:1), God tells Moses. Pharaoh remains obstinate throughout the ten plagues and never repents.

Chorazin and Bethsaida do not repent. Their lack of repentance is compared to Tyre and Sidon, pagan cities, which are denounced for their wickedness by the Old Testament prophets (cf. Joel 4:4-7; Isaiah 23, Ezekiel 26-28). If these cities had witnessed Jesus' "mighty deeds," they would have "repented in sackcloth and ashes" (11:21) as did the king of Nineveh and the whole city, including the animals, after but one day's preaching by Jonah (cf. Jonah 3:6).

On the day of judgment "it will be more tolerable for Tyre and Sidon" (11:22) than for Chorazin and Bethsaida because these latter two cities have witnessed "something greater than Jonah here" (12:41), yet they did not repent.

Capernaum's lack of repentance is compared to that of Sodom, an Old Testament town which was destroyed because of its grave sin (cf. Genesis 18:20 ff.). For the prophet Isaiah, Sodom was synonymous with depravity. Earlier in his Gospel, after recording the commission to the twelve, Matthew portrays Jesus as comparing the judgment on those towns which do not receive or listen to his disciples to be harsher than that for the city of Sodom (cf. Matthew 10:15).

By comparing Capernaum to Sodom, Matthew is pushing condemnation to the extreme. He is declaring that Capernaum is worse than Sodom because it has not repented. Jesus' "own town" has only illusions of grandeur which are similar to that of the king of Babylon, the place of Jewish captivity (cf. Isaiah 14:13-15)! "'Will you be exalted to heaven? You will be cast down to the netherworld'" (11:23).

According to Matthew, repentance is a key dimension of authentic discipleship. From the beginning of his ministry, Jesus in the Gospel of Matthew proclaims, "Repent, for the kingdom of heaven is at hand" (4:17). Those who hear Jesus and witness his "mighty deeds" and do not repent, are worse than Tyre, Sidon, and Sodom, the epitome of lack of repentance.

Meditation: In which ways have you repented after hearing the Gospel?

Prayer: God of repentance, you call all people to listen attentively to the good news of Jesus and to be converted from their old lives of sin to the new life he offers. Open our hearts to hear his preaching. Through our witness of his mighty deeds move us to authentic repentance of mind and heart. May we not be judged harshly but experience the depths of your mercy and love. We ask this through Christ our Lord, who lives and reigns with you and the Holy Spirit, one God, for ever and ever. Amen.

JOY
Matthew 11:25-27

Scripture: "I praise you, Father, Lord of heaven and earth, because you hid these things from the wise and the learned and revealed them to mere babes" (Matthew 11:25).

Reflection: Except for minor variations, Matthew 11:25-27 is identical to Luke 10:21-22; therefore, Matthew's source for this section is Q, a body of tradition concerning Jesus used by both Matthew and Luke.

While the verses preceding this section of the Gospel deal with the theme of unbelief, this section alters the "tone" to that of joy. Up to this point in the Gospel, Jesus finds his ministry basically rejected in Galilee. However, he nevertheless finds reason to praise his Father, the Lord (the master, the Creator) of heaven and earth for having hidden the mysteries of the kingdom from the religious experts and revealed them to the powerless.

At this point, three Matthean themes are brought together. First, it is the Father who does the hiding and the revealing. All depends on God's will. This theme is in keeping with the book of Exodus' view that "the Lord made Pharaoh obstinate" (Exodus 11:10). Since Matthew is uniquely interested in portraying Jesus as a new Moses, this theme fits nicely into this section of his Gospel; that is, it follows the verses describing the obstinacy of unbelief.

Second, those who should recognize God's revelation do not. These, of course, are the religious experts — the scribes and Pharisees for Matthew. They propose that obedience to the 613 precepts of the law is all that is necessary. Matthew characterizes them as arrogant and not open to revelation, and, therefore, not open to the possibility of authentic faith.

Third, those who should not recognize God's revelation do. These are the childlike — the poor, the tax collectors, and the sinners. They are not capable of obedience to the precepts of the law. Matthew characterizes these people as open to the new revelation of Jesus, and, therefore, also open to the possibility of authentic faith.

Matthew is telling his community that this is the "gracious will" (11:26) of the Father, who handed over this revelation to Jesus, who, in turn, passed it on to his disciples and those who were open to receive it.

In this section of his Gospel, Matthew establishes a new theme and an apocalyptic and Christological base for the rest of his Gospel. After Peter confesses that Jesus is "the Messiah, the Son of the living God," Jesus replies, "Flesh and blood has not revealed this to you, but my heavenly Father" (16:16-17). Before Jesus commissions the disciples, he tells them, "All power in heaven and on earth has been given to me" (28:18). According to Matthew, the Father handed over both the apocalyptic mysteries and all cosmic powers to Jesus. Therefore, Jesus and the Father are equal.

Meditation: Most recently, what has God revealed to you?

Prayer: Praise to you, Father of heaven and earth. From the wise and learned you have hidden the mysteries of your kingdom, but to the childlike you have revealed them through the ministry of your Son, our Lord Jesus Christ. Through the power of your Holy Spirit, continue to reveal your gracious will in our lives. Through Jesus, may we come to know you Father, as you live and reign with Jesus and the Holy Spirit, one God, for ever and ever. Amen.

WISDOM'S YOKE

Matthew 11:28-30

Scripture: "Take my yoke upon you and learn from me, for I am meek and humble of heart" (Matthew 11:29).

Reflection: The last three verses of chapter eleven (28-30) are unique to Matthew's Gospel, but they are similar to the invitation to learn wisdom given by the author of the book of Sirach: "Submit your neck to her (wisdom's) yoke, that your mind may accept her teaching. For she is close to those who seek her, and the one who is earnest finds her. See for yourselves! I have labored only a little, but have found much" (Sirach 51:26-27).

In this passage, Jesus invites those "who labor and are burdened" (11:28) to come to him. Who are these? Anyone who is overwhelmed by the law as taught by the scribes and the Pharisees. Matthew specifies this when Jesus denounces the scribes and Pharisees in chapter 23: "They tie up heavy burdens (hard to carry) and lay them on people's shoulders, but they will not lift a finger to move them" (23:4).

Like personified Wisdom in the book of Proverbs (8-9), Jesus teaches that rest can be had for all, especially those considered to be religious outcasts — those who were looked down upon by the scribes and Pharisees because they were not able to keep the law.

The wisdom-teacher, Jesus, echoes the prophet Jeremiah: "Thus says the Lord: Stand beside the earliest roads, ask the pathways of old. Which is the way to good, and walk it; thus you will find rest for your souls" (6:16). Jesus' "way to good" is a yoke, but it is "easy" and "light" (11:30) for it consists of obedience to Jesus' word. Matthew portrays Jesus as an example of this new yoke. To the paralytic, Jesus says, "rise and walk" (9:5). "Pick up your pallet, and go home" (9:6). The man is healed of paralysis and sin. He now proceeds on the "way to good." He has found rest.

The meekness and humility of Jesus are not discovered until later (chapter 21) in Matthew's Gospel, when he records Jesus' entry into Jerusalem. Echoing two prophetic texts (Isaiah 62:11 and Zechariah 9:9), Matthew records the reason why Jesus entered Jerusalem riding on an ass: "Say to daughter Zion, 'Behold, your king comes to you, meek and riding on an ass, and on a colt, the foal of a beast of burden'" (21:15). Jesus, who is being hailed as king by the crowd, does not sit on a horse, the beast of the triumphant conqueror; he rides the ass, the peasant's beast of burden. Furthermore, he enters Jerusalem, where he will be put to death. He is "meek and humble of heart" (11:29).

According to Matthew, the yoke of Jesus offers rest to those who assimilate and live Jesus' way — those who are authentic disciples — and not from practicing 613 precepts of the law. Matthew is interested in convincing his readers to adhere to Jesus, to be faithful, since his way, his yoke, is one that is much easier and much lighter than the law.

Meditation: Which kind of rest have you most recently experienced by taking Jesus' yoke and learning from him?

Prayer: God our Wisdom, you release the yoke of slavery to sin by your constant and gracious forgiveness. Through Jesus, you have called all people to take up the yoke of the gospel and experience your rest. Enable us to listen attentively to the wise teaching of your Son. Make us meek and humble of heart. We ask this through our Lord Jesus Christ, who lives and reigns with you and the Holy Spirit, one God, for ever and ever. Amen.

PEOPLE VERSUS LAW

Matthew 12:1-8

Scripture: "Have you not read what David did when he
and his companions were hungry, how he went into the
house of God and ate the loaves of offering, which neither he nor his companions but only the priests could law-
fully eat?" (Matthew 12:3-4)

Reflection: With some additions (verses 5-7) Matthew borrows
the narrative concerning the picking of grain on the Sabbath from
Mark's Gospel (2:23-28). This narrative and the one which follows (12:9-14, about the man with a withered hand which is
omitted from the daily Matthean cycle of Gospel selections) are
the only two places that Matthew (and Mark) deal with Jesus'
attitude toward the observance of the Sabbath.

The basic issue of the selection is Sabbath observance.

Because of their hunger, Jesus' disciples pick grain on the
Sabbath. This action is forbidden by the law: "For six days you
may work, but on the seventh day you shall rest; on that day you
must rest even during the seasons of plowing and harvesting"
(Exodus 34:21). Since picking heads of grain is considered to be
harvesting by the Pharisees, the action is deemed unlawful.

Jesus counters the Pharisees' argument by reminding them
of an Old Testament incident: the eating of the holy bread by
David and his men (cf. 1 Samuel 21:2-7).

This account, however, does not deal with the breaking of

129

the Sabbath rest but with a violation of the law because David and his men were hungry and without food.

This example is typical of Jesus' perspective on the law in the Gospel of Matthew. Human need, such as hunger (of the disciples and David and his men) takes precedence over the law. People are more important than the law.

The second counter to the Pharisees' argument is unique to Matthew. He has Jesus use a legal example which contradicts itself. "Regularly on each Sabbath day this showbread shall be set out afresh before the Lord, offered on the part of the Israelites by an everlasting agreement" (Leviticus 24:8), states the law. Furthermore, the law declares, "On the Sabbath day you shall offer two unblemished yearling lambs, with their cereal offering, two tenths of an ephah of fine flour mixed with oil, and with their libations. Each Sabbath there shall be the Sabbath holocaust in addition to the established holocaust and its libation" (Numbers 28:9-10).

In order to observe the Sabbath laws concerning their Temple duties, the priests must break the law concerning Sabbath rest from work. What Matthew is arguing is this: even the law recognized that Temple duty was more important than observance of the Sabbath rest. In other words, there is a hierarchy of mandatory observance built into the law. One part of the law can be violated — indeed, is mandated by the law itself! — in favor of a more important part of the law.

Therefore, the satisfying of a human need — food — cannot be a violation of the Sabbath observance. David demonstrated this. The Temple priests demonstrated this. The law itself demonstrated this. For Matthew, the presence of Jesus in the church (cf. 28:20) and the proclamation of the kingdom ("something greater than the Temple is here," 12:6) justify the conduct of Jesus' disciples and of the followers of Jesus at the time Matthew was writing this Gospel.

For Matthew, Jesus has authority over the law. "The Son of Man is Lord of the Sabbath" (12:8). Thus, this reemphasizes the reinterpreting of the law for the community, a project in which

Matthew has been engaged since the first sermon of Jesus (cf. 5:17-48).

One final point needs to be considered. Jesus tells the Pharisees, "If you knew what this meant, 'I desire mercy, not sacrifice,' you would not have condemned these innocent men" (12:7). The phrase, "I desire mercy, not sacrifice," was previously used in 9:13 as part of the narrative of the call of Matthew.

The phrase is taken from the prophet Hosea: "It is love that I desire, not sacrifice, and knowledge of God rather than holocausts" (6:6). Mercy is superior to the Temple sacrifices. Mercy is superior to the laws concerning ritual impurity (eating with tax collectors; cf. Matthew 9:9-13). Matthew also declares that mercy is superior to the law concerning picking heads of grain and eating them on the Sabbath. Anyone who proposes to know the mind of God (e.g., the Pharisees) should realize the importance of mercy.

Meditation: In which ways do you faithfully observe the Sabbath rest? Do any of these violate any higher laws?

Prayer: God of the Sabbath, after you completed the work of creation in six days, you rested from all that you had made on the seventh day. You have decreed that your people should imitate you and refrain from work on the day that you have made your own. Give us the rest we need, but also make us sensitive to the needs of our brothers and sisters. We ask this through our Lord Jesus Christ, the Son of Man and Lord of the Sabbath, who lives and reigns with you and the Holy Spirit, one God, for ever and ever. Amen.

SERVANT-SON

Matthew 12:14-21

Scripture: Jesus... withdrew from that place. Many people followed him, and he healed them all and commanded them not to make him known. This was to fulfill what was said by Isaiah the prophet (Matthew 12:15-17).

Reflection: Following the twin incidents of Sabbath violation — picking grain on the Sabbath and the healing of a man with a withered hand (12:1-13) — and the plot of the Pharisees to put Jesus to death (12:14) because of these violations, Matthew, unlike his Marcan source, presents a Jesus who knows what his enemies are doing. So, Jesus withdraws and heals all who follow him (12:15-16).

Because the power of Jesus cannot be limited, according to Matthew, he changes his Marcan source from "he had cured many" (Mark 3:10) to "he healed them all" (Matthew 12:15).

Because Mark is interested in preserving his "messianic secret" theme, Jesus in Mark warns those healed "not to make him known" (Mark 3:12). Matthew retains the phrase "he commanded them not to make him known" (12:16), since this fits nicely with the withdrawal motif. Also, Jesus can avoid other disputes for a while. Then using the longest Old Testament quotation found in his Gospel, Matthew interprets the action of Jesus through the prophet Isaiah. The evangelist is fond of "fulfillment" citations; however, throughout his Gospel, he never quotes any one accurately. This one based on Isaiah 42:1-4 is no exception. The quotation attempts to demonstrate that the meekness and humility of Jesus, which Matthew already portrayed (11:28-30), do not proceed from weakness or fear but from Jesus' divine mandate to fulfill the Old Testament. The reader must keep in mind that one of Matthew's basic presuppositions is that Jesus began nothing new (there is no "new covenant" in Matthew; he simply continued what was already in place — the "old covenant").

The (mis)quotation from the prophet Isaiah permits Matthew to bring together some of the themes that he has been working with up to this point in his Gospel.

First, Jesus is the Servant of the Lord: "Behold, my servant whom I have chosen, my beloved in whom I delight" (Matthew 12:18). Automatically, this sentence recalls the voice from the heavens at Jesus' baptism (3:17) and points ahead to the voice from the cloud in the transfiguration narrative (17:5). Jesus, the Servant-Son, is doing God's will.

Second, the Servant-Son receives the Spirit: "I shall place my Spirit upon him" (Matthew 12:18). Mary, according to Matthew, conceived Jesus "through the Holy Spirit" (1:20). At his baptism, "the Spirit of God" descended on Jesus "like a dove" and came upon him (3:16), after which "Jesus was led by the Spirit into the desert to be tempted by the devil" (4:1).

Third, the Servant-Son "will proclaim justice to the Gentiles and in his name the Gentiles will hope" (Matthew 12:18, 21). Justice for Matthew is righteousness, right behavior, doing God's will. Matthew has already presented Jesus' mission to the Gentiles through the healing of a centurion's servant (8:5-13) and the healing of the Gadarene demoniacs (8:28-34). He has reproached the unrepentant Jewish towns (11:20-24). Throughout the Gospel, Matthew warns his readers that those for whom the message of the kingdom is intended may find themselves rejected for not receiving God's Servant. However, the Gentiles, pagans, do receive him and heed his preaching.

Fourth, "He will not quarrel or shout out angrily, nor will

anyone hear his voice in the streets" (Matthew 12:19). For Matthew, this explains why Jesus withdraws from the dispute with the Pharisees after the violation of the Sabbath observance (12:15).

Fifth, anyone who is broken in body ("a bruised reed," Matthew 12:20) or anyone depressed in spirit ("a smoldering wick," Matthew 12:20) is healed by Jesus. The cure of the man with a withered hand (12:9-13) immediately precedes this section of the Gospel. The depressed in spirit are found in the first beatitude (5:3), which begins the Sermon on the Mount.

Sixth, the Servant-Son will bring "justice to victory" (Matthew 12:20). Here Matthew gives a glimpse of what will happen later in the Gospel — by doing the will of God (justice), Jesus will be victorious. Through his death and resurrection, the Servant of God will complete his mission and God's plan.

Meditation: In which ways are you a servant of God?

Prayer: God of Jews and Gentiles, you chose Jesus to be your Servant and proclaimed him to be your Son. You anointed him with your Spirit at his baptism and sent him forth to proclaim justice. Through our immersion in the waters of baptism, you have anointed us with the Holy Spirit. Place the right words on our lips that we may continue Jesus' mission of justice and peace. Bring justice to victory in us. We ask this through our Lord Jesus Christ, who lives and reigns with you and the Holy Spirit, one God, for ever and ever. Amen.

WHEAT AND WEEDS

Matthew 13:24-43

Scripture: "No, you might uproot the wheat at the same time you're gathering the weeds. Let them both grow together until harvest" (Matthew 13:29-30).

Reflection: The parable of the weeds among the wheat (13:24-30) and its explanation (13:36-43) is divided by the parable of the mustard seed (13:31-32), the parable of the yeast (13:33), and a summary statement with a quotation from Psalm 78 (13:34-35). The structure of this entire section of Matthew's Gospel is similar to the first half of the chapter where, following Mark's Gospel, Matthew narrates the parable of the sower (13:1-9) and then relates the purpose of parables and the privilege of discipleship (13:10-17) before explaining the parable of the sower (13:18-23). Therefore, this section of the Gospel (13:24-43) is obviously a Matthean arrangement of various pieces of material.

Only the parable of the weeds among the wheat and its explanation can be dealt with here. The parable of the mustard seed, the parable of the yeast, and the exhortation concerning the use of parables are examined on Monday of Week Seventeen.

While Matthew calls the weeds among the wheat a parable, it is more accurately labeled an analogy, since he later explains to the reader its exact meaning. The analogy concerns the appropriate behavior (righteousness; cf. 13:43) of members of the

Church during the time after Jesus' resurrection until his coming in glory. In other words, Matthew is telling the members of his community how to act and how to treat each other in this in-between time.

While members of the community await the harvest, a metaphor used by the prophets Jeremiah (51:33), Joel (4:13), and Hosea (6:11) for the time of God's judgment, they are not to judge each other as good (wheat) or as bad (weeds). The role of judge is reserved to the "Son of Man" (13:41), whose kingdom is mani-fested in the Church.

For Matthew, then, the kingdom is mixed; it consists of wheat and weeds. The weeds cannot be uprooted because the wheat might also be uprooted. In Jesus' first sermon Matthew made it clear that Christians should not judge each other (7:1-5). If they do not judge each other, then they do not separate them-selves. Matthew is concerned with preserving the unity of his community, as demonstrated in the setting of the explanation of the parable: "Then, dismissing the crowds, he (Jesus) went into the house. His disciples approached him and said, 'Explain to us the parable of the weeds in the field'" (13:36). Jesus breaks with the crowds, who represent unbelieving Israel. He focuses his attention on the disciples. This is Matthew's way of focusing his attention on his community, the early Church.

The parable and its explanation ("the field is the world," 13:38) presuppose the resurrection of Jesus and the granting to him "all power in heaven and on earth" (28:18). The twice-used "Son of Man" in the explanation also points to a post-resurrec-tional composition date for this parable and its explanation and clearly places its current form in the hands of the author of this Gospel.

Jesus has already sowed his teaching about and preaching of the kingdom of heaven. The "good seed" are those who have believed. The "weeds" are the unbelievers. No one knows who the "wheat" are. No one knows who the "weeds" are. In other words, no one can judge another person as either being in or outside of the kingdom. This is reserved to the Son of Man alone at the "end of the age" (13:39, 40), a unique Matthean reference to the time of judgment.

According to Matthew, on the day of harvest (judgment) the angels (harvesters) will collect the weeds (evildoers) and burn them in the fiery furnace, "where there will be wailing and grinding of teeth" (13:42), a favorite Matthean description for the doom of unbelievers. "Then, the righteous will shine like the sun in the kingdom of their Father" (13:43). With the use of the word "righteous," Matthew reemphasizes his central theme — behavior. Those who hear God's word and do God's will are righteous. In varied and many ways from the beginning of the Gospel Matthew has focused on this theme. Therefore, "whoever has ears ought to hear" (13:43).

Meditation: How do you separate people from each other? What does Matthew's parable about and explanation of the weeds among the wheat say about this activity?

Prayer: God of the kingdom, you permit both wheat and weeds to grow together in your Church until the day of judgment. Preserve us from judging the members of the Church, so that we may not bring about division. Open our ears and keep us faithful to the preaching and teaching of Jesus until the day of harvest. Count us among the righteous in your kingdom, where you live and reign with our Lord Jesus Christ and the Holy Spirit, one God, for ever and ever. Amen.

A DESERTED PLACE

Mark 6:30-34

SUNDAY
of Week

16

Cycle B

Scripture: "Come away privately, just yourselves, to a desert place and rest a while." His (Jesus') heart was moved with pity for them, for they were like sheep without a shepherd; and he began to teach them many things (Mark 6:31, 34).

Reflection: The section of Mark's Gospel which narrates the return of the twelve (6:30-34) from their mission (6:7-13) follows Mark's description of the death of John the Baptist at the request of Herodias' daughter and leads into the narrative of the feeding of the five thousand in "a desert place" (6:35). By placing this section in this location Mark is able to call upon two Old Testament themes.

The first of these themes is that of the desert as a place where God can speak to and hear from the hearts of his people. By portraying Jesus as calling the apostles together "to a desert place" (6:31) in order to hear their report of their ministry, Mark is echoing the Exodus and the ensuing wandering in the desert, where God formed a people after his own heart.

Jesus and the disciples "went off alone in the boat to a desert place" (6:32). This recalls the forty years in the desert where God was with the twelve tribes. Jesus, however, unlike Moses, leader of the chosen people, draws many others to hear his teaching. For Mark, all people have been called by God to be his chosen people through Jesus. Those who follow Jesus are people of a new exodus.

The second Old Testament theme that Mark uses reflects God as shepherd of his people. The author of the book of Num-

141

bers puts this prayer on the lips of Moses: "May the Lord, the God of the spirits of all mankind, set over the community a man who shall act as their leader in all things, to guide them in all their actions; that the Lord's community may not be like sheep without a shepherd" (Numbers 27:15-17). After Moses' prayer, God directs him to lay his hand upon Joshua, who became Moses' successor, leader of the Israelites and escort of the Israelites into the promised land after Moses' death.

It is no accident that Mark alludes to this passage. The Hebrew name "Joshua," which is rendered "Jesus" in English, means "Yahweh saves" and "Yahweh helps." Thus, Mark views Jesus as the new Joshua, who saves, helps, and leads the new exodus of all people.

Another allusion to the shepherd theme is present in this section of the Gospel; it is derived from the prophet Ezekiel, who devotes a whole chapter to his parable of the shepherds. After castigating the shepherds (leaders) of Israel for pasturing themselves instead of their sheep (Israelites), Ezekiel portrays God as saying, "I myself will pasture my sheep; I myself will give them rest, says the Lord God" (34:15).

For Mark, Jesus is this new shepherd. He calls his people to rest. He is "moved with pity for them" (6:34) and pastures them with his teaching. In other words, Mark is proclaiming that Jesus is functioning as God, the shepherd. This role will become clearer in the narrative of the feeding of the five thousand, which immediately follows this section of the Gospel and reminds the reader of God's gift of manna in the desert.

In his own unique way, Mark is proclaiming Jesus to be God. Jesus is Ezekiel's faithful shepherd of God's chosen people.

Meditation: Where is your desert — that place of rest, where God speaks to your heart? In which ways is Jesus your shepherd?

Prayer: God of the desert, once you called a people from the slavery of Egypt. Through Moses you guided them into the desert where you gave them rest, taught them, and formed them after your own heart. Through Jesus you have led us from the slavery of sin to the desert of rest, where he has taught us and given us new hearts. Make of us faithful sheep, who follow the shepherd through death to resurrection. We ask this through our Lord Jesus Christ, your Son, who lives and reigns with you and the Holy Spirit, one God, for ever and ever. Amen.

MARTHA, MARTHA!

Luke 10:38-42

Scripture: "Martha, Martha, you are anxious and upset about many things, but only one thing is necessary. Mary has chosen the better part and it will not be taken from her" (Luke 10:41-42).

Reflection: The short narrative about Jesus' visit with Martha and Mary follows the parable of the good Samaritan and precedes Luke's version of the Lord's Prayer. The location of the Martha-Mary story within the context of Luke's Gospel discloses the function of the narrative and its meaning.

The emphasis of the parable of the good Samaritan is on appropriate action. The scholar of the law asks Jesus, "What must I do to inherit eternal life?" (Luke 10:25). The answer to this question is given in the parable: "Go and do likewise," (Luke 10:37), which means that the lawyer is to act as his mortal enemy, the Samaritan, and show compassion. In other words, the good Samaritan is an example of one who does or practices the word (teaching) of Jesus.

The Martha-Mary story presents the other side of the coin of doing the word — namely, hearing the word. In contrast to John's Gospel, Lazarus is not mentioned in Luke's Gospel. Martha and Mary occupy a home in a village which is visited by Jesus as he continues on his journey to Jerusalem.

Martha is characterized as the sister "burdened with much

serving" (10:40). In being busy with the details of hospitality, Martha is functioning according to Semitic custom, which was geared to lavish expenditure on the guest. The reader need only recall Abraham's hospitable welcome of three visitors and the ensuing promise of a son in order to understand the importance of hospitality in the Semitic world.

Mary, on the other hand, is characterized as the inhospitable type. She "seated herself at the Lord's feet listening to him speak" (10:39). According to custom, she should have been busy with the details of hospitality like her sister, Martha. Mary was not being a good host.

Therefore, when Martha requests that Jesus tell Mary to help her, she is invoking the social custom of the time. Jesus, of course, knows the social custom and what hospitality requires, but he does not order Mary to act like Martha. He violates the custom of hospitality and turns things upside down. In this way, the unexpected twist at the end of the story makes it parabolic in form.

Jesus' response, "Only one thing is necessary. Mary has chosen the better part and it will not be taken from her" (10:42), places an emphasis on hearing the word. Mary had been listening to Jesus speak. Mary's inaction is praised by Jesus; she chose the better part. Hospitality takes second place to the teaching (word) of Jesus, according to Luke.

Jesus is functioning as the host. He is Luke's Servant, who is delivering the word of God. Mary chose to permit Jesus to be the host and receive from his hand. Martha failed to recognize who the real host was.

Luke is demonstrating the necessary balance between hearing the word (Mary) and doing the word (Martha, good Samaritan). Both are necessary for followers of Jesus in Luke's community. The way of Mary is the way to become a better Martha. The section of the Gospel, which deals with prayer, will give Luke an opportunity to further explore the relationship between hearing and doing the word of God.

It is important to note Mary's physical position in this uniquely Lucan account. Mary sits beside the Lord at his feet.

She assumes the posture of a male disciple (cf. Luke 8:35). Throughout his Gospel, Luke is very interested in the role of women. Through his portrayal of women in the Gospel, he reflects what he believes their role to be in the Christian community and what their role was at the time that he was writing this Gospel.

He mentions Mary, called Magdalen; Joanna, the wife of Herod's steward Chuza; Susanna, and many others who provided for Jesus and the Twelve out of their resources (8:2-3). When Jesus is crucified, these women stand at a distance (23:49). Mary Magdalen, Joanna, and Mary the mother of James, and others who accompanied them bear witness to the resurrection (24:10). This association of women with the ministry of Jesus is very unusual in the light of the culture of the time. It reflects a uniquely Lucan view.

Meditation: When do you, like Mary, hear the word of God? When do you, like Martha, practice (do) the word of God?

Prayer: God of hospitality, you once visited Abraham and Sarah and gave them the promise of a son. You have visited us in the person of Jesus, your own Son. He has taught us the good news of your kingdom. He has shown us how to put into practice the good news that we hear. Give us an open heart, like Mary, that we may sit at his feet and listen to him speak. Give us the willingness of Martha, that we may serve others in his name. We ask this through the same Jesus Christ our Lord, who lives and reigns with you and the Holy Spirit, one God, for ever and ever. Amen.

LIKE JONAH
Matthew 12:38-42

Scripture: "Just as Jonah was in the belly of the whale for three days and three nights, so will the Son of Man be in the heart of the earth for three days and three nights" (Matthew 12:40).

Reflection: The weekday lectionary cycle omits Jesus' discussion with the Pharisees about driving out demons "by the power of Beelzebul" (12:24) as well as the analogy between a tree and its fruits (12:33-37) which follows it. Likewise, the section which follows the demand for a sign (12:38-42) — the return of the unclean spirit (12:43-45) — is omitted in the weekday course of readings. To adequately understand the demand of the Pharisees for a sign, the reader must place it within the context of Matthew's discussion of exorcism.

The source for this section is Q (cf. Luke 11:29-32). Matthew has already portrayed Jesus as defeating the devil (4:1-11). The discussion between Jesus and the Pharisees concerning Beelzebul serves only to confirm Satan's defeat.

But the scribes and Pharisees want a sign from Jesus that will authenticate his claims, his power. The "scribes and Pharisees," of course, are the unbelievers in Matthew's community; they want a reason to believe that Jesus, who had been put to death and raised from the dead, is the Messiah.

In this passage Jesus refers to unbelievers as an "unfaithful (literally "adulterous") generation" (12:39). Both the prophet Hosea (2:4-15) and the prophet Jeremiah (3:6-10) refer to the covenant between God and Israel as a marriage bond. When the Israelites were unfaithful, that is, when they broke the covenant through idolatrous practices, these prophets spoke of them as being adulterous. Matthew is declaring that those who do not believe in Jesus are like the idolaters of old.

The sign that Matthew chooses to give to unbelievers is that of Jonah, for two reasons.

First, by referring to Jonah's three day and three night stay in the belly of the whale (cf. Jonah 2:1) Matthew is implicitly echoing the resurrection of Jesus, which at the time of the writing of this Gospel had already taken place.

Second, after getting to Nineveh, Jonah preached but one day and the whole city repented. Therefore, according to Jesus, "The men of Nineveh will stand in judgment against this generation and will condemn it, because they repented at the preaching of Jonah; but, behold, one greater than Jonah is here" (12:41). The people of Nineveh were pagans, but they repented. The present generation has Jesus risen from the dead — the "one greater than Jonah [who] is here" — but they fail to repent. On judgment day the pagans (Gentiles), who have repented, will condemn those who should believe (for Matthew, members of his own community) and condemn them.

Matthew gives another example of why unbelievers in his community should believe in Jesus: "The queen of the south will rise up at the judgment against this generation and condemn it, because she came from the ends of the earth to hear the wisdom of Solomon; and behold, one greater than Solomon is here" (12:42). In other words, Sheba, the queen of the south (cf. 1 Kings 10:1-13), was a pagan who traveled to Israel to hear the wisdom of Solomon. Matthew's community has Jesus, the Wisdom of God incarnate — the "one greater than Solomon [who] is here" — and yet they do not believe. On judgment day the queen of the south will condemn this "unfaithful generation" who have rejected Jesus.

As usual, Matthew is attempting to hold his community to-gether. He does not want the Jewish unbelievers to continue in their unbelief. But he also knows that the Gentiles are becoming believers. Through the power of Jesus' resurrection, both groups can become one community of believers. The signs have been given. Evil has been conquered. It is up to every generation to repent.

Meditation: What most recent signs has God given to you that indicate that you need to repent?

Prayer: God of signs, through the preaching of your prophet Jonah, you converted the entire city of Nineveh to yourself. Through the teaching and preaching, death and resurrection of Jesus, you converted the entire world to yourself. Through the power of your Holy Spirit, convert our hearts. May we never be unrepentant, but always recognize the greatest one among us — Jesus, who lives and reigns with you and the Holy Spirit, one God, for ever and ever. Amen.

GOD'S WILL

Matthew 12:46-50

Scripture: "Here are my mother and my brothers. For whoever does the will of my Father in heaven is my brother and sister and mother" (Matthew 12:49-50).

Reflection: The section of the Gospel referred to as the true family of Jesus appears in all of the synoptics. Matthew's source is Mark (3:31-35). However, he has omitted the occasion for this section of Mark's Gospel — namely, the fact that Jesus' family had declared, "he is out of his mind" and "set out to seize him" (Mark 3:21). By omitting the Marcan setting for the narrative concerning the true family of Jesus, Matthew is able to give the narrative a new setting and a slightly different meaning.

Matthew presumes that Jesus and his disciples are inside a house, while his mother and his brothers appear outside (cf. 12:46). In Mark, there is a crowd "seated in the circle" (Mark 3:34) around Jesus. Matthew changes the group in the inner circle for two reasons.

First, Mark portrays the disciples as slow to comprehend throughout the Gospel; they never come to understand who Jesus is. For Matthew, disciples are members of his community. He is not interested in portraying them as ignorant, but as the inner group who know who Jesus is, understand his teaching and preaching, and put his words into practice.

Second, Matthew has already specified the conditions for

151

discipleship (cf. 8:18-22; 10:37-39) — the breaking of family ties. Now Matthew's Jesus, the Master, must demonstrate that no family ties can get in his way either. In other words, what Jesus asks of his disciples, the breaking of family ties, he himself does.

Natural kinship with Jesus counts for nothing. What does count? For Matthew, it is doing the will of the heavenly Father. This, of course, is Matthew's theme of righteousness, correct behavior, emphasized once again. The authentic family of Jesus is composed of those people who behave as God wants. This new family is Matthew's community, his church.

Those who are baptized into the community (cf. 28:19) become brother, sister, and mother to Jesus. By doing the will of the heavenly Father, people become sons and daughters of God and brothers and sisters and mothers of Jesus.

Meditation: Do you find that you are inside the house with Jesus (his authentic disciple, a member of his new family) or standing outside (a member of his natural family)?

Prayer: Father of Jesus, you call all men and women to do your will by practicing the word you spoke through your only Son, Jesus. From the outside world of disbelief bring us into the inner circle of authentic disciples. Make of us brothers and sisters and mothers of Jesus, who lives and reigns with you and the Holy Spirit, one God, for ever and ever. Amen.

EARS TO HEAR

Matthew 13:1-9

Scripture: "Whoever has ears, let them hear" (Matthew 13:9).

Reflection: The thirteenth chapter of Matthew's Gospel begins the third of five sermons of Jesus. The entire chapter, which consists of seven parables, is commonly called the parables discourse. Matthew borrows two of Mark's parables and adds five others from Q and his own unique special source. The first parable of this chapter, the parable of the sower, is borrowed from Mark (4:1-9).

The setting for the third sermon is the seashore (13:1). Jesus leaves the house, crowds follow, and he gets into a boat and sits down (13:2), while the crowd stands along the shore. Jesus assumes the same physical position — seated — as he does for the first discourse, the Sermon on the Mount. That is, he assumes the customary position of a teacher of the times (cf. 5:1; 13:3).

The parable of the sower illustrates a typical Palestinian way of planting seed. Often, the sowing preceded the ploughing. The sower casts seed everywhere in an extravagant fashion. He is not able to tell what may be under the thin topsoil of the region, so he takes a risk and throws seed everywhere — on the path, on rocky ground, among thorns, and on rich soil.

For Matthew, Jesus is the sower of the seed. Just like the sower goes out to sow, Jesus goes out of the house to speak to the crowd. In parables, Jesus speaks about God and his kingdom in extravagant ways.

At first sight, it seems that much seed is wasted; three-fourths of the seed produces no results. As Matthew has shown up to this point of his Gospel, three-fourths of those who hear Jesus do not believe. Only the disciples — the remaining one-fourth — believe, but even then they question (cf. 13:10 ff.).

Moreover, the one-fourth of the seed that does grow produces fruit in various measures — "a hundred or sixty or thirty fold" (13:8). Through this amazing result, Matthew is expressing in these words of Jesus his own confidence that God's kingdom will be proclaimed and that God's will (righteousness) will be done.

To those community members who doubted in the face of three-fourths failure, Matthew is offering abundant hope. All it takes, he is saying, is for one-fourth of the seed to produce. This one-fourth can yield as much as the whole amount planted — a hundred or sixty or thirty fold. Just as the seed is sown extravagantly, so it produces extravagantly.

Therefore, "whoever has ears, let them hear" (13:9). In other words, since it is presumed that everyone has ears, every person should listen attentively to this teaching and put it into practice. The parable, then, was not only meant for the disciples and the crowd at the seashore but for everyone who reads Matthew's Gospel.

Meditation: Which one-fourth of the seed produces an abundant harvest in your life?

Prayer: God of farmers, through your patriarchs and prophets you have sowed your word extravagantly. Through your prophets you have revealed your mercy to your people. Jesus has sown the word of your kingdom in our hearts. Through the working of your Holy Spirit bring the seed to fruition in us. May we produce a hundred or sixty or thirty fold according to your will. We ask this through our Lord Jesus Christ, your Son, who lives and reigns with you and the Holy Spirit, one God, for ever and ever. Amen.

GRACE AND FREE-WILL
Matthew 13:10-17

Scripture: "Amen, I say to you, many of the prophets and the righteous longed to see what you see but did not see it, and to hear what you hear but did not hear it" (Matthew 13:17).

Reflection: Following his Marcan source (4:10-12) and adding a section from Q (Matthew 13:16-17), Matthew follows up the parable of the sower with an explanation of the purpose of parables. Matthew's explanation is much longer than Mark's, and it displays some unique Matthean characteristics.

In Matthew's Gospel the disciples are portrayed as believers; they understand who Jesus is. Therefore, their eyes are blessed, because they see what "many prophets and righteous people longed to see... but did not see it" (13:17), and their ears are blessed, because they hear what "many prophets and righteous people longed to hear... but did not hear it" (13:17). Clearly, Matthew has contrasted his believing disciples to Mark's unbelieving disciples.

In this section of his Gospel, Matthew also theologically works out his perspective on the parables. The problem that the parables illustrate, for Matthew, is Israel's lack of faith. Israel, God's chosen people who are awaiting the Messiah, should have believed but did not; the Gentiles, who were not awaiting a Messiah, should not have believed but did.

155

In Matthew, Jesus speaks to the crowds in parables because they have already refused to see and to hear his message. Matthew, the author, through the words of Jesus, is speaking to his own audience; he is both urging them to believe and warning those who do believe to be careful that they do not lose the precious gift that they have received. This perspective can be contrasted to the Jesus we find in Mark's Gospel, who speaks to the crowds in order that they may not understand.

Matthew is relying on an Old Testament understanding; namely, that God has everything under control. "Isaiah's prophecy is fulfilled in them" (13:14). One of the best descriptions of God's over-all control is found in the book of Exodus, where Pharaoh's obduracy in refusing to permit the Israelites to leave Egypt is credited to God. God says, "I will make Pharaoh so obstinate that, despite the many signs and wonders that I will work in the land of Egypt, he will not listen to you" (Exodus 7:3-4).

Why does God harden some hearts and not others? Why does God make Pharaoh obstinate and Moses' and Aaron's task so difficult? If God is in control, then God must be in control of sin too. There is no attempt by the biblical authors to reconcile this problem. Grace is active in the world; sin is active in the world. It is a paradox that Matthew is using to deal with the faith of the Gentiles and the disbelief of Israel. He has no answer to the problem.

To some, God grants "knowledge of the mysteries of the kingdom of heaven" (13:11). To others, "it has not been granted" (13:11). "To anyone who has, more will be given and he will grow rich" (13:12). In other words, God will give further understanding to the person who accepts the revealed mystery, the grace of God. "Anyone who has not" accepted the mystery, "even what he (or she) has will be taken away" (13:12). In other words, God will take away the offer, because everything is in God's control. Who can understand the mind of God?

The people of the present age (at the time of Matthew's writing as well as now) are blessed because they can see and they can hear what those who longed to see and hear (prophets and righteous people) never saw and heard. The present age is being offered by God the possibility of believing and understanding. They can either accept it or reject it, and, according to Matthew, whatever they choose to do must be done because of God's will, righteousness.

Meditation: How do you reconcile the paradox between grace and free-will in your life?

Prayer: God of grace, you never cease to seek out your people and to reveal to them the mysteries of your kingdom. Yet, you also have endowed your people with freedom of will so that they may choose to grow in knowledge of your ways. In the silent moments of our lives, permit us to contemplate the parables of Jesus. Give us ears to hear and eyes to see that we might be named blessed in the kingdom, where you live and reign with your Son, our Lord Jesus Christ, and your Holy Spirit, one God, for ever and ever. Amen.

FOUR TYPES OF PEOPLE

Matthew 13:18-23

Scripture: "Listen, then, to the parable of the sower" (Matthew 13:18).

Reflection: After narrating his version of the parable of the sower, and after explaining Jesus' purpose of speaking in parables, Matthew follows Mark (cf. 4:13-20) and, with a few peculiar Matthean editing features, offers an explanation of the parable of the sower. Since Matthew is fond of allegory, Mark's interpretation of the parable of the sower fits neatly into his Gospel.

The focus of the parable of the sower is the sower. The focus of Matthew's explanation of the parable is the seed, of which there are four kinds, each corresponding to four types of persons (soils) in Matthew's community. The seed grows depending on the soil, the disposition of the person upon whom it falls.

First, some people hear the "word of the kingdom" (13:19), but they never truly understand; they never become authentic disciples. Here, the reader should notice the Matthean emphasis on hearing and understanding, which ties into the privilege of discipleship section (13:16-17) which immediately precedes this explanation. Authentic disciples are those who hear the word and understand it.

Second, some people hear "the word and receive it at once with joy" (13:20). However, "when some tribulation or persecution comes because of the word," these "immediately fall away"

(13:21). In Matthew's community, there were people who were followers of Jesus as long as it was convenient. When their faith proved to be inconvenient in the face of persecution, they apostatized; they denied their faith.

Third, some people hear the word, "but then worldly anxiety and the lure of riches choke the word and it bears no fruit" (13:22). In Matthew's church, there were people who heard the word of the kingdom, but they chose the world and riches. The best example of this type of person is given by Matthew later in his Gospel — the rich young man (19:16-30). There, Jesus declares, "Amen, I say to you, it will be hard for one who is rich to enter the kingdom of heaven" (19:23).

Fourth, the authentic disciple or follower of Jesus reflects Matthew's three-fold characteristic of authenticity. He or she "hears the word and understands it" and "bears fruit" (13:23). For Matthew, righteousness is hearing, understanding, and doing (practicing) the word. The author is encouraging the members of his community to continue to do God's will (to bear fruit, to be righteous) no matter what comes their way. In each member, the word, heard, understood, and done, produces accordingly — "a hundred or sixty or thirty fold" (13:23).

Meditation: When did you hear the word but not understand it? When did you hear the word but abandon it in the face of problems? When did you hear the word but exchanged interest in it for consumer goods and services? When did you hear the word, understand it, practice it, and discover a rich yield?

Prayer: God our sower, you plant the word of your kingdom in the soil of our lives. Through the working of your Holy Spirit, give us attentive hearts, understanding minds, and wills to put your word into practice. Bring forth a generous yield from our lives. We ask this through our Lord Jesus Christ, your eternal Word and Son, who lives and reigns with you and the Holy Spirit, one God, for ever and ever. Amen.

GROWING TOGETHER

Matthew 13:24-30

Scripture: "The kingdom of heaven may be compared to a man who sowed good seed in his field. While everyone was sleeping his enemy came and sowed weeds all through the wheat, and then went off" (Matthew 13:24-25).

Reflection: The parable of the weeds among the wheat is unique to Matthew's Gospel. The author compares the kingdom of heaven to the situation narrated in the entire story — the growing together of wheat and weeds. For Matthew, his church reflects the kingdom, which "now" is composed of wheat and weeds.

The analogy of wheat and weeds works well for an agricultural society. The weed, darnel, is a poisonous plant. In the early stages of its growth it looks like wheat. Therefore, by the time both wheat and weeds reach a stage of differentiation, the roots of each are so intertwined that any attempt to pull up the weeds would result in pulling up the wheat also. The best solution is to permit both weeds and wheat to grow together. After the harvest, when the wheat is separated from the weeds, the weeds can be burned.

Matthew is attempting to hold together a community. By narrating this story, he is telling the members of his church that not one of them has any authority to judge the difference between wheat and weeds. This is not a new Matthean theme; it is found throughout the first sermon of Jesus and in other places in the Gospel.

There is only one judge, one harvest master; he is the Son of Man. When he comes (the parousia), then wheat and weeds will be separated. Until that time, the kingdom is composed of saints (wheat) and sinners (weeds). No one knows who is a saint and who is a sinner, since the demands of righteousness entail doing God's will — whatever that may be.

What doesn't look like God's will may, in fact, be God's will. The reader needs to remember Joseph, who broke the law in order to do God's will and take Mary as his wife!

Likewise, what looks like God's will may not be God's will. The reader needs to remember the Pharisees, who adhere strictly to the law but are condemned around every corner by the Matthean Jesus! The definitive separation of saints and sinners will take place "when the Son of Man comes in glory" (25:31; cf. 31-46).

To attempt to separate the wheat from the weeds before the harvest is to take on the role of God, and this is the sin of idolatry. God will send the Son of Man, when God deems it time for the harvest. Until that time, the role of the members of the community (composed of wheat and weeds) is to patiently seek reconciliation with each other.

This parable begins the second section of Jesus' third sermon in Matthew's Gospel. The author has created an almost-identical sequence which parallels the first section of the Gospel. In that first section the parable of the sower is followed by the discourse on the purpose of parables and the privilege of discipleship before the explanation of the parable of the sower.

The parable of the weeds among the wheat is followed by two shorter parables, a short explanation as to how Jesus used parables, and the explanation of the parable of the weeds.

Meditation: What do you think are the difficulties involved in permitting the wheat (saints) and the weeds (sinners) to grow together (coexist) until the harvest (second coming of Jesus)?

Prayer: God of the harvest, you plant the good seed of your word throughout the world. However, the enemy often comes and plants weeds among your wheat. We cannot understand your wisdom in ordering that they be permitted to grow together until the harvest. Help us refrain from lifting our hand in judgment. On the day when you send your Son to gather the wheat into your kingdom, count us among your loyal servants. We ask this through Christ our Lord. Amen.

TREASURE, PEARLS, NET

Matthew 13:44-52

Scripture: "The kingdom of heaven is like a treasure buried in a field..., like a merchant searching for fine pearls..., like a net thrown into the sea, which collects fish of every kind" (Matthew 13:44, 45,47).

Reflection: Matthew concludes the third sermon of Jesus, commonly known as the discourse in parables, with three uniquely Matthean parables (13:44-53). These very short stories function to reemphasize the author's theological perspective, which was presented in earlier parables in the same chapter (13).

First, "The kingdom of heaven is like a treasure buried in a field, which a person finds and hides again, and out of joy goes and sells all he has and buys that field" (13:44).

For Matthew, the kingdom is a treasure, which a person may accidentally discover — like money hidden in a field.

Because of the political problems in Palestine, people often hid their valuables in fields. If the rich person was killed, then the treasure remained hidden until someone accidentally discovered it.

A field hand finds the hidden treasure — the kingdom — and hides it again. The man deceives the original owner by covering up the treasure and buying the field. For Matthew, once one has discovered the kingdom of God, one should do anything in order to obtain it. The treasure of the kingdom is worth any price. Discovering the kingdom means being totally committed to it.

Second, "The kingdom of heaven is like a merchant searching for fine pearls. When he finds a pearl of great price, he goes and sells all that he has and buys it" (13:45-46).

In this parable the kingdom is compared to a merchant, who, unlike the farmer who accidentally discovers the kingdom actively goes in search of it. He is searching for fine pearls (the reader should notice the plural). However, when he finds only one pearl, he realizes its value, sells all else that he has, and buys the one valuable pearl.

Again, the point is commitment. The merchant invests his life, like the farmer, in one commitment — the kingdom.

Investment brokers would never urge or direct investors in such a direction. However, when it comes to the kingdom of heaven, one gives up whatever is necessary in order to possess that which has been the object of one's lifetime search.

Third, "The kingdom of heaven is like a net thrown into the sea, which collects fish of every kind. When it is full they haul it ashore and sit down to put what is worthwhile into buckets. What is not they throw away. Thus it will be at the end of the age" (13:47-49).

This parable echoes the parable of the weeds among the wheat and emphasizes Matthew's understanding that the church, his community (the sea), is made up of both good (what is put in buckets) and bad (what is thrown away). The kingdom is a net, which is filled with every kind of fish.

It is only at the end of the age that any separation will take place. Until that time, Matthew is exhorting the members of his community not to label each other as good or bad; this responsibility belongs to God alone. When the day of judgment (separation) comes, the wicked will be divided from the righteous, those who have done the will of God.

The righteous will inherit the kingdom. The wicked will be thrown away into the fiery furnace, "where there will be wailing and grinding of teeth" (13:50). The last phrase is one of Matthew's favorite ways of describing eschatological punishment and concluding a parable which deals with it.

The treasure and the pearl are favorite Old Testament images for wisdom, understanding. "Every scribe who has been instructed in the kingdom of heaven is like the head of a household who brings from his storeroom both the new and the old" (13:52). In Matthew's community, the scribe is a leader. Such a person knows both the new, the teaching of Jesus concerning the kingdom, and the old, the law and the prophets. The old informs the new, and the new informs the old.

"When Jesus finished these parables, he went away from there" (13:53). This is how Matthew ends the third of Jesus' sermons.

Meditation: When did you accidentally discover the kingdom of heaven? When did you find the kingdom of heaven after searching for it? To what can the kingdom of heaven be compared today?

Prayer: God of the household, you bring from your storeroom both the old and the new. You have given us the treasure of your law and the prophets and the pearls of wisdom of your Son, our Lord Jesus Christ. Through the power of your Holy Spirit, give us a deep understanding of these mysteries that we may be counted among the righteous in the kingdom, where you live and reign with Jesus and the Holy Spirit, one God, for ever and ever. Amen.

PASSOVER FOODS

John 6:1-15

Scripture: Jesus went up on the mountain, and there he sat down with his disciples. The Jewish feast of Passover was near. Jesus took the (barley) loaves (from a boy), and after blessing them, he distributed them to those who were reclining, and likewise with the fish (which the boy had), as much as they wanted (John 6:3-4, 11).

Reflection: For five continuous Sundays, the Marcan cycle of readings is interrupted by selections from chapter six of John's Gospel. This chapter contains the Johannine account of the multiplication of the loaves and the fishes, the bread of life discourse, and the disciples' attestation that Jesus has the words of eternal life.

The first section of chapter six (verses 1-15) of John's Gospel narrates the multiplication of the loaves and the fishes. This is the fourth of seven signs in John. While this same basic account appears twice in Mark, twice in Matthew, and once in Luke, it has been reshaped by the Johannine author to reflect his own concerns.

The setting for the story is a mountain. Jesus in the Gospel of John, unlike in the synoptic Gospels, takes the initiative and asks Philip, "Where can we buy enough food for them (the crowd) to eat?" (6:5). The mountain setting is not only reminiscent of many of the great events of Israel's past, but it specifically points to Moses, who met God in a burning bush on a mountain, who led the Israelites to worship God on a mountain, and who received the law from God on a mountain.

Jesus' question to Philip echoes Moses' question to God, "Where can I get meat to give all this people" (Numbers 11:13), after the escape from Egypt and during the wandering in the desert. John pictures Jesus as a new Moses, the new leader of people from slavery to freedom, the provider of food for people.

The time for this narrative is near Passover, the feast celebrating the exodus from Egypt. "There was a great deal of grass in that place" (6:10). In other words, it is Springtime.

Beside the paschal lamb needed for the feast, unleavened bread is also used. The author of this Gospel includes no eucharistic institution narrative, as do the synoptics. However, he does understand Jesus to be the new passover lamb, whose bones are not broken (cf. Exodus 12:46).

The bread given to the crowd is in the form of barley loaves, according to John. Bread made from barley was the food of the poor. Also, John echoes the multiplication of the barley loaves at the hands of the prophet Elisha (cf. 2 Kings 4:42-44). Elisha feeds a hundred men with twenty barley loaves, and there is some left over. Jesus feeds five thousand people with five barley loaves.

Therefore, the crowd, the reader, can conclude, "This is truly the Prophet, the one who is to come into the world" (6:14). Jesus is the Prophet like Moses (cf. Deuteronomy 18:15); Jesus is the prophet like Elijah, who has come into the world before the day of the Messiah (cf. Malachi 3:1, 23).

For John, this story proclaims to the reader that Jesus is the new food for people. He is readily available. He leads people out of the slavery of sin to the freedom of being sons and daughters of God; a new exodus takes place in him. During the time of this exodus (each person's lifetime) Jesus offers himself as food. He continues to replicate this sign every time the Eucharist is celebrated. He is "the lamb of God," who takes away the sins of the world.

Meditation: When has Jesus recently taken the loaves of your life and multiplied them for others?

Prayer: God of bread, in the desert when your people were hungry, you rained down manna for them to eat. Through Moses, your prophet, you led your chosen people from the desert of hunger to the promised land of plenty. Jesus, our bread of life, has chartered a new exodus. He has led us from the slavery of sin to the promised land of your kingdom. Make us always hunger for the bread that Jesus gives. Multiply the loaves of our lives that we might be able to share with others what he has given to us. We ask this through our Lord Jesus Christ, your Son, who lives and reigns with you and the Holy Spirit, one God, for ever and ever. Amen.

PERSISTENT PRAYER

Luke 11:1-13

Scripture: "Ask and you shall receive; seek and you shall find; knock and it shall be opened to you. For everyone who asks, receives; and whoever seeks, finds; and to those who knock, it shall be opened" (Luke 11:9-10).

Reflection: Immediately following the parable of the good Samaritan and the Martha and Mary story, Luke relates three teachings concerning prayer. These teachings further emphasize the Lucan theme of hearing the word of God (Mary) and doing the word of God (the good Samaritan).

The first of these three teachings presents the Lord's Prayer. Matthew uses the occasion of the first sermon of Jesus (on the mount; Matthew 6:9-15) to present this prayer, while Luke sets it within the context of Jesus' own act of praying. The Matthean version of the prayer is the one most familiar to Christians.

Typical of Lucan settings, Jesus is found to be "praying in a certain place" (11:1). Before any major decision or any major teaching, Luke portrays Jesus at prayer. In this way, Jesus serves as a model for Luke's readers. Before any major decision, Christians should engage in prayer, according to Luke.

Just as John the Baptizer taught his disciples to pray, so Jesus teaches his disciples to pray. The formula which Jesus gives is the one which was being prayed by Christians at the time that Luke was writing his Gospel. It stresses the fatherhood of God and asks that the kingdom come speedily. It petitions God for daily needs, for forgiveness, and for deliverance from the final test — the final judgment.

The second teaching focuses on the effectiveness of persistent prayer. No father would "hand his son a snake when he asks for a fish" (11:11). No father would hand his son "a scorpion when he asks for an egg" (11:12). If no wicked human being would do such a thing, then certainly God would never do such a thing. Parents give only good gifts to their children. The Father gives a gift that is better — "the Holy Spirit to those who ask him" (11:13).

The gift of the Holy Spirit is clearly a Lucan emphasis. Throughout his Gospel and the Acts of the Apostles, the Holy Spirit plays a major role. For Luke, Jesus is the model who teaches Christians how to pray persistently and get results. The Holy Spirit guides the members of the Church in their prayer requests and in their persistence.

Meditation: In which recent situation did you find yourself persistent in prayer and guided by the Holy Spirit?

Prayer: "Father, hallowed be your name, your kingdom come. Give us each day our daily bread and forgive us our sins for we ourselves forgive everyone in debt to us, and do not subject us to the final test" (Luke 11:2-4). Amen.

A MUSTARD SEED AND YEAST

Matthew 13:31-35

Scripture: "The kingdom of heaven is like a mustard seed that a man took and sowed in his field.... The kingdom of heaven is like yeast that a woman took and mixed with three measures of wheat flour until all of it was leavened" (Matthew 13:31, 33).

Reflection: Matthew borrows the parable of the mustard seed from Mark's Gospel (4:30-32). Most scripture scholars agree that this parable probably originated in oral tradition with Jesus because it is provocative and reverses usual expectations.

At the time of Jesus the proper metaphor for the kingdom was greatness — not smallness. For Jesus to say that the kingdom is like a mustard seed contradicts the established comparisons of the time. Anyone who heard such a figure of speech would not only be confused but upset. Who would dare compare the greatness of God to a tiny mustard seed?

In time the original intent of the parable was altered by the writers of the Gospels. Matthew's version reflects Mark's alteration of the parable. The smallness of the mustard seed comes to represent the small beginnings of the kingdom (which exists in the Church, for Matthew the community), but which results in greatness.

The mustard seed "is the smallest of all the seeds, yet when full-grown it is the largest of plants. It becomes a large bush, and the 'birds of the sky come and dwell in its branches'" (13:32).

This latter comparison and application of the parable was influenced by Nebuchadnezzar's vision: "I saw a tree of great height at the center of the world. It was large and strong, with its top touching the heavens, and it could be seen to the ends of the earth. Its leaves were beautiful and its fruit abundant, providing food for all. Under it the wild beasts found shade, and in its branches the birds of the air came to nest..." (Daniel 4:7-9).

Daniel interprets Nebuchadnezzar's vision: "The large, strong tree that you saw, with its top touching the heavens, that could be seen by the whole earth and which had beautiful foliage and abundant fruit, providing food for all, under which the wild beasts lived, and in whose branches the birds of the air dwelt — you are that tree, O king, large and strong. Your majesty has become so great as to touch the heavens, and your rule extends over the whole earth" (Daniel 4:17-19).

Through their use of the book of Daniel, the writers of the Gospels have extended Nebuchadnezzar's kingdom to the kingdom of heaven.

Another Old Testament influence on reinterpreting the parable of the mustard seed is the prophet Ezekiel. The Lord God says, "I will take from the crest of the cedar, from its topmost branches... a tender shoot, and plant it on a high and lofty mountain; on the mountain heights of Israel I will plant it. It shall put forth branches and bear fruit, and become a majestic cedar. Birds of every kind shall dwell beneath it, every winged thing in the shade of its boughs" (Ezekiel 17:22-23).

Later, Ezekiel presents the allegory of the cypress: "Behold, a cypress (cedar) in Lebanon, beautiful of branch, lofty of stature, amid the very clouds, lifted its crest. Thus it grew taller than every other tree of the field, and longer of branch because of the abundant water. In its boughs nested all the birds of the air, under its branches all beasts of the field gave birth, in its shade dwelt numerous peoples of every race" (Ezekiel 31:3, 5-6).

Under the influence of Ezekiel, the promise of messianic restoration made to Israel is seen as taking place in the kingdom of heaven, which was preached by Jesus. The original parable of Jesus was a parody of the great cedar (representing Israel), which the Gospel writers transformed into an allegory for the growth of the kingdom.

The parable of the yeast is from Q (cf. Luke 13:20-21). However, like the parable of the mustard seed, this parable reflects a genuine saying of Jesus. It contains an unlikely metaphor for the kingdom, and it provokes the audience to see reality in a new way.

To say that the kingdom of heaven is like yeast (more accurately translated as "leaven") is to compare the good kingdom to something which corrupts. In the ancient world, leaven was considered to be corrupting. When Passover was celebrated, no leaven could be found in Jewish homes. What was holy was untouched by leaven.

The corrupting agent, the leaven, is mixed (more accurately translated as "is hidden") in three measures of wheat flour (or dough). Three measures is not only about a bushel of flour, but an Old Testament sign of theophany, an unexpected appearance of God.

When Abraham receives three visitors, he tells Sarah to make rolls out of three seahs of fine flour (cf. Genesis 18:6). Later, Abraham and Sarah receive a promise of a son and discover that the three visitors were God.

As a test of his call from God, Gideon prepares an offering of a kid and an ephah of flour in the form of unleavened cakes (cf. Judges 6:19). An ephah of flour is three seahs or three measures. His offering is consumed by God's fire, and his call to be a leader of the Israelites is validated.

When Hannah offers her son, Samuel, to God, she offers an ephah of flour (cf. 1 Samuel 1:24) among other items. Samuel is the answer to her prayers for a son, whom she promised to dedicate to God if he would answer her prayer.

When the reader puts all this information together into one bowl of understanding, the thrust of the parable suddenly becomes apparent. The kingdom of heaven (the presence of God) is hidden in the world which it will change gradually, corrupting and destroying the old and making the whole world new.

Meditation: Using the style of Jesus, to what can you compare the kingdom of heaven today?

Prayer: God of mustard seeds and leaven, what is small in our sight is large in your eyes. What is corrupt in our understanding is good in your mind. Through the parables of Jesus, teach us your ways. He has announced what has lain hidden from the foundation of the world. May his words not fall on deaf ears. We ask this through our Lord Jesus Christ, your Son, who lives and reigns with you and the Holy Spirit, one God, for ever and ever. Amen.

THE WORLD-FIELD

Matthew 13:35-43

Scripture: "The one who sowed good seed is the Son of Man, the field is the world, the good seed the children of the kingdom. The weeds are those who belong to the Evil One, and the enemy who sowed them is the Devil" (Matthew 13:37-39).

Reflection: Since the parable of the weeds among the wheat is unique to Matthew's Gospel, the explanation of the parable of the weeds among the wheat is also peculiar to the same author. The setting is inside the house, after Jesus dismisses the crowd, indicating that a break has taken place between unbelieving Israel and the believing disciples.

Matthew supplies a list of equivalences so that the disciples (and the reader) can understand the parable, which is really an allegory. The parable concentrates on having patience with the wicked and permitting both good and bad to co-exist until the time of judgment. The explanation of the parable focuses on the doom awaiting the wicked.

The Son of Man sows good seed. This is the risen Jesus at work in the world through his followers (cf. 28:16-20). Matthew understands that Jesus is always at work — teaching, preaching, baptizing, etc. — through his disciples.

The disciples are sent to all nations; "the field is the world" (13:38). Matthew possesses an interest in spreading the message of the kingdom throughout the whole world. He has a particular interest in holding together his community, his church, but he views the mission to the Gentiles as being of equal importance.

The "children of the kingdom" are the authentic disciples of Jesus. They are the "righteous," who "will shine like the sun in the kingdom of their Father" (13:43). They behave according to the will of God. Some of these may not belong to the Church.

"The weeds are those who belong to the Evil One, and the enemy who sowed them is the Devil" (13:38-39). For Matthew, "all who cause others to sin and all evildoers" (13:41) exist throughout the world — both inside and outside the Church.

At harvest time, "the end of the age" (13:39), a phrase found only in Matthew's Gospel, the angel-harvesters will collect the weeds and burn them. "They will throw them into the furnace of fire, where there will be wailing and gnashing of teeth" (13:42), a favorite Matthean descriptive for eternal punishment.

Matthew distinguishes between the kingdom of the Son of Man and the kingdom of the Father. The Son of Man's kingdom co-exists with the Father's, but it continues only until the "end of the age." Once the age ends and judgment is complete (cf. Matthew 26:31-46), the Son of Man will hand over the righteous to the kingdom of the Father, which is brought about in stages.

Through his interpretation of the parable of the weeds among the wheat, Matthew reminds the members of his community that the world and the Church are made up of both good and bad in the present. Both will be judged at a later date. Both are called to repentance while there is still time. Therefore, "whoever has ears, let them hear" (13:43).

Meditation: Do you see yourself as good seed or weeds, or both? Explain.

Prayer: Heavenly Father, you have sown the seed of the good news of your kingdom throughout the world. From the beginning of time you have spoken your words of life to your creation — Adam and Eve, Abraham and Sarah, Isaac and Rebekah, David, the prophets, and Jesus, your own Son. Protect us from the weeds of the enemy that we may survive the harvest at the end of the ages. Count us among the righteous in the kingdom where you live and reign with Jesus and the Holy Spirit, one God, for ever and ever. Amen.

SYMBOLS OF WISDOM

Matthew 13:44-46

Scripture: "The kingdom of heaven is like a treasure hidden in a field... Again, the kingdom of heaven is like a merchant seeking fine pearls..." (Matthew 13:44-45).

Reflection: After the explanation of the parable of the weeds among the wheat, Matthew puts three more parables on the lips of Jesus. The parable of the treasure and the parable of the pearl are the first two of these three uniquely Matthean stories.

Both treasure and pearls are symbols of wisdom in the Old Testament. The kingdom of heaven is like wisdom, according to Jesus; it is found accidentally. Once it is found, the finder realizes the value of what he has discovered and sells everything else in order to own it.

There is a definite dedication to the task of acquiring the treasure. The finder is willing to deceive the owner by hiding it again in order to have it. Such is the value of finding the kingdom of heaven.

In Palestine at the time of Jesus, it was not uncommon for the wealthy to bury their treasure in order to protect it from invasions and revolt. If the owner died, then the treasure remained hidden until someone accidentally found it.

In this parable, the emphasis is on finding treasure in an employer's field, hiding it, buying the field, and laying claim to it. It may take some deception in order for one to possess the kingdom of heaven.

The parable of the pearl, like that of the treasure, has a high probability of being told orally and originally by Jesus. Matthew, of course, has left his editorial marks on both.

Unlike the man who accidentally discovers the treasure hidden in the field, the merchant actively searches for fine pearls. In the ancient world, pearls were more valuable than gold. While the wealthy merchant is in search of pearls, he finds one "pearl of great price" and sells all that he has in order to buy it.

His response is like that of the poor day laborer — immediate. The value of the one pearl — of the kingdom — is greater than any number of other pearls. He does whatever is necessary to possess it. He makes himself poor by selling all that he has in order to have the one pearl.

Real wealth, according to Matthew, is the kingdom of heaven. The poor field worker sells what little he has to own the treasure of the kingdom. The wealthy merchant strips himself of his riches in order to own the pearl of the kingdom. Their investments are total, but the treasures bring joy to their owners. Both the field hand and the merchant are committed to the kingdom of heaven. This is the type of commitment demanded of authentic followers (the righteous) of Jesus.

Meditation: What hidden heavenly treasure have you most recently found? What heavenly pearl have you most recently sought?

Prayer: Hidden God, you are the treasure we seek. You are the pearl of wisdom we need to guide us on our way. Open our ears to hear the message of Jesus. Give us the will to make the necessary investment and commitment to the good news he proclaimed. Show us the way to the kingdom of heaven, where you live and reign with Jesus and the Holy Spirit, one God, for ever and ever. Amen.

LIKE A NET

Matthew 13:47-53

Scripture: "Again, the kingdom of heaven is like a drag-net cast into the sea, which collected fish of every kind. When it was filled they hauled it ashore and sat down to put what was good into containers. What was bad they threw out" (Matthew 13:47-48).

Reflection: The parable of the fishnet is the last of the seven parables of the third sermon of Jesus in Matthew's Gospel. This particular parable is only found in Matthew's Gospel, and it reflects the same concern as that found in the parable of the weeds among the wheat and its explanation — namely, the good and bad exist together until the end of the age, when the Son of Man will make the final judgment.

Typical Matthean language is used in the parable of the fishnet. The angels (previously "harvesters," now "fishermen") separate the good fish (people) from the bad. The righteous, those who have done the will of God and behaved correctly, are merely separated from the wicked. The emphasis is on the punishment which the wicked will receive. They will be thrown "into the furnace of fire, where there will be wailing and gnashing of teeth" (13:50), Matthew's favorite descriptive phrase for eternal damnation.

The third discourse is brought to an end by an acknowledgment of understanding on the part of the disciples.

Unlike the Marcan disciples, the Matthean followers of Jesus understand the parables. They are like scribes who have been instructed in the kingdom of heaven (13:52). The storerooms of their lives contain what is new — the teaching of Jesus — and what is old — the law and the prophets.

In typical Matthean fashion, a reference is made to the first discourse where Jesus declares, "Do not think that I have come to abolish the law or the prophets. I came not to abolish but to fulfill" (5:17).

Also, keeping the Matthean balance between the old and the new, reference is made to the previous section, which dealt with the question of fasting, where Jesus declares, "You do not put new wine into old skins, for then the skins burst and the wine is spilled, and the skins are ruined. Instead, you pour new wine into fresh skins, and both are preserved" (9:17).

This final image of the scribe who is like the head of a household who brings from his storeroom both the new and the old is one of the many issues that Matthew deals with throughout the Gospel. It reflects his in-between position. He is attempting to define what it means to be a Jewish-Christian without a synagogue but with a Torah. This author believes that the words of Jesus form a true interpretation of the old law, but the followers of Jesus must take Jesus' words and put them into practice. Each person, then, is a storeroom, filled with the new and the old.

Meditation: In which ways are you like a storeroom — a repository of the new and the old?

Prayer: God of heaven and earth, through the law and the prophets, you teach your people your way of holiness. Through Jesus, your Servant and your Son, you show your people how to practice the words they hear. Make us storerooms of your wisdom that we may be able to bring forth both the new and the old at the end of the age. We ask this through our Lord Jesus Christ, who lives and reigns with you and the Holy Spirit, one God, for ever and ever. Amen.

KNOWING JESUS

Matthew 13:54-58

Scripture: "Isn't this the carpenter's son? Isn't his mother called Mary and his brothers James and Joseph, Simon and Judas? Aren't his sisters all among us here? Where did he get all this wisdom?" (Matthew 13:55-56).

Reflection: The concluding verses (54-58) of chapter thirteen of Matthew's Gospel are borrowed from Mark (6:1-6) and begin another narrative section of the Gospel. Jesus' "native place" (13:54) becomes the first stop of Jesus' itinerant ministry around Galilee.

As Matthew portrays the scene, the presumption of those people from Jesus' native place (Nazareth) is that they know who Jesus is. Unlike Mark, Jesus is not the carpenter, but the "carpenter's son." Unlike Mark, Jesus is not called the "son of Mary," a Jewish slur, but his mother's name is simply given. Also, the Nazarenes know his brothers and sisters (relatives). By knowing all this about Jesus, they presume to know Jesus.

For Matthew, however, this cannot be true. A person can know about Jesus and still not know him. Here, Matthew is warning the members of his community. He is telling them that they, like the Nazarenes, may know about Jesus but still not know him.

The true family of Jesus consists of those who do the will of the heavenly Father (cf. 12:49-50).

Therefore, "A prophet is without honor only in his home-

town and in his own house" (13:57). Matthew has omitted the
Marcan reference in this quotation to "among his own kinsmen"
(Mark 6:4) in order to soften Mark's seemingly harsh reference
to Jesus' family.

For Matthew, the issue is authentic faith and not family ties.
Those who may have known or known about any of Jesus' relatives have no advantage over those who have not. Every person
has the capacity to know Jesus. His family is not composed of
blood relatives; it is made up of members of the Church who seek
righteousness, authentic discipleship.

Meditation: What do you know about Jesus? In which ways do
you know Jesus?

Prayer: God of the family, through your prophets of old you called
countless men and women to be members of your chosen people.
Through Jesus, the greatest of the prophets, you have called us
to be counted among the members of your family. Through the
working of your Holy Spirit, guide us to do your will and give us
the faith we need to be righteous in your sight. Enable us to recognize the mighty deeds which you work in our midst. We ask
this through Christ our Lord. Amen.

BEHEADING OF JOHN

Matthew 14:1-12

Scripture: (Herod the tetrarch) had John beheaded in prison. His head was brought in on a platter and given to the girl (the daughter of Herodias), who took it to her mother (Matthew 14:10-11).

Reflection: Matthew's source for the narrative concerning Herod's opinion of Jesus and the death of John the Baptist (14:1-12) is Mark's Gospel (6:14-29). However, Matthew not only edits the length of the story, but he makes some significant changes in the narrative. The placement of the story, immediately following Jesus' rejection at Nazareth, is important to notice.

Mark's Gospel portrays Herod as one who "feared John, knowing him to be an upright and holy man.... When he listened to him, he was greatly disturbed, and yet he liked to listen to him" (Mark 6:20). Matthew portrays Herod as one who "wanted to kill" John (Matthew 14:5).

In chapter two (16-18), Matthew presented Herod the Great, who was responsible for the slaughter of so many innocent children in his attempt to murder the infant Jesus. In this section, the author presents Herod the tetrarch (Herod Antipas), the son of Herod the Great, who kills John the Baptist. For Matthew, the martyrdom of John, who was regarded by the people "as a prophet" (14:5), prefigures the death of the greatest of the prophets, Jesus, on a cross.

Matthew is interested in rejection. He is calling his community to pay attention to what happened in the past — John the Baptist was rejected; Jesus was rejected; the Church will be rejected. He is calling the members of his community to pay attention to what was taking place in the present — some of them were being rejected and some were rejecting others. According to Matthew, those who follow Jesus can expect to experience rejection.

Meditation: How have you experienced rejection because of your faith?

Prayer: God of the prophets, you called holy men and women to speak your good news to your people and to summon them back to you. Your prophet, John the Baptist, prepared the way for the greatest of the prophets, Jesus, who continues to call all people to repentance. Give us open ears and hearts that are moved by his message to take up our daily crosses and follow in the footsteps of Christ, your Son, who lives and reigns with you and the Holy Spirit, one God, for ever and ever. Amen.

WITHDRAWING

Matthew 14:13-21

Scripture: Jesus… left there privately in a boat for a desert place. And when the crowds heard this they followed him on foot from the cities. When he disembarked and saw the large crowd, he was moved with pity for them, and he healed their sick (Matthew 14:13-14).

Reflection: Matthew's source for the narrative of the feeding of the five thousand (14:13-21) is Mark's Gospel (6:34-44). Matthew, however, edits Mark's account of this miracle, which is the only one found in all four Gospels.

Following the narrative which explained the death of John the Baptist, Jesus withdraws in a boat "for a desert place" where he could be alone (14:13). This action of Jesus is unique to Matthew, and it forms a pattern. Following John's arrest, Jesus, "withdrew to Galilee" (4:12). Before this, Joseph had taken the child and his mother and "withdrew to Egypt," when Herod threatened the life of the child (2:13-15). Throughout Matthew's Gospel, Jesus "withdraws" from danger until the set time when "the Son of Man will be handed over to be crucified" (26:2).

Matthew's emphasis on a "desert place" (14:13, 15) echoes the setting for the "manna in the desert" event of the book of Exodus. Just as God, after Moses' intercession, once fed his chosen people in a "desert place," so Jesus, the new Moses, feeds the new community of the faithful in a desert place. However,

Jesus feeds the Church not only with bread, but with his teaching, his pity, and his ability to cure (cf. 14:14).

In Matthew's Gospel, the disciples understand who Jesus is and what he teaches, unlike in Mark's Gospel where they are portrayed as "slow to grasp." This author sees the disciples as mediators. Jesus tells them, "There's no need for them to go away: you give them some food to eat" (14:16). Once the loaves and fish are multiplied, they are given "to the disciples, who in turn gave them to the crowds" (14:19).

Thus, in Matthew's church, those who break bread in memory of Jesus are validated and appointed to do so by Jesus himself.

For Matthew, this narrative of the feeding of five thousand represents the fullness of the kingdom of heaven. When the members of Matthew's church gather together for the breaking of the bread, they represent the unity for which this author strives. The five thousand men, who are fed, does not include "women and children" (14:21). This theme will be echoed later in the Gospel with the parable of the wedding feast (22:1-14) and the parable of the ten virgins (25:1-13).

Other aspects of this narrative are discussed on Monday of Week Eighteen.

Meditation: To where do you withdraw in order to be healed and fed?

Prayer: God of mercy, you call your people to withdraw in order that you might speak to their hearts and feed them with your word. Be moved with pity for us. Call us to quiet places. Feed us with your word and the body and blood of your Son, Jesus, who lives and reigns with you and the Holy Spirit, one God, for ever and ever. Amen.

BREAD OF LIFE

John 6:24-35

Scripture: "I am the bread of life; whoever comes to me shall not hunger, and whoever believes in me shall never thirst" (John 6:35).

Reflection: A section (6:25-35) of the Johannine Jesus' bread of life discourse forms the second part of a five-week series of selections from John's Gospel. The account of the multiplication of the loaves (John 6:1-15) formed the first part of the series on Sunday of Week Seventeen, Cycle B. Through this long discourse, John is able to make some important theological points which reveal who he believes Jesus to be.

First, Jesus tells the crowd in this passage to "labor not for food that perishes but for food that remains for eternal life" (6:27). The food of which Jesus speaks is not the physical bread, which was multiplied in the last narrative, but is similar to the water offered to the Samaritan woman — "water welling up to eternal life" (6:27).

In both cases, John understands Jesus to be offering faith to people. Faith is food which nourishes people throughout their lives to eternal life. Water is drink which quenches the thirst for God that people have throughout their lives to eternal life. Through faith in Jesus, people have their hunger and thirst satisfied.

Second, the food and drink of faith does not have to be worked for, as one would work for money to buy physical bread or as one would work by carrying water or making money to pay a bill. When the crowds ask, "What can we do to accomplish the works of God?" Jesus tells them, "This is the work of God, to

189

believe in the one he sent" (6:28-29). In other words, faith does not have to be earned; it is a free gift offered by God through Jesus.

Third, the crowd thinks that it needs a sign in order to believe in Jesus. After all, there was the sign of manna in the desert in the past. Through Moses' intercession, God had given his people bread from heaven to eat. God worked a whole series of signs and the people believed in him.

Jesus in John's Gospel takes the focus off of Moses and reminds the people that "it was not Moses who gave you bread from heaven. On the contrary, my Father gives you the true bread from heaven" (6:32).

The "true bread from heaven" is not physical bread, like the manna of the past. "The bread of God is that which comes down from heaven and gives life to the world" (6:33).

John understands Jesus to be this bread which sustains life. Bread is a staple of life. Jesus is the staple of eternal life. Just like the manna sustained the lives of the Israelites in the desert, so now those who believe in Jesus will find that their lives are sustained for eternal life.

For John, Jesus is bread. All people need to do is to ask: "Lord, give us this bread always" (6:34). However, they have to understand that what they are asking for is not a loaf of physical bread but the faith to believe that Jesus will satisfy their hunger and their thirst forever.

Meditation: In which ways is your faith your food and your drink?

Prayer: Heavenly Father, once you rained down bread from heaven for your people to eat in the desert, and thus you satisfied their hunger. Through the incarnation of Jesus, your Son, you have given us the true bread from heaven, and, thus, shared your life with the world. Strengthen the work of our faith that we may never hunger or thirst again. We ask this through our Lord Jesus Christ, who lives and reigns with you and the Holy Spirit, one God, for ever and ever. Amen.

GREED

Luke 12:13-21

Scripture: "Watch out for and guard against all greed, because your life doesn't consist in the abundance of your possessions" (Luke 12:15).

Reflection: Luke has a particular bent against riches. His position concerning wealth is that it is given to a person in order to be shared with others. One has wealth so that one can give it away.

The parable of the rich fool, which is introduced by a dialogue between someone in the crowd asking Jesus to tell his brother to share the inheritance with him, illustrates the uselessness of trust in material riches as compared to dependence upon God. The narrative setting of the parable has been provided by Luke, and this parable is found only in his Gospel.

The introductory dialogue is reminiscent of that found in the story of Martha and Mary (Luke 10:38-42). Jesus is asked to intervene in a family problem. He, however, replies with a question, which removes him from the position of arbitrator.

Luke's focus is not on inheritance but on greed, the accumulation of wealth. Therefore, Jesus warns the crowd to "watch out for and guard against all greed, because your life doesn't consist in the abundance of your possessions" (12:15).

In the culture of the time, riches were considered to be a sign of God's blessing. If you were rich, it was because God fa-

191

vored you. Being poor was considered a sign of being cursed by God. You were poor because you or one of your relatives had done something displeasing to God.

In the parable the rich man's land "produced a bountiful harvest" (12:16). Therefore, he was considered to be exceedingly blessed by God. The only logical thing for him to do was to tear down his barns and build larger ones in which to store all his grain and other goods. Then, he would be secure "for many years" (12:19). His security was to be found in his riches.

But a surprising reversal of events takes place. The rich man dies, like all other human beings. His material riches are not enough security to preserve his life. Nothing can insure life. Amassing material things is futile. "God said to him, 'You fool, this night your life will be demanded of you; and the things you have prepared, whose will they be?'" (12:20).

The answer to this question is left to the crowd — and the reader. Riches cannot guarantee life. Only God can provide life. Furthermore, riches are not a sign of God's blessing, and being poor is not a sign of being cursed by God.

Jesus in Luke's Gospel reverses this cultural understanding. For his middle class (rich) audience, this parable came as quite a shock. It is important to note that Jesus does not condemn riches in this passage; he condemns covetousness and greed. As long as wealth is being given away, being used to help those who are in need, it is good. When it is hoarded, then it becomes bad.

Authentic wealth is found in God, who alone can guarantee life. Every single person is dependent upon God. To be attached to riches instead of being attached to God is useless and futile. Every single person will die and leave his or her wealth to be inherited by others. There is nothing wrong with receiving one's share of an inheritance, as long as that share is used to help better the state of those who have nothing.

Presuming that some people forming the crowd were poor, this parable shocked them as much as the rich. They found themselves no longer cursed because of their poverty. Furthermore, they found themselves being heirs to the riches of others, who are obligated to help them. The answer to the question at the end of the parable, "The things you have prepared, whose will they be?" (12:20), is now given: they will belong to the poor.

To title this story the "parable of the rich fool" is an oxymoron; "rich fool" is a combination of contradictory words. In the culture of the time, the person who was rich was certainly not a fool. However, this title was typical of other unique Lucan parables, such as the "good Samaritan" and the "dishonest steward."

Meditation: What is your attitude toward riches? Explain.

Prayer: God of the universe, your creation is your gift to be shared by all people. Guard us against all greed. Protect us from covetousness. Through the working of your Holy Spirit, help us to respond to those who are in need that we may continuously share what belongs to you with everyone. Make us rich in what really matters in your sight. We ask this through our Lord Jesus Christ, your Son, who lives and reigns with you and the Holy Spirit, one God, for ever and ever. Amen.

WHOLENESS

Matthew 14:13-21

Scripture: He took the five loaves and the two fish, and looking up to heaven, (Jesus) said the blessing, and after breaking them, gave the loaves to the disciples, who in turn gave them to the crowds (Matthew 14:19).

Reflection: The narrative of the feeding of the "five thousand men, not counting women and children" (Matthew 14:21) follows Matthew's story about the death of John the Baptist at the hands of Herod Antipas. Matthew borrows the story of the feeding from Mark's Gospel (6:34-44), but he abbreviates some of his original material and expands other parts of it.

The small amount of food, five loaves and two fish, is borrowed from Mark's Gospel. When the five loaves and the two fish are added together the sum is seven, which represents totality or completeness. For Matthew, then, the food that Jesus gives — his teaching, preaching, the curing of the sick, etc. — restores people to wholeness; it is all the food they need.

Jesus' actions with the loaves and the fish — looking up to heaven, saying the blessing, breaking the loaves, and giving them to the disciples to give to the crowds — echo the same actions of Jesus at the Last Supper (26:26). While this series of actions was usual at any Jewish meal, Matthew's style would indicate that he is interested in the eucharistic overtones present in the feeding of the five thousand. For Matthew, Eucharist is taking what little one has, sharing it, and watching it multiply.

It is also important to note that the action of "looking up to heaven," while not connected to the Last Supper institution narrative, made it into Eucharistic Prayer I (Roman Canon) of the Roman Missal. The words which introduce the institution narrative of the bread state, "The day before he suffered he took bread in his sacred hands and looking up to heaven, to you, his almighty Father, he gave you thanks and praise."

Matthew omits the Marcan reference to Jesus' dividing the fish among the people (Mark 6:41). His interest is not in the multiplication of fish but the multiplication of loaves with its eucharistic overtones. In other words, he has reduced Mark's miracle account by refocusing the narrative toward the Eucharist.

The abundance of left-over fragments — "twelve baskets full" (14:20) — is reminiscent of the miracle worked by Elisha (2 Kings 4:42-44). Taking twenty barley loaves, Elisha fed a hundred men. All ate, and there was some left over, as the Lord had said there would be. For Matthew, Jesus is a prophet like Elisha. However, he is greater than Elisha; he only needs five loaves to feed five thousand, whereas Elisha needed twenty loaves to feed one hundred.

Throughout most of the narratives which lead to Peter's confession about Jesus at Caesarea Philippi (16:13-20), Matthew mentions bread in one form or another. Bread is the gift which the Messiah gives to those who believe. And, this bread comes in many forms.

Meditation: What kind of bread has Jesus given to you recently?

Prayer: God of bread, you feed us with the finest wheat of your Son, our Lord Jesus Christ, who is the bread of life. May we always hunger for this food. May we always be willing to share it with all we meet. At the end of the age, bring us into the banquet of the kingdom, where you live and reign with Jesus and the Holy Spirit, one God, for ever and ever. Amen.

ON THE WATER

Matthew 14:22-36

Scripture: Peter got out of the boat and began to walk on the water toward Jesus. But when he saw how (strong) the wind was he became frightened; and as he began to sink, he cried out, "Lord, save me!" At once Jesus stretched out his hand and caught him, asking, "O you of little faith, why did you doubt?" (Matthew 14:29-31).

Reflection: The narrative of Jesus walking on the water (Matthew 14:22-36) is borrowed by Matthew from Mark (6:45-52). However, Matthew has expanded the story by adding a section concerning Peter (14:28-31), who, until he begins to doubt, also walks on the water with Jesus. Matthew has taken and kept a Marcan epiphany while at the same time shaping it into an allegory of the Church.

In Matthew's previous water-miracle (8:23-27), Jesus was portrayed as the God of the Old Testament who calmed the chaotic waters. In this section of his Gospel, Matthew portrays Jesus with the power to walk on the chaotic waters. This scene echoes Psalm 77:20, where it is said of God, "Through the sea was your way, and your path through the deep waters, though your footsteps were not seen."

A similar image is found in the book of Job. In his second reply, Job declares that God "alone stretches out the heavens and treads upon the crests of the sea" (9:8). Clearly Matthew, by por-

197

traying Jesus as walking on the water, understands him to be powerful, like the God of the Old Testament.

The epiphany dimension of this story is found in the "It is I" (14:27) response of Jesus to the fright of the disciples. When Moses encounters God in the burning bush and asks God for his name, God replies, "I am who I am" and "I AM" (Exodus 3:14). Thus, the divine is revealed. Matthew's "It is I" serves the same purpose; Jesus is here to save the disciples, just as God was there to save the Israelites. The hidden identity of Jesus as Son of God, which is found in the Marcan source, becomes public with Matthew's note: "Those who were in the boat did him homage, saying, 'Truly, you are the son of God'" (14:33).

Through Matthew's special section concerning Peter, an allegory of the Church is established in this section. The disciples in the boat represent Matthew's community, which is threatened by evil (the fourth watch of the night) and the turmoil (tossed about by the waves) of the times (persecution?). However, when the Church is in need and all seems lost, Jesus is there. Matthew will reinforce this point at the end of the Gospel, where Jesus declares, "I am with you always, until the end of the age" (28:20).

Peter, the first leader of the Church, plays an important role in Matthew's Gospel. He addresses Jesus as "Lord," and he momentarily walks on the water like his master. His cry, "Lord, save me!" (14:30) is the same as that of the cry of the Church. "The disciple is not above his teacher, nor the servant above his master. It is enough for the disciple to become like his teacher, and for the servant to become like his master" (10:24-25).

Like God in the Old Testament, Jesus stretches out his hand and saves Peter, who later will be named the foundation of the Church (16:18). However, Peter does not escape without a rebuke for his lack of faith: "O you of little faith..." (14:31). This uniquely Matthean phrase is used through the Gospel to indicate those disciples whose faith in Jesus is not as deep as it should be.

Matthew rounds off this story of Jesus' power and the disciples' confession of his divine Sonship by portraying Jesus as the great healer. "They brought all those who were sick to him and begged him to just let them touch the hem of his cloak, and as many touched it were healed" (14:35-36). This section is an edited version of a similar Marcan account (6:53-56). For Matthew, Jesus is no hidden miracle-worker; he is clearly the Son of God.

Meditation: When did you experience the boat of your life being tossed about by the waves of problems, indecisions, moral issues, etc. and discover Jesus calming the sea of your fear and calling you to walk through the problems, indecisions, moral issues. etc., with him?

Prayer: God of the sea, your power extends over the chaos of our lives and brings calm in the midst of strife. When we least expect him, Jesus comes walking through our lives with his healing and strength. Through your Holy Spirit, calm our fears. Strengthen our faith. When our boats begin to sink, save us. We ask this through our Lord Jesus Christ, your Son, who lives and reigns with you and the Holy Spirit, one God, for ever and ever. Amen.

DOG FOOD

Matthew 15:21-28

Scripture: (The Canaanite woman) came and knelt before (Jesus) and said, "Lord, help me." But in answer he replied, "It is not right to take the children's bread and throw it to the dogs." But she said, "Please, Lord — even the dogs eat the crumbs that fall from their master's table!" (Matthew 15:25-27).

Reflection: Matthew's source for this narrative is Mark's Gospel (7:24-30). However, the original Marcan account has been reworked quite extensively by Matthew to focus on his own particular concerns. The story follows Matthew's version of the distinction between what is clean and what is unclean, that which keeps Jews and Gentiles apart. Therefore, it is appropriate that in the passage from his Gospel he show how Jesus put into practice his own teaching through contact with a Gentile, a Canaanite woman.

This story, similar in form to that of the healing of a centurion's servant (8:5-13), is Matthew's way of further justifying the mission to the Gentiles. Matthew's community was haunted with a Jesus who claimed to have been "sent only to the lost sheep of the house of Israel" (15:24). When Gentiles accepted Jesus and his way, some clarification had to be made regarding the limitations of Jesus' ministry.

The Canaanite woman addresses Jesus as "Lord, Son of David" (15:22). The title "Lord" is used of the risen Christ. The title "Son of David" is used of the triumphant Jesus, who enters the city of Jerusalem to suffer and die.

201

"O woman, great is your faith!" (15:28) states Jesus. Like the story of the healing of the centurion's servant, Matthew attributes Jesus' granting the woman's request to her faith. Gentiles believe too.

Another interesting point to note about this story is the tenacity of the woman. A Canaanite, an image of Israel's ancient enemy, she and other Gentiles are referred to as "dogs" by Jesus, the one "sent only to the lost sheep of the house of Israel." She dutifully acknowledges her unworthiness and the fact that "it is not right to take the bread of the children (Israel) and throw it to the dogs" (15:26). In other words, the woman acknowledges the privileged position of Israel.

But she uses the derogatory remark to her advantage. "Even the dogs eat the crumbs that fall from their master's table!" (15:27). The privileged position of Israel is not accessible, but there must be other openings. Surely, the Gentiles can share in the crumbs. In this way, the woman gets a crumb, and her daughter is healed.

The woman is a model of humility and faith. She, like others throughout Matthew's Gospel, calls out, "Have pity on me..." (15:22). She is a Gentile who believes. She is an example, held up by Matthew, of how the mission of Jesus to Israel had to be expanded to the Gentiles. She also functions as a confirmation for Matthew's church that the mission to the Gentiles must continue. At the end of the Gospel of Matthew Jesus declares, "Go..., make disciples of all nations" (28:19).

Meditation: How is your faith like that of the Canaanite woman? Or, how would you respond if someone called you a "dog"?

Prayer: God of all nations, through the ministry of Jesus, your Servant and your Son, you have called all people to yourself. Guide to unity both Jew and Gentile, man and woman, free person and slave. Bring your people together in one communion of faith. We ask this through our Lord Jesus Christ, who lives and reigns with you and the Holy Spirit, one God, for ever and ever. Amen.

ROCK

Matthew 16:13-23

Scripture: Peter replied, "You are the Messiah, the Son of the living God." And in response Jesus said to him, "Blessed are you, Simon son of Jonah. For flesh and blood has not revealed this to you, but my heavenly Father. And so I say to you, you are Peter, and upon this rock I will build my Church" (Matthew 16:16-18).

Reflection: The weekday cycle of semi-continuous Matthean readings omits the summary statement concerning the healing of many people (15:29-31) and the narrative of the feeding of the four thousand (15:32-39), both of which follow the story of the Canaanite woman's faith (15:21-28) — yesterday's Gospel account.

Also omitted is the Matthean scene consisting of the demand for a sign by the Pharisees and Sadducees (16:1-4) and Jesus' warning to his disciples to "Take care and guard against the leaven of the Pharisees and Sadducees" (16:6). These two accounts precede Peter's confession about Jesus (16:13-20) and the first prediction of the Passion (16:21-23), which make up today's section of Matthew's Gospel.

The narrative concerning Peter's confession about Jesus is derived from Mark (8:27-30), where it functions as the turning point of the whole Gospel. Up to this point in Mark's Gospel, Mark has portrayed Jesus as a man of power. From this point on, he subverts that theme; Jesus demonstrates that discipleship involves powerlessness and includes suffering and death.

Matthew has significantly modified Mark's story. The setting of Caesarea Philippi is the same, but the question, "Who do people say that I am?" (Mark 8:27) becomes, "Who do people say that the Son of Man is?" (Matthew 16:13).

Three of Mark's answers are given: John the Baptist, Elijah, one of the prophets. These have been kept because they echo Matthean themes. The answer, "John the Baptist," serves as a reminder of Herod's opinion of Jesus: "This man is John the Baptist. He has been raised from the dead" (14:2).

The answer, "Elijah," echoes the description of John the Baptist: "John wore clothing made of camel's hair and had a leather belt around his waist. His food was locusts and wild honey" (3:4). There existed a popular expectation that Elijah would return to prepare for the final manifestation of the kingdom of God. Throughout his Gospel, Matthew understands John the Baptist as fulfilling this function (cf. 11:14; 17:11-13).

"One of the prophets" is Mark's third answer to Jesus' question. Because of his teaching, preaching, and mighty deeds, Jesus was regarded by Matthew as a great prophet, like Moses.

This author, however, adds a fourth answer to the Marcan list: "Jeremiah." This answer points to the first prediction of the Passion, as well as the rest of the Gospel. Jeremiah is considered to be the suffering prophet, who was rejected and martyred at the hands of his own people — a fate which would likewise befall Jesus.

None of these answers adequately reveal the true identity of Jesus. So, the Matthean Jesus asks his disciples (and every believer after them), "Who do you say that I am?" (16:15).

Mark's "Peter" becomes Matthew's "Simon Peter," who responds, "You are the Messiah, the Son of the Living God" (16:16). Thus, three Matthean titles for Jesus — the heart of the author's Christology, his understanding of who Jesus is — are brought together in one story: Son of Man, Messiah, Son of the living God.

"Son of Man" refers to Jesus in three ways: He is the earthly man with a specific ministry of teaching and preaching the kingdom of heaven. As the suffering servant of God, he will go to Jerusalem, where he will suffer and die. Finally, he is the judge, who will separate the wheat and the weeds, the sheep and the goats, on the last day.

As "Messiah," Jesus is the anointed of God, the one promised to the chosen people. He is the fulfillment of all past hopes and expectations.

Finally, as "Son of the living God," Jesus is transcendent. In Mark's Gospel, no human confesses Jesus as Son of God until after his death on the cross (the Marcan messianic secret). Matthew, probably employing a post-resurrectional, early Church confessional formula, identifies Jesus as the Son of God. Jesus is the embodiment of the life which God has in himself and which he shares with others.

Once Peter has identified Jesus and bestowed on him these three Christological titles (a revelation which had come from the heavenly Father: 16:17), Jesus bestows a title upon Peter: rock.

The English translation of this section does not adequately convey the play on words of the Aramaic original. The word for rock and Peter are the same. Therefore, the better translation would be rendered, "You are the Rock and upon this rock I will build my Church."

The significance of bestowing the title "rock" on Simon is found earlier in the Gospel in the first sermon of Jesus: "Everyone who listens to these words of mine and acts on them will be like a wise man who built his house on rock. The rain fell, the floods came, and the winds blew and buffeted the house. But it did not collapse; it had been set solidly on rock" (7:24-25).

Only in Matthew's Gospel is the word "Church" used. It appears two other times in 18:17. For Matthew, "Church" is the community of believers, who have been gathered together after the resurrection. The leader of this early community is Simon Peter, who, unlike Mark's Peter, builds it on the confessional foundation of Jesus as Son of Man, Messiah, and Son of God.

The authority of Peter is confirmed by the handing over of the "keys to the kingdom of heaven" (16:19). Borrowing an image from the prophet Isaiah (22:15-25), Matthew portrays Peter as receiving the authority to teach and to include or exclude people from the community. Now, Matthew has completed the foundation account of the Church, explained the role of Peter, and he has established the identity of Jesus for his community.

The first prediction of the Passion follows. Matthew's source is Mark (8:31-33), where the story serves to orient the rest of the Gospel toward powerlessness — the suffering and death of Jesus. Matthew uses the narrative in somewhat the same way. It serves as a balance to the glory and triumph found in the Christological titles in the section preceding it. As Messiah, Jesus suffers and dies; this is a fact with which Matthew must contend. Also, Peter did betray Jesus. So, after his fantastic confession of faith and confirmation of leadership, Peter is portrayed as one who gets it all wrong.

Discipleship involves suffering and death and resurrection. Anyone who fails to recognize this is an obstacle. Such a person thinks "not as God does, but as human beings do" (16:23). The next section of Matthew's Gospel appropriately launches into the conditions of discipleship.

Meditation: After confessing Jesus as Son of Man, Messiah, and Son of God, in which ways do you find that you revert to thinking as human beings do and deny the suffering and death aspects of discipleship?

Prayer: God our rock, you build your Church on the frailty of human beings and entrust to them the keys of your kingdom. Make us good stewards of your countless blessings. Keep us from becoming an obstacle to authentic discipleship. Enable us to freely accept suffering and death in the promise of entering the kingdom, where you live and reign with Jesus, your Son, and the Holy Spirit, one God, for ever and ever. Amen.

SELF-DENIAL

Matthew 16:24-28

Scripture: "If anyone would come after me, let him deny himself, take up his cross, and follow me.... The Son of Man will come in the glory of his Father with his angels, and then he will pay each one according to his conduct" (Matthew 16:24, 27).

Reflection: Immediately following Simon Peter's confession about Jesus and the first prediction of the passion, Matthew, following his Marcan source (8:34-38), presents the conditions of discipleship (Matthew 16:24-28).

Matthew expands his Marcan source and echoes some of his earlier material, which is found in the second discourse of Jesus (10:33, 37-39). The conditions for discipleship presented in this section of the Gospel are not necessarily the precise conditions laid out for the historical disciples of Jesus but for the members of Matthew's community.

First, an authentic follower of Jesus is willing to deny self. For Matthew, to deny means that one is willing to disown self (cf. 10:33; 26:34-35). One's self cannot be the center of one's existence. Only Jesus can be the center of one's existence.

The denial of self is another important Matthean theme. It reaches its high point on the cross, where Jesus denies himself as the Son of God, and suffers and dies a less than human death. Therefore, the authentic disciple (Christian) is one who is willing to take up the cross — the one who is willing to give up his or her life, like Jesus did.

The second condition of discipleship, then, is a willingness to stand firm in faith to death. In this way, one follows Jesus. Such self-denial and cross-carrying and following Jesus might look like death at first. However, "whoever would save his life will lose it, while whoever loses his life for my sake will find it" (16:25). God's ways are the total reversal of human ways. If one denies Jesus, disowns faith in him when faced with persecution, in order to preserve earthly life, such a person will forfeit eternal life in the kingdom of heaven. If, on the other hand, one stands firm in faith when faced with persecution (as did Jesus) and ends up giving up his or her life, then this person will share in the everlasting life of the kingdom of heaven.

Winning and losing are given new meanings by Jesus in the Gospel of Matthew. Winning is not preserving one's life at the cost of one's faith. "What good would it do to gain the whole world but forfeit your life? Or what could you give in exchange for your life?" (16:26). Winning is freely giving up one's life because faith is more important. Losing is preserving one's earthly life and giving up one's faith in Jesus.

When "the Son of Man will come in the glory of his Father with his angels, he will pay each one according to his conduct" (16:27). This verse points toward the judgment of the nations scene (27:31-46), where the sheep are separated from the goats. The basis for separation is faithfulness to Jesus and to the community, the Church, his body. Behavior, conduct, righteousness — a theme used throughout the Gospel — is the supreme mark of and condition for discipleship.

Meditation: Recently, in which way have you denied yourself, taken up your cross, and followed Jesus (that is, lost your life) only to discover that you found authentic life?

Prayer: God our Father, your ways are not our ways, and our ways are not your ways. Through Jesus you have taught us the mystery of saving life by losing it and losing life by saving it. Send us your Holy Spirit to guide us to self-denial, to help us to take up the cross, and to lead us in the footsteps of Jesus. Count us among the authentic disciples in the kingdom where you live and reign as perfect Trinity — Father, Son, and Holy Spirit — one God, for ever and ever. Amen.

LITTLE FAITH

Matthew 17:14-20

Scripture: "O unbelieving and perverse generation, how long will I be with you? How long will I put up with you? Bring him (the boy) here to me." Jesus rebuked it and the demon went out of him, and from that very hour the boy was cured (Matthew 17:17-18).

Reflection: The healing of the boy with a demon (Matthew 17:14-20) follows the narrative of the transfiguration of Jesus (17:1-8) and the discussion between Jesus and the disciples about the coming of Elijah (17:9-13). Both of these accounts are omitted from the daily cycle of reflections from Matthew's Gospel. Matthew's source for the narrative concerning the healing of the boy with a demon is Mark's Gospel (9:14-29).

Matthew, however, has greatly shortened the Marcan account by leaving out some of the details concerning the boy's illness and refocusing the story on the need for faith on the part of the disciples — instead of the boy's father.

The father of the boy addresses Jesus as "Lord" and requests that he "have pity" on his "son, for he is a lunatic and suffers terribly" (17:15). Matthew states that the man "knelt down before" Jesus (17:14). Clearly, then, Matthew portrays the father as a believer — he kneels (worships) and begs for mercy by addressing Jesus as "Lord" instead of the usual "Teacher."

A uniquely Matthean feature is the father's reference to his son as a "lunatic" (17:15), literally, "one affected or struck by the moon." Matthew reflects the belief of ancient physicians that the phases of the moon affected epileptic seizures. Jesus' disciples have not been able to cure the boy. This inability is credited to their "weak faith" (17:20).

At the same time, Jesus takes the occasion to rebuke the present generation for its faithlessness. Matthew is alerting the members of his church that the ministry of Jesus is drawing to a close (in fact, it is always drawing to a close), and that the time to profess faith in Jesus is now.

In private, the disciples learn that all it takes is a "little faith." A person doesn't have to have a basket full of faith; "faith the size of a mustard seed" (17:20) is sufficient. With little faith, one "will say to this mountain, 'move from here to there,' and it will move. Nothing will be impossible" (17:20). For Matthew, authentic faith can move mountains.

The last verse of this section of the Gospel (17:20) is a combination of a Q saying (cf. Luke 17:6) and a Marcan saying (cf. Mark 11:23). Mark omits the reason for the disciples' inability to heal the boy, namely, their "weak faith." This is a uniquely Matthean phrase used to describe those disciples whose faith is not as deep as it should be. Those of "weak faith" in Matthew's community were at one and the same time being warned and encouraged. They are being warned to not abandon the little faith they have. They are being encouraged to use it to move mountains (hyperbolically)!

Meditation: To what can you compare the size of your faith? What "mountain" have you recently moved with it?

Prayer: Faithful God, you never despise the little faith of your people, but you foster a trust that has the ability to suffer and to die and to remain firm in you. Have pity on us. Make of us authentic disciples of Jesus, your Son. Make our mustard seed size of faith strong enough to move mountains. We ask this through our Lord Jesus Christ, who lives and reigns with you and the Holy Spirit, one God, for ever and ever. Amen.

TOSSED BY PROBLEMS

Matthew 14:22-23

Scripture: (Jesus)… made his disciples get into the boat and go on ahead of him to the other side, while he sent the crowds away. After doing so, he went up on the mountain by himself to pray. When evening came on he was there alone, while the boat was already several miles away, tossed about by the waves, for the wind was against it (Matthew 14: 22-24).

Reflection: Matthew's narrative concerning the walking of Jesus on the water and Peter's walking on the water (14:22-33) immediately follows the account of the feeding of the five thousand (14:13-21). For Matthew, this story, which has been borrowed and enhanced from Mark's Gospel (6:45-52), is the author's way of speaking about the Church and her problems after the resurrection of Jesus.

The boat represents the Church. When Matthew was writing his Gospel, his community was being tossed about by dissension, persecution, betrayal, and a host of other problems. Thinking herself all alone on the wind-and-wave-tossed sea, the Church, according to Matthew, has the risen Lord with her. He is with her "always, until the end of the age" (28:20). In the midst of fear, however, the community often forgets this fact.

Some fear breeds more fear. Fear keeps the Church from recognizing the continual presence of Jesus with her. The disciples, like the Church, think they see a ghost, which only causes more fear. Matthew is alerting his community to the fact that in the face of problems courage is needed — not fear. "Take courage, it is I; do not be afraid" (14:27), Jesus tells the disciples and Matthew tells the Church.

The "It is I" response recalls the revelation of the divine name to Moses in the desert. When Moses was given his mission by God,

211

his first response was fear. Then God told Moses his name, "I am" (cf. Exodus 3:14). Moses' fear was turned into courage. With the presence of Jesus with the Church, Matthew declares that the members of the community have nothing to fear.

In Matthew's Gospel, Peter occupies an important role. Following the exhortation to courage, Matthew inserts some of his own unique tradition concerning Peter, the leader of the early, fear-filled Church (cf. 14:28-32).

For Matthew, Peter represents the human dimension of the Church. He is ready to follow Jesus by walking on the water, once Jesus calls him to leave the boat. He can walk on the water, until he becomes frightened. Then, he begins to sink and cries, "Lord, save me!" (14:30).

Matthew is demonstrating to the members of the community what they can do with the presence of Jesus with them and also how vulnerable they are in the state of fear. Fear is not compatible with faith. "O you of little faith," Jesus says to Peter, "why did you doubt?" (14:31).

The "little faith" aspect of believers is one of Matthew's unique and favorite phrases to describe those who profess faith in Jesus but aren't as strong as they should be. Of course, those of "little" or "weak faith" is descriptive of every member of the Church for Matthew. No one, except Jesus, has perfect faith.

Like the Matthean disciples, believers can declare of Jesus, "Truly, you are the Son of God" (14:3). They are in the Church and the wind has died down; the problems are momentarily solved. However, such a declaration of faith often does not hold up when fear of the unknown comes on board. Matthew is exhorting his faith-professing fearful community to trust in the presence of the risen Jesus, who is present with the Church until the end of time.

Meditation: When has fear so overcome you that you failed to believe in the presence of Jesus?

Prayer: God of water, wind, and waves, you never abandon your people in times of trouble. When the problems of our lives cause us to fear and doubt, strengthen us with the presence of Jesus. Make of us an authentic community of believers who profess that Jesus is the Son of God, who lives and reigns with you and the Holy Spirit, one God, for ever and ever. Amen.

STOP MURMURING!
John 6:41-51

Scripture: The Jews complained about him because he said, "I am the bread that came from heaven...." Jesus answered and said to them, "Stop murmuring among yourselves.... I am the bread of life..., the living bread that came down from heaven. Whoever eats this bread will live forever; and the bread that I will give is my flesh for the life of the world" (John 6:41, 43, 51).

Reflection: The third selection from John's Gospel (6:41-51) in the midst of the Marcan Gospel cycle is taken from the bread of life discourse (6:22-71). Since John's Gospel has no eucharistic institution story — only a washing of feet account — like the Synoptic Gospels do, the author of this Gospel presents a long sermon by Jesus on the bread of life. This discourse is filled with eucharistic overtones and Old Testament imagery.

The original "bread that came down from heaven" was the manna, which God gave his people in the desert. For the Johannine author to write that Jesus is the "bread that came down from heaven" is to claim that Jesus is food for God's people to eat, like the manna they ate in the desert. However, anyone who eats this new "manna" come down from heaven will never die.

The murmuring of the crowds echoes the grumbling of the Israelites in the desert. Once they had escaped Egyptian slavery, the Israelites began to grumble against Moses and Aaron and wished that they had stayed in Egypt where there was food rather than die in the desert. Moses and Aaron tell the people that they are not grumbling against them but against the Lord. After hearing their grumbling, the Lord gives manna to his people so that they can have their fill of bread (cf. Exodus 16:1-15).

Just as the Israelites come to know that it is God who feeds them in the desert, so those who listen to Jesus come to understand that he is God and he feeds people with "living bread," his flesh, which gives life to the world.

Some of those who listen to him, and those who read the Gospel with faith, recognize the eucharistic overtones and Old Testament imagery. Others see that Jesus is the "son of Joseph." They ask, "Do we not know his father and mother?" (6:42).

For John, it all depends on faith. Faith is the window through which a person views Jesus. If one believes, then he or she sees the new manna that has come down from heaven "so that one may eat it and not die" (6:50). If one does not believe, then all one sees is "the son of Joseph."

Meditation: Examine your faith. Of what does it consist? In other words, what do you believe about Jesus that influences how you see him?

Prayer: Father of Jesus, when your people grumbled against you in the desert, you gave them manna from heaven to eat. When your people murmured against Jesus near the sea, you gave them the bread of life. Draw us to this living bread that we may eat of it and live forever. On the last day, raise us up to be with you, your Son, our Lord Jesus Christ, and the Holy Spirit, one God, for ever and ever. Amen.

VIGILANCE

Luke 12:32-48

Scripture: "Blessed are those servants who, when he comes, the lord will find still vigilant. Amen, I say to you, he will gird himself, have them recline at table, and proceed to wait on them" (Luke 12:37).

Reflection: In Luke's Gospel, the parable of the rich fool (12:16-21) directly leads into an explanation of how believers are dependent on God (12:22-34) and a discussion concerning vigilance (12:35-48). Today's selection (12:32-48) consists of the last few verses of the section on dependence on God and the full section on vigilance and the characteristics of faithful servants.

Luke continues to foster the belief that there will be a second coming of Jesus (cf. Acts 1:11), and therefore he exhorts the members of his community to be faithful to the teaching of Jesus until he returns. However, the time between the first and second coming of Jesus — the time of the Church — is a long period for Luke. Those who are faithful followers of Jesus have their loins girded. For Luke, this represents readiness.

The metaphor recalls the instruction given by God to Moses in preparation for the exodus from Egypt (cf. Exodus 12:11). Followers of Jesus are on a journey — an exodus — with Jesus. Luke emphasized this in his transfiguration account: "Moses and Elijah… spoke of his exodus that he was going to accomplish in

215

Jerusalem" (9:31). Believers follow Jesus through suffering and death to resurrection and new life.

Faithful followers are also watchful for Jesus' return. It is not a watchfulness that bespeaks an imminent second coming of Jesus, but it is one of vigilance during the historical period of the Church. "Those servants whom the master finds vigilant on his arrival" are blessed (12:37); they are prepared for the coming of the Son of Man (cf. 12:40).

Those who are prepared will receive a surprise. The master "will gird himself, have them recline at table, and proceed to wait on them" (12:37). All will be reversed in the kingdom of God. Servants will no longer be servants, and masters will no longer be masters. This so-called eschatological reversal theme is frequently found in the parables.

Those who are not prepared, that is, those who are not vigilant are like stupid thieves, who most likely will get caught by the master of the house into which they try to enter. The delay of the master, the delay of the second coming of Jesus, is not reason, according to Luke, to act irresponsibly (cf. 12:45-48). People who believe in Jesus and follow him on his journey have a responsibility to be vigilant and faithful until Jesus comes in glory — no matter how long the delay.

Meditation: How do you practice vigilance and faithfulness as you wait for the second coming of Jesus?

Prayer: Master God, you exhort your people to have their loins girded and their lamps ready for the promised second coming in glory of Jesus, your Son. Through the working of your Holy Spirit, make of our lives a vigil of expectation. Keep us faithful to the teaching of Jesus, and fill us with an eagerness for the day when he will come and wait on us. Never let us waver in prudence as we wait in joyful hope for the coming of our Savior, Jesus Christ, who is Lord for ever and ever. Amen.

TAXES

Matthew 17:22-27

Scripture: "What do you think, Simon? The kings of the earth — from whom do they collect tax or tolls? From their subjects or from others?" (Matthew 17:25)

Reflection: Matthew's unique narrative concerning the payment of the Temple tax (17:24-27) follows Jesus' second prediction of the Passion (17:22-23), which, unlike disciples in Mark's Gospel, is understood by the disciples here, so that they are "overwhelmed with grief" (17:23). Like his two previous sections (14:28-31 and 16:16-19), the account of the payment of the Temple tax comes from Matthew's own special material about Peter.

The issue of paying the Temple tax has two levels of meaning for Matthew. First, according to Jewish law (cf. Exodus 30:11-16; Nehemiah 10:33), every male Jew over nineteen years of age was obligated to pay the tax, which was used for the upkeep of the Temple. This practice continued until the Temple was destroyed in 70 A.D.

Priests and rabbis often claimed exemption to the tax. Since Jesus is considered a "teacher" by the collectors of the Temple tax, the question is: Will Jesus pay the tax? The question, "Doesn't your teacher pay the Temple tax?" (17:24), indicates that Jesus was obliged to pay it.

The second level that Matthew is dealing with in this section of the Gospel concerns the paying of the tax for the Temple of Jupiter Capitolinus, which was levied on the Jews after the Jerusalem Temple was destroyed. Indeed, this is the more important issue on which Matthew wants to guide his church.

Just as subjects are not bound by the same laws as foreigners, neither are Jesus and his disciples — Matthew's church — who belong to the kingdom of heaven, bound by the duty of paying the Temple tax, which is imposed by those who are not of the kingdom (pagan Romans). Those who belong to the kingdom of heaven are free — free of the Temple tax, free from the Temple itself (which represents the past), and free from the Law, which imposed the tax.

But while the followers of Jesus are free from such a tax, they are not free to give offense to others. Peter's answer to Jesus' question is right, but it is right for a different reason. One does not pay the tax because it is the law; one pays the tax because not doing so will give offense to others.

Matthew, as he did in the first sermon of Jesus, presents his community with a "higher" law or reason or motivation. Those who have been freed by Jesus trust in the Father's care, like Peter who goes fishing in order to "earn" the coin to pay the tax. Then Peter pays the tax for Jesus and for himself.

By portraying Peter as paying the tax, Matthew establishes an example for his church. All followers of Jesus pay the tax, but not because it is a law to pay it.

They pay the tax in order to avoid giving scandal, a Matthean theme which becomes prominent in chapter 18, which immediately follows this narrative.

Reflection: For which reasons do you pay your taxes? Make a list of these reasons (motivations). Which of them came close to Matthew's reason?

Prayer: God of freedom, you made all people your sons and daughters through the suffering, death, and resurrection of Jesus. You have given them a freedom beyond all imagining. However, you have also given them a responsibility to not give any offense or scandal to each other. Keep us conscious of our freedom, but also make us aware of our responsibilities to each other. Hear our prayer through our Lord Jesus Christ, your Son, who lives and reigns with you and the Holy Spirit, one God, for ever and ever. Amen.

ONE STRAY

Matthew 18:1-5, 10, 12-14

Scripture: "If a man has a hundred sheep and one of them strays away, will he not leave the ninety-nine in the hills and go in search of the one who went astray? And if he finds it, amen, I say to you, he rejoices more over it than over the ninety-nine that did not go astray. Likewise, it is not the will of your Father in heaven that one of these little one be lost" (Matthew 18:12-14).

Reflection: Chapter 18 of Matthew's Gospel comprises the fourth sermon of Jesus, often called the "Church Order Discourse," in this Gospel. In this sermon, Matthew deals primarily with the relations that must exist between the members of his church. The first fourteen verses deal with a warning against greatness (18:1-5), an instruction about not causing weak members of the community to sin (18:6-9), and the parable of the lost sheep (18:10, 12-14), which shows how straying members of the community are to be sought out. The section on not causing weak members of the community to sin (18:6-9) is omitted by the weekday lectionary cycle.

Matthew's source for his section on the greatest in the kingdom (18:1-5) is Mark's Gospel (9:33-37). The author has already set the stage for this teaching in the previous narrative concerning the payment of the Temple tax, wherein the followers of Jesus are told to avoid giving offense to anyone (17:27). One of the ways that offense can be given is by assuming an air of great-ness.

The question posed by the disciples (in Mark's Gospel, the question is posed by Jesus), "Who is the greatest in the kingdom of heaven?" (18:1), is answered with the presence of a child, who, in the culture of the time, represents complete dependence.

"Unless you turn and become like children, you will not enter the kingdom of heaven" (18:3), is the answer Jesus gives to the disciples' question. In other words, the kingdom of heaven is for those who are completely dependent on and fully trust in God. There is no one who is greater than anyone else. The question is not an authentic question for followers of Jesus; all au-thentic followers are equally dependent on God.

To use a child as an example of authentic discipleship is shocking to great, dominant men! The child represents the exact opposite of the meaning of greatness. This, however, is Jesus' way, according to Matthew. "Whoever receives one child ..." in Jesus' name receives him (cf. 18:5). In Matthew's community, all mem-bers are equal; no one is greater than anyone else.

This teaching reduces all people to one common denomi-nator, and it eliminates some of the strife that Matthew was en-countering in his church. By reducing all persons to equality, he can hold together his fledgling community.

The parable of the lost sheep (18:10, 12-14) comes from Q (cf. Luke 15:3-7). Luke employs the parable to justify Jesus' table fellowship with sinners; Matthew uses this parable to teach the members of his community that they have an obligation to seek out fellow members who go astray and, if possible, bring them back to the Church.

Matthew's unique addition to the parable is found in his reference to "these little ones" (18:10, 14), who represent authen-tic and equally-dependent disciples, as seen from the teaching on the greatest in the kingdom.

The parable itself (18:12-13) is typical of other parables of Jesus. It is extravagant insofar as no decent shepherd would leave ninety-nine sheep on a mountainside and go and search for one that had gone astray. This a ridiculous chance, which, after careful weighing, should not be taken.

However, the exaggeration serves to make the point: members of the Church cannot leave a fellow member, who, for whatever reason, wanders away from the community. Everyone in the Church is obligated to care for and not to neglect everyone else. This is the way of Jesus, according to Matthew. It will be echoed later in the Gospel, when the disciples hear Jesus say, "Whatever you did for one of these least brothers (or sisters) of mine, you did for me" (26:40).

Meditation: Since there is no greatest in the kingdom, in which ways do you treat all people equally? In which ways do you seek out those who may have strayed from the Church?

Prayer: Heavenly Father, you will that all people come to share in the joys of your kingdom. Move our hearts to become like children. Open our eyes to see that all people are equal in your sight. Help us to seek out those who stray, so that not a one of your little ones will ever be lost. Hear our prayer through our Lord Jesus Christ, your Son, who lives and reigns with you and the Holy Spirit, one God, for ever and ever. Amen.

BINDING AND LOOSING

Matthew 18:1-20

Scripture: "Whatever you bind on earth shall be bound in heaven, and whatever you loose on earth shall be loosed in heaven.... Where two or three are gathered together in my name, I am there among them" (Matthew 18:18, 20).

Reflection: This section (Matthew 18:15-20) of Matthew's fourth sermon of Jesus is uniquely Matthean with a trace of Q. It presents the procedure for dealing with a fellow disciple who sins within the community but has no intention of leaving the Church or ceasing to sin.

The first step is taken privately: "If your brother sins (against you), go and show him his error between you and him alone" (18:15). By providing this first step, Matthew's Jesus empowers every member of the community to attempt to eliminate sin in the Church by engaging in private correction. "If he listens to you, you have won over your brother" (18:15); that is, one has gained him back for the community.

If this first step does not work, then step two involves taking "one or two others along... so that 'every statement may stand on the testimony of two or three witnesses'" (18:16). The need for witnesses is founded on the law in the book of Deuteronomy (cf. 19:15), which states that a person can be accused of a crime only with the support of two or three witnesses.

If the second step fails, the church is convened. This is

223

Matthew's second of only two uses of the word "church" (the first is in 16:18), which means the local congregation. The local church, in Matthew's understanding, is the final appeal.

The local church is given the authority to bind and to loose, much as Peter was given the same authority earlier in the Gospel (cf. 16:19). Jesus promises that "if two… agree on earth about anything for which they are to pray, it shall be granted to them by (the) heavenly Father" (18:19). Thus, Matthew endows the local church with power to admit or to exclude people from the community. And the use of this power is ratified by God.

If the sinner "refuses to listen even to the church" (18:17), then the sinner is excommunicated and is to be treated like a Gentile or a tax collector. A Gentile is a pagan, who is not a member of the community. A tax collector is a person, who was a member of the community, but turned traitor. The local church, then, is instructed to separate itself from the sinner, when he or she refuses to repent after being confronted by the community.

By the time that Matthew is writing this, the understanding has evolved that the members of his church are no longer Jewish-Christian or Gentile-Christian; they are members of a new and separate people, who follow the ways of the risen Jesus. He has promised to be with them until the end of the age (cf. 28:20).

The last verses of this section (19-20) were probably independent sayings, which Matthew wove together and attached to the order for dealing with a sinner. The last verse reflects a claim by rabbis that when two pious Jews sat together to discuss the word of the law, the *shekinah* (the divine presence) was with them.

By reworking this Jewish idea into a Christian understanding, Matthew replaces the Law with "in my (Jesus') name" (18:20). The *shekinah* is replaced with "there am I in the midst of them" (18:20). In Matthew's understanding, the church gathers around the words of Jesus, who, after being raised from the dead, continues to be with and to guide his community of followers. The local church acts in Jesus' name.

Meditation: What order do you follow when confronting a member of the community (local church) who sins (against you)?

Prayer: Heavenly Father, you have given the Church the power to bind and to loose through the resurrection of your Son, Jesus. Give us the wisdom to use wisely this great gift. Give us the courage to seek out those who sin, urge them to reform, and bring them back. Make us always aware that when we gather, Jesus is present with us, even as he lives and reigns with you and the Holy Spirit, one God, for ever and ever. Amen.

FORGIVENESS WITHOUT LIMIT

Matthew 18:21-19:1

Scripture: Peter… asked Jesus, "Lord, how many times can my brother sin against me, and I'll have to forgive him? Up to seven times?" Jesus said to him, "I don't say to you up to seven times but up to seventy-seven times" (Matthew 18:21-22).

Reflection: The last section (18:21-19:1) of the fourth sermon of Jesus in Matthew's Gospel deals with the need for constant forgiveness in the Church. The scene is composed of two parts: a question about forgiveness and the parable of the unforgiving servant.

Peter, representing the community, asks Jesus how often a member of the community should forgive a fellow member who sins. Seven times, Peter's suggested answer to his own question, was assumed to be enough, since seven represented fullness. Jesus, however, pushes the instances of forgiveness into infinity by declaring that one member of the Church must be willing to forgive another member "seventy-seven times" (18:22) or "seventy times seven times."

In other words, forgiveness is to be offered without limit. A community that is willing to forgive is easily held together. Such forgiveness reverses Lamech's "seventy-sevenfold" promise of vengeance (cf. Genesis 4:23-24).

The parable of the unforgiving servant, which is unique to Matthew's Gospel, stresses the extravagance and unlimitedness of forgiveness. When the king decides to settle accounts, one debtor is brought to him who owes him "a huge amount" (18:24), literally, "ten thousand talents." The debtor is unable to pay, but begs for mercy and wins the compassion of his master, who forgives him the loan.

When the forgiven debtor meets a fellow servant, who owes him "a much smaller amount" (18:28), literally, "a hundred denarii," he demands repayment and is not moved to mercy, even though his fellow servant falls to his knees and begs for it.

The emphasis is on the wide difference between the two amounts which were owed. The first debtor, for the sake of comparison, owed the king $100 million dollars, while the second debtor owed his fellow servant only $100. Followers of Jesus have received God's great forgiveness; it is absurd for them to refuse to offer it to each other, when their offenses against God are far greater than the offenses of their fellow follower against them.

In the kingdom of heaven, God's forgiveness is without limit. Therefore, the followers of Jesus, who have received God's forgiveness, should offer it to those who sin against them — without limit. Failure to do so will result in the withdrawal of God's forgiveness from those who have failed to offer it to others.

Meditation: In which ways do you offer unlimited forgiveness to others as God has offered it to you?

Prayer: Heavenly Father, your forgiveness is without limit. Your compassion is beyond measure. Your pity is without comparison. When a fellow member of our community sins against us, make us a people of unlimited forgiveness. Through the power of your Holy Spirit, enable us to forgive each other from our heart. Bring us to the joy of the kingdom of heaven, where you live and reign with your Son, our Lord Jesus Christ, and the Holy Spirit, one God, for ever and ever. Amen.

HARD HEARTS

Matthew 19:3-12

Scripture: Some Pharisees came up to him (Jesus), and tested him.... He said to them, "Because of the hardness of your hearts Moses allowed you to divorce your wives, but from the beginning it was not so. I say to you, whoever divorces his wife — unless the union is unlawful — and marries another commits adultery" (Matthew 19:3, 8-9).

Reflection: Matthew's discussion concerning marriage, divorce, and celibacy follows the conclusion of the fourth sermon of Jesus and begins the section of the Gospel concerned with Jesus' ministry in Judah and Jerusalem. The source for the discussion concerning marriage and divorce is Mark's Gospel (10:2-12). The part about celibacy is unique to Matthew.

In Judaism there were two schools of debate concerning marriage and divorce. One of these was the school of Shammai, which held a strict position on no divorce. The other school, that of Hillel, was more lenient when it came to the question of divorce. The question posed to Jesus by the Pharisees, "Is it lawful for a man to divorce his wife for any cause whatever?" (19:3) reflects a debate concerning marriage and divorce in Matthew's community.

Jesus answers the question by quoting the book of Genesis. "Have you not read that from the beginning the Creator 'made them male and female' and said, 'For this reason a man shall leave his father and mother and be united to his wife, and the two shall become one flesh'? Therefore, what God has joined together, let man not separate" (19:4-6). Thus, he makes clear that the will and the purpose of God from the beginning in creating human beings male and female is that they be joined together in a permanent union; this bond is cemented by the Creator himself, and no one can undo it. Divorce is illegal.

But such an answer is too simple, especially when one recalls that Matthew's audience is primarily Jewish and it knows the Hebrew Bible (Old Testament). In the book of Deuteronomy (24:1-4), Moses lists the reasons why a man may divorce his wife. Jesus discounts these reasons for Matthew's community by declaring that it was "because of the hardness of their hearts (that) Moses allowed... divorce" (19:8).

This is a severe charge, for it declares Israel's unwillingness to listen to God's word, a sin often spoken of by the prophets. The provision for divorce in the law, then, according to Jesus, does not reflect the will of the Creator, but the rebelliousness and sinfulness of human beings. The Church, the community of believers, is where the Creator's original will is re-established.

Jesus goes on to declare, "Whoever divorces his wife — unless the union is unlawful — and marries another commits adultery" (19:9). The "unless the union is unlawful" clause does not weaken the absolute prohibition of divorce. It refers to unions contracted by members of Matthew's community before they were baptized. In Matthew's church, an "unlawful" marriage cannot be continued after Baptism into the Church.

The last part of this section (19:10-12) deals with the question of celibacy. The question of celibacy was an important one in the early Church, especially in a Jewish-Christian community which highly upheld and, in some sense, mandated the marriage of its members for the continuation of the human race and to provide descendants to inherit the promises made to the patriarchs.

According to Matthew, celibacy is to be freely embraced; marriage is freely renounced "for the sake of the kingdom of heaven" (19:12). It is not for all "but only those to whom that is granted" (19:11).

There are three types of celibacy presented by Matthew.

The first is that of one who is "incapable of marriage" (19:12), literally a "eunuch," due to a sexual birth defect.

The second is that of one who has been castrated, made incapable of marriage "by others" (19:12). Neither of these two groups has freely embraced celibacy for the sake of the kingdom.

The third type is one who has "renounced marriage for the sake of the kingdom of heaven" (19:12). This person has freely made himself a eunuch in order to devote himself entirely to the service of the kingdom. This way of life is not for everyone. "Let whoever can accept this accept it" (19:12), according to the Matthean Jesus.

Meditation: In which ways are marriage and celibacy complementary?

Prayer: Creator God, in the beginning you made people male and female and willed that they leave their parents and be united as one in order to support each other and to continue the human race. You decreed that what you had joined together no one should separate. Later in time, you upheld the dignity of a life of celibacy and called people to renounce marriage for the sake of your kingdom. Help both married couples and celibate men and women to be signs of your infinite love and to work together for the coming of the kingdom, where you live and reign with Jesus, your Son, and the Holy Spirit, one God, for ever and ever. Amen.

LET THE CHILDREN COME

Matthew 19:13-15

19

Scripture: Jesus said, "Let the children be, and don't stop them from coming to me; for the kingdom of heaven belongs to such as these" (Matthew 19:14).

Reflection: Matthew's source for his blessing of the children section (19:13-15) is Mark's Gospel (10:13-16). However, Matthew has toned down the Marcan Jesus' indignation with his disciples and shortened the narrative. Also, this section echoes the narrative concerning the greatest in the kingdom (18:1-5), wherein a child is held up as an example of what a person must be like in order to enter the kingdom of heaven.

The child is an example of powerlessness in Matthew's community. At the time of the composition of this Gospel, the cultural mentality dictated that children had no rights; they were considered the property of their fathers. Since they were not adults, they were not persons.

But Jesus rejects that kind of thinking. Children are worthy of respect for "the kingdom of heaven belongs to such as these" (19:14). In Matthew's church, then, children are no longer treated as if they had no human dignity or value. Rather, in the Matthean community, they are for adults models of those who will inherit the kingdom of heaven.

Such obvious cultural reversals are common in Matthew's

Gospel. Members of his church no longer are to live by the old values, but by the higher standards set by Jesus.

Meditation: What image would Jesus use today in order to communicate the higher standards required of those who wish to enter into the kingdom of heaven?

Prayer: God our Father, you call all people to be your children. You lay your hands on us and heal us. You hold up those who are considered the least among us as examples of those who will inherit your kingdom. Give us the trust of children that we may come to share in the kingdom where you live with your Son, our Lord Jesus Christ, and the Holy Spirit, one God, for ever and ever. Amen.

A SCRAP OF HELP

Matthew 15:21-28

Scripture: Behold, a Canaanite woman of (the district of Tyre and Sidon) came and cried out, "Have mercy on me, Lord, Son of David! My daughter is terribly tormented by a demon" (Matthew 15:22).

Reflection: Matthew's source for the narrative concerning the Canaanite woman's faith is Mark's Gospel (7:24-30). Matthew has both shortened and altered the original story to fit his own needs.

For Matthew the story serves to show how the mission of Jesus is to be extended from the Jews to the Gentiles. Establishing this mission for his community is one of Matthew's favorite themes throughout the Gospel. He begins it with the visit of the magi to the infant Jesus and carries it throughout the Gospel with such instances as the healing of a centurion's servant (8:5-13) and the healing of the Canaanite woman's daughter (15:21-28).

In Matthew's community there is a remembrance of Jesus' ministry being "only to the lost sheep of the house of Israel" (15:24). However, by the time that Matthew was writing his Gospel, the ministry of Jesus had been extended to the Gentiles through the preaching and witness of his disciples and later followers. Therefore, this story serves to both confirm the mission to the Gentiles as well as to validate that mission.

Jesus is portrayed as being unsympathetic to the woman.

She refers to him by important Matthean Christological titles: Lord and Son of David. Her request, "Have mercy on me..." (15:22), reminds us of the pleas of the two blind men who were healed (cf. Matthew 9:27; 20:30). Jesus "did not say a word in answer to her" (15:23).

After a request from his disciples to send her away, the woman again says, "Lord, help me" (15:25). Then, Jesus uses a derogatory term for Gentiles — dogs. "It is not right to take the children's bread and throw it to the dogs" (15:26).

The children are "the lost sheep of the house of Israel" (15:24), the Jews. The dogs are the Gentiles, the unbelievers.

But even Jesus cannot outwit the woman. "Please, Lord, for even the dogs eat the crumbs that fall from their master's table" (15:27). In other words, she acknowledges her Gentile status, but requests a crumb of help nevertheless.

For Matthew, this story becomes a opportunity for teaching his community something very important. "O woman, great is your faith!" Jesus declares (15:28). Because Jesus acknowledges that this woman, a Gentile, has great faith — is a believer like the others, the mission to the Gentiles in Matthew's community has a well established precedent to follow in recruiting other Gentiles.

Meditation: Which people or groups of people are classified by many as "dogs" today? How are they authentic believers?

Prayer: God of every people and race and nation, you invite all men and women to believe in your Son, Jesus. Give us the craft of the Canaanite woman that we may never give up when confronted with difficulties. Give us her courage to confront human indignity. Give us a share in her great faith that we may spread your name, the name of Jesus, and the name of your Holy Spirit throughout the world. We ask this through Christ our Lord. Amen.

TRUE FOOD AND TRUE DRINK

John 6:51-58

Scripture: "Unless you eat the flesh of the Son of Man and drink his blood, you will not have life within you. Whoever feeds on my flesh and drinks my blood has eternal life, and I will raise him on the last day. For my flesh is true food, and my blood is true drink" (John 6:53-55).

Reflection: This section (6:51-58) of John's Gospel is the fourth of five parts of chapter six which interrupt the semi-continuous cycle of Gospel readings from Mark. Verses 51-58 form part of the bread of life discourse, which follows the Johannine account of the multiplication of the loaves and the fishes and the walking on the water narrative.

Flesh and blood are used with double meaning in this selection. The Jews (John's favorite way of providing opponents for dialogue with Jesus) understand flesh to be human flesh. To eat Jesus' flesh, then, is to engage in cannibalism. Likewise, to drink blood is not only cannibalistic, but it is to defile life itself. The culture of the time believed that life was found in blood. Therefore, blood was sacred.

The verb for feeding is also used in two ways. It means to munch or to gnaw, as an animal eats the prey it has caught. However, it can also refer to human eating in terms of providing nourishment for one's body.

The author of this Gospel is drawing a parallel between eating flesh and eating the bread of life and drinking blood and drinking the wine of eternal life. When the members of the Johannine community gathered to break bread and to share the cup in memory of Jesus, the author wanted them to be aware that the food they ate and the wine they drank were real nourishment for eternal life.

The meaning of "flesh," "blood," and "feed" that one chooses depends on faith. Faith is the window through which one looks; it determines what one sees. The man or woman of faith sees bread and wine, which are the flesh and blood of Jesus. The person who does not believe sees only bread and wine.

By eating the flesh and blood of Jesus, a believer remains united to God's life. "Just as the living Father sent" Jesus, and he has "life because of the Father, so also the one who feeds on" Jesus "will have life because of" him (John 6:57). Jesus is the food and drink that provides eternal life, just as bread and wine provide nourishment for earthly life.

People of the past ate the "bread that came down from heaven" — the manna — but they died. By eating the flesh and blood of Jesus, people can now live forever.

Meditation: In which ways, other than the Eucharist, do you eat and drink of the eternal life of Jesus?

Prayer: God of flesh and blood, from the clay of the earth you fashioned man and woman in your image and likeness and blew into them the breath of your Spirit. You have given humankind the flesh and blood of Jesus, your Son, as food and drink that nourish the spirit. Give us an intense hunger for his body and blood that we may one day be raised up to share eternal life in the kingdom where you live and reign with Jesus and the Holy Spirit, one God, for ever and ever. Amen.

PEACE VERSUS DIVISION

Luke 12:49-53

Scripture: "Do you think that I have come to establish peace on the earth? No, I tell you, but rather division" (Luke 12:51).

Reflection: The section of Luke's Gospel which deals with Jesus as a cause for division (12:49-53) follows the example of the vigilant and faithful servants and Peter's question concerning the application of the story. For Luke, the faithful servant, that is, the faithful disciple of Jesus, may be a source of division. In Luke's community, those who were faithful often found that they caused division within their own family.

A Christian enters the community through baptism, which plunges one into the life-long journey with Jesus. "There is a baptism with which I must be baptized, and how great is my anguish until it is accomplished!" (Luke 12:50). A person's life-long journey with Jesus may lead to death and will probably cause division before this.

Baptism initiates a person into a new family, of those "who hear the word of God and keep it" (11:28). In order to be faithful to the word of God, believers may have to separate themselves from their own families. This is one of the prices of Christian discipleship, and it touches every member of one's family — father and son, mother and daughter, mother-in-law and daughter-in-law (cf. 12:53).

The authentic Christian is on fire with faith. "I have come to set the earth on fire, and how I wish it were already blazing!" Jesus states (12:49). Faith is like a fire which burns in a person's heart. It continues to burn even when one is faced with the strong possibility of separation from family and death. A clear sense of values and priorities can keep the Christian faithful to his or her mission.

Meditation: What kind of fire and faith burns within you? How has it led to division in your family?

Prayer: God of fire, you once revealed yourself to Moses in the form of a burning bush. You strengthened him to be the leader of your people. In the fullness of time you sent your Son, Jesus, as a fire on the earth. We have been baptized into his death and resurrection and received the fire of the Holy Spirit. Strengthen us in our work. When we are confronted with division, keep us faithful and give us your peace. We ask this through our Lord Jesus Christ, who lives and reigns with you and the Holy Spirit, one God, for ever and ever. Amen.

RICHES VERSUS PERFECTION

Matthew 19:16-22

Scripture: Jesus said to (the young man), "If you want to be perfect, go, sell your possessions and give to the poor, and you will have treasure in heaven. Then come, follow me." When the young man heard this, he went away sad, because he had many possessions (Matthew 19:21-22).

Reflection: The account concerning the rich young man (19:16-22) and the instruction of Jesus concerning riches and the disciples' reward (19:23-30) is divided into two sections in the daily lectionary cycle of Gospel selections. Matthew's source for the first of these selections, the rich young man, is Mark (10:17-31); however, Matthew has reworked the Marcan account to suit his own purposes.

The man addresses Jesus as "teacher," a title used throughout by Matthew to indicate those who do not believe in Jesus. His question concerns "eternal life," which is one of many phrases used by the author of this Gospel to indicate salvation and the kingdom of heaven.

The contrast in the story is set up between following the law and being perfect (being righteous, doing God's will). The young man has kept the commandments: "All of these I have observed" (19:20). As has been demonstrated many times before by Matthew, keeping the law is not sufficient for his community. What is lacking is perfection, doing God's will to the very best of one's ability. In his first sermon, Jesus said, "Be perfect, as your heavenly Father is perfect" (5:48).

The young man's obstacle to perfection is his riches. "He had many possessions" (19:22). In the culture of the time, riches was considered a sign of God's favor. A person who was rich was also considered to be blessed by God. A person who was poor was considered to be cursed by God because of his sin or that of his parents.

For the man to strip himself of his riches and reduce himself to utter poverty would not be easy. The cultural understanding of riches as a blessing, though, is being reversed by Matthew. He is instructing the rich in his church; they have nothing over those who are poor. In fact, their riches present a problem to their entrance into the kingdom. God has a special predilection for the poor; riches are not necessarily a sign of being favored by God.

In this passage, Jesus instructs the rich man to disassociate himself from his riches, that is, to reduce himself to the state of poverty, so that he might follow Jesus unencumbered. By following Jesus, the man has the opportunity to reach perfection, to fulfill God's will perfectly. The man is to give his riches to the poor, those who have nothing, those who were considered to be cursed by God.

Once the rich young man gives away his wealth, he can follow Jesus, who is on his way to the cross. Those who are rich have an obligation to use their wealth to help those who have none, and, in doing so, to discover God's will for them. Riches are more often than not an obstacle to the kingdom. Keeping the law will not bring one into the kingdom; only authentic righteousness can do that. For the rich, authentic righteousness involves selling what they have and giving the proceeds to the poor and having treasure in heaven (cf. 19:21).

Meditation: In which ways do you disassociate yourself from your wealth in order to give to the poor?

Prayer: God of perfection, everything that exists belongs to you, and your will is that everything be shared among your people. Let us never forget that merely keeping your commandments is not sufficient. You call us to do your will and to use our wealth for the good of others. Make us righteous in your sight that we may share in the fullness of the kingdom where you live and reign with Jesus, your Son, and the Holy Spirit, one God, for ever and ever. Amen.

RICHES VERSUS SALVATION

Matthew 19:23-20

Scripture: "It is easier for a camel to pass through a needle's eye than for one who is rich to enter the kingdom of God" (Matthew 19:24).

Reflection: The instruction of Jesus concerning riches (19:23-20) forms the second part of the narrative concerning the rich young man in Matthew's Gospel. Once the young man hears Jesus say, "If you wish to be perfect, go, sell what you have and give to (the) poor, and you will have treasure in heaven. Then come, follow me" (19:21), he goes away sad, "for he had many possessions" (19:22). For Matthew, the young man's departure offers Jesus an opportunity to instruct the church about riches.

Throughout the Old Testament riches or wealth is considered to be a sign of God's favor. The person who owns possessions is considered to be blessed by God. However, Jesus reverses this understanding. Riches, he declares, is a hindrance to entrance into the kingdom of God. The basic presupposition of the community is wrong. "With difficulty will the rich enter the kingdom of heaven" (19:23).

In order to emphasize this point, Matthew uses some of his typical extravagant language: "It is easier for a camel to pass through a needle's eye than for one who is rich to enter the kingdom of God" (19:24). In other words, it is impossible for a person who is rich to gain entrance into the kingdom if he or she is attached to wealth.

The argument then proceeds to the next question, which is posed by the disciples: "Who then can be saved?" (19:25).

If riches are no longer a guarantee of God's favor or blessing, then what is? The answer is that there is no guarantee. Human beings cannot save themselves. Only God can save them. "For God all things are possible" (19:26). Salvation is God's gift to us; it is not determined or guaranteed by riches.

The followers of Jesus "in the new age" (19:28) are those who have "given up everything and followed" him (19:27); these are contrasted to the rich man who in the present age has given up nothing and abandoned Jesus. On the day of judgment, authentic followers will receive the status of the patriarchs and "sit on twelve thrones, judging the twelve tribes of Israel" (19:28).

In other words, just as riches are no longer and necessarily a sign of blessing from God, in the new age of the kingdom, the followers of Jesus will judge Israel — a reversal, typical of Matthew. Borrowed from Q (cf. Luke 22:29-30), the verse indicating this reversal (19:28) illustrates the role of the church in the new age.

However, as soon as Matthew has indicated the role of the Church in the new age, he cautions the members of the Church that salvation remains God's gift. "Many who are first will be last, and the last will be first" (19:30). One's place in the kingdom is left to God.

Meditation: What have you given up in order to follow Jesus?

Prayer: God of the kingdom, salvation is a gift, which you freely offer to your people. Make us aware of the fleeting quality of material things. May we never find security in riches. Guide us in the footsteps of Jesus, your Son, that we may come to share the joys of the kingdom, where you live and reign with him and the Holy Spirit, one God, for ever and ever. Amen.

ENVY VERSUS GENEROSITY

Matthew 20:1-6

Wednesday
of Week
20

Scripture: "When evening came the owner of the vineyard said to his foreman, 'Call the workers and pay them their wages, beginning with the last and ending with the first.' Thus, the last shall be first, and the first, last" (Matthew 20:8, 16).

Reflection: The parable of the workers in the vineyard (Matthew 20:1-16) is unique to Matthew. It is connected to the preceding section about riches and the reward promised to those who give up everything to follow Jesus through the use of a reversal refrain: "The last will be first, and the first will be last" (Matthew 20:16: cf. 19:30; 20:8).

In Matthew's church, the image of a vineyard would have been readily recognized. The vineyard represented Israel. The landowner represented God. "The kingdom of heaven is like a landowner who went out at dawn," nine o'clock, noon, three o'clock, five o'clock, "to hire laborers for his vineyard" (20:1). In other words, the vineyard owner goes into the marketplace repeatedly in order to hire workers. In Matthew's understanding, God never ceases to invite his people into his kingdom.

However, no one invited to the kingdom is any greater than anyone else. God rewards not according to any kind of human standard, but according to God's own standards of equality. In order to demonstrate this, those who worked only one hour received the same pay as those who worked all day. Those who worked all day "thought they would receive more" (20:10). In other words, their presumption was false. They had agreed upon "the usual daily wage" (20:13); therefore, they were not being cheated unjustly. Nevertheless, they are envious because of the owner's generosity (cf. 20:15).

There is also a surprise for those who worked only one hour and received a full day's pay. However, they voice no complaint! Because of this dual surprise ending, which is characteristic of many of the authentic parables of Jesus, many scholars believe this to be one of Jesus' original parables.

The moral of the parable, added by Matthew, consists of a warning to the members of his church. No one in the community can claim a greater reward than anyone else. "Did you not agree with me for the usual daily wage? Take what is yours and go. What if I wish to give this last one the same as you?" (20:13-14). God, who is just, distributes his gifts as he wills and not according to any pre-determined human concept of equality. In God's kingdom, God is free to do as he wishes!

When viewed from characteristic human terms of equality, it looks like the last are first and the first are last. It makes no difference in reality, though, when one responds and becomes a follower of Jesus — just as long as one responds. In the end, all followers will inherit the kingdom and its benefits as pure gifts from God. No one, no matter how long he or she has been a follower of Jesus, is more important than anyone else.

In Matthew's view, then, all laborers, followers of Jesus, are equal. This fact helps reduce any strife in the community and holds it together. Those who work long hours will inherit the kingdom alongside those who come into the vineyard late.

Meditation: How does Matthew's view of God's system of reward (as exemplified in the parable of the workers in the vineyard) conflict with your views of reward and equality?

Prayer: God of the vineyard, you never cease to call people to follow your Son, Jesus, and to spread the good news of your kingdom. Give us untiring feet and hands as we labor. Protect us from envy. Keep us from ever presuming that one laborer is greater than another. In your generosity, we trust that we will inherit the kingdom, where you live and reign with Jesus and the Holy Spirit, one God, for ever and ever. Amen.

INVITATION TO THE FEAST

Matthew 22:1-14

Scripture: "(The king)… said to his servants, 'The wedding feast is ready, but those who were invited weren't worthy to come. So go to the main roads and invite to the feast whomever you find.' The servants went out into the streets and rounded up everyone they found, bad and good alike, and the hall was filled with guests" (Matthew 22:8-10).

Reflection: A large section of Matthew's Gospel (20:17-21:46) is omitted by the daily cycle of readings. This section includes the third prediction of the Passion (20:17-19), the request of the mother of James and John for places on Jesus' right and left (20:20-28), another healing of two blind men account (20:29-34; cf. 9:27-31), the entry into Jerusalem (21:1-11), the cleansing of the Temple (21:12- 17), the cursing of the fig tree (21:18-22), the questioning of Jesus' authority (21:23-27), the parable of the two sons (21:28-32), and the parable of the tenants (21:33-46).

Matthew's source for the parable of the wedding feast is Q (cf. Luke 14:15-24). However, Matthew has so allegorized the parable that most of its original thrust has been lost. This should come as no surprise to the reader, since Matthew has employed allegory throughout his Gospel.

The setting of the allegory is a wedding feast, an Old Testament metaphor for the time of final salvation. The prophet Isaiah best illustrates this metaphor: "On this mountain the Lord of hosts will provide for all peoples a feast of rich food and choice wines, juicy, rich food and pure, choice wines" (Isaiah 25:6). With this setting, the allegory becomes a detailed account of salvation history.

The king who gives the wedding feast is God. The son for whom the feast is given is Jesus. The people of Israel, the invited guests, refuse to come to the wedding feast, when the servants, the prophets, convey the king's invitation. "Some ignored the invitation and went off, one to his farm, another to his business. The rest seized his servants, treated them shamefully, and killed them" (22:5-6).

Because of the actions of the invited guests, the king is enraged and sends his troops to destroy the murderers, and to burn their city. Here Matthew reflects the historical destruction of Jerusalem by the Romans in 70 A.D. and gives the reason why he believes the city was destroyed — Israel's unfaithfulness. Then, the king says to his servants, "The feast is ready, but those who were invited were not worthy to come. So go into the main roads and invite to the feast whomever you find" (22:9). Since Israel refused to come to the wedding feast, the Gentiles have now been invited. They accept the invitation and come to the feast. Here Matthew reflects a theme which he has worked with throughout the Gospel — Gentiles are invited to the kingdom.

Both the "bad and good alike" (22:10) enter the wedding feast. For Matthew, until the end of final judgment, the kingdom of heaven is made up of the bad and the good. Like the parable of the weeds among the wheat (13:24-30; 36-43), followers of Jesus are not to anticipate the final judgment by deciding who is bad and who is good. Judgment is God's responsibility.

Besides this warning against judgment, Matthew adds a warning to his community in terms of a story about a man who entered the banquet hall not properly dressed. Just presuming that one is included in the kingdom is not enough; a lifestyle of repentance and a change of mind and heart is necessary. A life of good deeds must be continued. The proper wedding garment refers to this type of lifestyle. Matthew's warning is aimed at those members of his community who entered the church but then were backsliding into their old lifestyle.

Authentic discipleship demands a continuity of conversion of life. Otherwise, the king, God, will throw the person "into the darkness outside, where there will be wailing and grinding of teeth" (22:13). In other words, they will be condemned.

While many Israelites have been invited to the wedding feast, most of them have refused the invitation, Matthew is saying, whereas the Gentiles, although few in number, have been admitted into the kingdom. Matthew's warning to his community is at once harsh and, understood in context, an attempt to urge the members to authentic discipleship.

Meditation: With what role do you identify best in the parable of the wedding feast: the king, the servants, the first invited guests, the bad and good guests, the man without a wedding garment? Explain.

Prayer: God of the wedding feast, you have prepared a banquet of rich food and choice wines for those who faithfully follow your Son, Jesus. Move us to accept the invitation of your servants, the prophets. Enable us to see our excuses. Dress us in the wedding garment of continual conversion of life. Only with your help will we be able to enter the kingdom, where you live and reign with Jesus and the Holy Spirit, one God, for ever and ever. Amen.

LOVE IS GREATEST

Matthew 22:34-40

Scripture: "You shall love the Lord, your God, with all your heart, with all your soul, and with all your mind. This is the greatest and the first commandment. The second is like it: You shall love your neighbor as yourself. The whole law and the prophets rest on these two commandments" (Matthew 22:37-40).

Reflection: The daily lectionary omits the discussion concerning the paying of taxes to the emperor (22:15-22) and the discussion concerning the question about the resurrection (22:23-33), both of which follow the parable of the wedding feast and precede Matthew's version of the greatest commandment. Matthew's source for the discussion concerning the greatest commandment is Mark (12:28-34), which has been severely edited and sharpened by Matthew.

The one who questions Jesus is a "scholar of the law" (22:35) or scribe, one who is well-trained in the law of Moses. The man is an unbeliever, as he uses Matthew's favorite unbeliever's form of address, "Teacher."

The question is not about the first commandment, as in Mark, but about the "greatest" commandment. Jesus recites the heart of all the commandments — the *Shema* (Deuteronomy 6:4-5). The greatest commandment centers on love of God with all one's heart (the center of knowing, willing, and feeling), with all one's soul (life), and with all one's mind (energy). In other words, love engages the total person.

And because love involves the whole person, it extends to one's neighbor. "You shall love your neighbor as yourself" (22:39). God comes first, but one cannot love God without loving the neighbor.

Throughout the Gospel, this has been one of Matthew's favorite themes. "The whole law and the prophets rest on these two commandments" (22:40) — the love of God and the love of neighbor. God's will is found in love, according to Matthew. Authentic discipleship is measured against love and not against a series of 613 commandments.

Matthew refuses to give a new set of commandments: to do so would be to fall into the very trap he has been trying to spring. Authentic discipleship involves love of God and neighbor. Any other commandment or law must be measured against love, which at the same time binds people to the heart of God's will and frees them from the law when it degenerates into the mere keeping of the law for the sake of keeping it. For Jesus in the Gospel of Matthew it is not a matter of merely keeping the Law; it is a matter of why one keeps it.

Meditation: In which ways do you authentically love God and neighbor as you love yourself?

Prayer: God of love, you have instructed your people to love you with all their heart, with all their soul, and with their mind, and to love their neighbor as they love themselves. Keep us faithful to this great commandment of love. Help us to see that the whole law and the prophets depend on it. May we put into practice what we know. We ask this through our Lord Jesus Christ, your Son, who lives and reigns with you and the Holy Spirit, one God, for ever and ever. Amen.

PREACHING VERSUS PRACTICING

Matthew 23:1-12

Scripture: "The scribes and the Pharisees sit on the chair of Moses. So do and observe all that they tell you, but do not follow their example. For they preach but do not practice" (Matthew 23:2-3).

Reflection: The question about Jesus being David's son (22:41-46) is omitted from the semi-continuous daily reading from Matthew's Gospel. In the following chapter (23), Matthew presents an introductory section (23:1-12), which consists of the denunciation of the scribes and Pharisees. This is followed by seven "woes" (23:13-36).

Matthew's source for this introductory section (23:1-12) is Mark (12:38-39) and Q (cf. Luke 11:37-52; 13:34-35). However, most of the material is peculiar to Matthew, and it represents specific problems with which he was concerned in the church for which he wrote this Gospel.

For Matthew, "scribes and Pharisees" is a code phrase for Judaism, which Matthew's community is at once facing, in dialogue with, and slowly breaking away from. Since the scribes and Pharisees "sit on the chair of Moses" (23:2), they are to be listened to, but their example is not to be followed. In other words, Matthew does not abolish the law; he only abolishes those who misinterpret it.

Throughout the Gospel, Matthew has proposed that followers of Jesus are righteous; that is, that they do God's will not because of the law but because it is the right thing to do. The scribes and Pharisees observe the law but for the wrong reasons. They do not practice what they preach. In fact, they make it more difficult. "All their works are performed to be seen" (23:5). They are not authentic. Matthew exhorts his readers to be authentic and not to imitate the scribes and Pharisees.

Furthermore, those who are leaders in Matthew's church are to avoid anything which separates them or sets them apart from the rest of the community, especially titles. No one is to be called "rabbi," which means "my great one." Likewise, no one is to be called "father" or "master." "The greatest among you must be your servant" (23:11).

Authentic discipleship involves service — service of equals by equals. This has been one of Matthew's favorite themes; it has been one of the ways that he has been able to preserve his community and avoid factionalism and division. Among the followers of Jesus, anything that hints of the superiority of one person over another is to be avoided. In this way, the members of Matthew's church will avoid the problems which possessed Pharisaic Judaism.

Meditation: In what ways might you identify attitudes or judgments as being similar to that of the "scribes and Pharisees" today?

Prayer: God of Moses, you gave your law to your people in order to teach them how to live and how to be pleasing in your sight. However, forgetting the spirit of the law, your people kept its letter and forsook you, the Law-giver. Jesus, your Servant and your Son, has given us the law of love. Through the working of the Holy Spirit enable us to both preach and put into practice this law. Make us authentic followers of Jesus, who is Lord for ever and ever. Amen.

ROCK AND KEYS

Matthew 16:13-20

Scripture: "I say to you, you are Peter, and on this rock I will build my church, and the gates of hell shall not prevail against it. I will give you the keys to the kingdom of heaven" (Matthew 16:18-19).

Reflection: Matthew's source for Peter's confession about Jesus (16:13-20) is Mark's Gospel (8:27-29) and Matthew's own unique tradition concerning Peter. The author's emphasis in this section of his Gospel is on the identity of Jesus and a validation of the role of Peter in the early Church.

Jesus' identity is revealed in this section through a series of correct and incorrect titles. The first of the correct titles is "Son of Man," which is associated with the suffering, dying, and rising Jesus. The second correct title is "Messiah," which means "the anointed one," the one chosen by God. The third correct title is "Son of the living God," which is most likely a title used in the context of a post-resurrectional confession of faith.

The first of the incorrect titles is "John the Baptist," which represents Herod's opinion of Jesus' identity (cf. 14:2). The second incorrect title is "Elijah," whom Matthew equates with John the Baptist (cf. 3:1-6; 11:14; 17:11-13). The third incorrect answer is "Jeremiah," a unique addition to Matthew's Marcan source, which may function as a signpost toward Jesus' ultimate betrayal on the cross.

Knowing the correct titles is not attributed to Peter's natural abilities but to God's revelation. By portraying the scene this way, Matthew validates God's election of Peter as early leader of the community.

Because of God's choice of Peter, Peter becomes the foundation for the community. He is a rock; his name means rock. The community, with Peter as its leader, will be one that listens to Jesus' words and acts on them. This community will be "like a wise man who built his house on rock. The rain fell, the floods came, and the winds blew and buffeted the house. But it did not collapse; it had been set solidly on rock" (7:24-25).

As leader of the early Church, Matthew must also justify Peter's authority. He is given the "keys to the kingdom of heaven" (16:19). Even though Matthew shies away from anyone being more important or having more authority than anyone else in the Church throughout his Gospel, he also realizes that there must be some ultimate authority, some final appeal. This person was Peter (and his successors). So, whatever was ruled on earth would also be ruled in heaven.

For Matthew's community, this section of his Gospel revealed the complete identity of Jesus and the role of Peter. It answered the question, "Who is Jesus?" and it answered the question, "What is the role of Peter in the community?"

Meditation: What title do you use most frequently for Jesus? What does the title mean for you? In which ways is the Church continuing to be built on Peter?

Prayer: Living God, Father of Jesus, the Messiah, the Christ, you have revealed your divinity through the flesh and blood of humanity. You have called us together to be your Church, and you have appointed leaders to guide our way. Keep us faithful to your word. Give us deacons, priests, and bishops who are on fire with your truth. We ask this through our Lord Jesus Christ, your Son, who lives and reigns with you and the Holy Spirit, one God, for ever and ever. Amen.

SPIRIT AND LIFE

John 6:60-69

Scripture: "The words I speak to you are spirit and life." Jesus then said to the Twelve, "Do you too wish to turn back?" Simon Peter answered him, "Lord, to whom would we go? You have the words of eternal life. We have come to believe and are convinced that you are the Holy One of God" (John 6:63, 67-69).

Reflection: The last section of chapter six of John's Gospel (6:60-69) forms the fifth and final selection from this Gospel and the interruption of the Marcan cycle. Next Sunday, the Gospel of Mark is resumed.

Throughout the Johannine discourse on the bread of life there has been a debate between Jesus, who claims to be the bread of life, and the Jews, who understand this claim as cannibalism. Once these points are made, the author of the Gospel separates some of the disciples of Jesus, unbelievers, from the Twelve, who do believe.

Some disciples were murmuring, "This saying (concerning eating the flesh and drinking the blood of the Son of Man) is hard; who can accept it?" (6:60). Unique to John's Gospel is the portrayal of Jesus as always being in charge and knowing what is going on. So, Jesus asks, "Does this shock you?" (6:61). As the author already knows, far greater shocks are in store!

The bread that Jesus gives is not for the nourishment of the body but for the feeding of the spirit. "The words I speak to you are spirit and life" (6:63). One's understanding of the difference between bread for the body and bread for the spirit distinguishes believers from unbelievers. Therefore, "many (of) his disciples returned to their former way of life and no longer went about with him" (6:66). In John's community, there were some who could not accept this teaching and they were leaving the Church.

In this Gospel, the Twelve are portrayed as believers. Through Simon Peter, their spokesman, they profess their belief in the "words of eternal life" (6:68) of Jesus. Thus, in the Johannine scheme of things, they are held up as examples of faith for John's community. There is no one else to whom one can turn except Jesus.

Meditation: Have you ever thought of no longer following Jesus? Why? Why not?

Prayer: Father, you have given us Jesus, your Son, as the bread of life and the drink of eternal salvation. May we always cling to his words of spirit and life. Draw us into the circle of his friends and keep us faithful. We ask this through our Lord Jesus Christ, who lives and reigns with you and the Holy Spirit, one God, for ever and ever. Amen.

SALVATION

Luke 13:22-30

Scripture: "There will be wailing and gnashing of teeth when you see Abraham, Isaac, and Jacob and all the prophets in the kingdom of God and you yourselves cast out" (Luke 13:28).

Reflection: The sayings concerning salvation (Luke 13:22-30) follow Luke's version of the parable of the mustard seed (13:18-19) and the parable of the yeast (13:21-21). The emphasis of this section is placed on the effort that is necessary for entrance into the kingdom of God. The Lucan setting for this section is Jesus' traveling to Jerusalem (13:22).

Salvation is an important theme in Luke's Gospel. The question, "Lord, will only a few people be saved?" (13:23) not only reflects the author's concern but that of his middle class Gentile community. Salvation is a present reality for Luke; it is not something coming in the future. Salvation is present now in the person and ministry — especially the proclamation of the kingdom of God — of Jesus.

Therefore, readers should "strive to enter through the narrow gate" (13:24). This takes effort. And those who get into the kingdom will do so because of their effort.

Luke wants to make sure that his Gentile audience understands that entrance into God's kingdom will not be based on whom they may or may not have known.

The master in the mini-parable closes and locks the doors, and knocking on the outside and shouts of "we ate and drank in your company and you taught in our streets" (13:26) will not motivate him to get up and unlock the door. Luke is saying that even though Jesus was Jewish, those who are Jewish have no advantage. In fact, Jesus' own contemporaries may have more of a disadvantage than the Gentiles. Salvation is not dependent on having known Jesus; it is dependent on following him to Jerusalem.

Some people will be surprised when they "see Abraham, Isaac, and Jacob and all the prophets in the kingdom of God" and find themselves "cast out" (13:28). This statement serves as a warning to those who presumed salvation by association. "Some are first who will be last" (13:30).

In Luke's understanding, the kingdom of God, salvation, is open to all people. They will come "from the east and the west and from the north and the south and will recline at table in the kingdom of God" (13:29). The invitation is extended to both Jews and Gentiles. Entrance is not based on presumptive association but on following Jesus.

Meditation: In which ways do you presume salvation?

Prayer: God of Abraham, Isaac, and Jacob, and all the prophets, your Son, Jesus has shown us the way to your kingdom — through the narrow gate. Continue to call people from the north and the south and the east and the west to your banquet. May we be numbered among those deemed worthy to recline at your table. We ask this through our Lord Jesus Christ, your Son, who lives and reigns with you and the Holy Spirit, one God, for ever and ever. Amen.

WOE TO YOU WHO SWEAR
Matthew 23:13-22

Scripture: "Woe to you, scribes and Pharisees, you hypocrites" (Matthew 23:13, 15).

Reflection: After the introduction (23:1-12) to the denunciation
of the scribes and Pharisees section of his Gospel, Matthew lists
seven "woes," the first three of which form this section (23:13-
22) of the Gospel. His sources for these "woes" are Mark, Q, and
his own unique material.

The "woe" is borrowed from the prophets and various
apocalyptic types of literature. It expresses both the speaker's
horror concerning sin, and it proclaims the punishment that
awaits those who commit such sin.

Throughout the Gospel, Matthew has been interested in the
theme of righteousness — doing God's will for the right reason,
being authentic. "Scribes and Pharisees" is Matthew's generic
term for those who pride themselves on being self-righteous. They
know the law, but they do not act on it. They appear to be righteous, but they are not righteous. The authentic (righteous) person is one who hears the word (law) and does (practices) it. Any
split between hearing and doing is hypocrisy.

In effect, Matthew is rejecting Pharisaic Judaism in the Gospel and in his community. His church, composed primarily of
Jewish-Christians, could easily fall into the trap of the past —
keeping the law for its own sake, which is self-righteousness.

Matthew wants the members of his community to keep the law because it is the right way to behave. By hearing the word and acting according to what is heard, one does God's will. Matthew refuses to offer guidelines, to specify exactly what correct behavior is, for to do so would be to create another law, which in Matthew's opinion doesn't work.

In the first woe, the scribes and Pharisees are accused of locking "the kingdom of heaven before human beings" (23:13). The charge is that those who are designated the leaders, the facilitators, the guides to the kingdom have locked the doors so that neither they nor anyone else can enter. In other words, the scribes and Pharisees are a living contradiction. Matthew is warning his community not to become a living contradiction themselves.

The second woe accuses the scribes and Pharisees of corrupting others through missionary endeavors. Jewish missionaries did "traverse sea and land to make one convert" (23:15) among the Gentiles, who sometimes accepted circumcision and all the details of the law. However, in Matthew's estimation, it was not conversion that was accomplished; it was corruption. The convert became "a child of Gehenna" (23:25), one belonging to the garbage dump. Authentic conversion, Matthew is saying, involves much more than circumcision and adherence to the Law.

The third woe is an attack on taking oaths; this was already made earlier in the Gospel (cf. 5:33-37). The argument reduces the practice to one of absurdity or hyperbole, as is usual for Matthew. Values are presented as upside down. One could swear by the Temple and not be obligated, but one could swear by the gold of the Temple, because it was considered to be of greater value, and be obligated.

Likewise, a person could swear by the altar, and it would not mean anything, but a person could swear by the gift on the altar and be obligated, because the gift was considered to be sacred. What Matthew is proposing is that Temple and altar are basic to Judaism; gold and gifts are not.

The basic values of religion had become inverted. The Temple made the gold sacred, not vice versa. The altar made the gift sacred, not vice versa. Religious integrity, in Matthew's view, doesn't involve any swearing at all. It calls for authenticity — the doing of God's will.

Oaths created secure places for the scribes and Pharisees. They could claim to be leading and guiding, but they blinded others and themselves. They hid behind religious distinctions and never gave themselves over to the will of God. Matthew is warning his community not to fall into this trap. No swearing is necessary. Only doing God's will, being righteous, being authentic, is necessary.

Meditation: In which ways are you (a) a living contradiction, (b) a corrupter of others, (c) and an oath-taker? What can you do to begin to change?

Prayer: God of righteousness, you have called all people to integrity of life. You have opened your kingdom and invited every person to enter. Remove our hypocrisy and our blindness. Through the gift of the Spirit, guide us in the footsteps of Jesus, who is Lord for ever and ever. Amen.

WOE TO YOU WHO SWALLOW CAMELS

Matthew 23:23-26

Scripture: "You pay tithes on mint and dill and cumin, yet have neglected the weightier things of the law: justice and mercy and faithfulness" (Matthew 23:23).

Reflection: This section of Matthew's Gospel (23:23-26) forms the fourth and fifth of a series of "woes," which are addressed to "scribes and Pharisees," Matthew's generic reference for anyone who espouses a religion which is based solely on teaching rules and regulations without ever practicing or keeping them. Matthew is strictly opposed to self-righteousness. Authenticity consists of hearing the word and doing it.

The fourth woe, an expression of a speaker's horror concerning sin and a proclamation of the punishment awaiting those who sin, contrasts things of lesser importance (tithes on herbs) with things of great importance (justice, mercy, and faithfulness) for Matthew. The scribes and Pharisees were preoccupied with trivial matters. The real issue, as Matthew presents it, is not whether one should pay tithes but "the weightier things of the law" (23:23).

The first of these "weightier things" is justice. Matthew has consistently argued against any member of the community judging any other member; judgment belongs to the Son of Man, when he comes in glory. Here, Matthew reemphasizes this as well as urging his church to be just.

Mercy is the second "weightier thing." Like justice, mercy refers to the proper disposition of one member of the community towards another member. Just as God is merciful toward all, we are to show mercy to each other.

Finally, faithfulness or fidelity, the third of the "weightier things," refers to the trust and total surrender to God that righteousness demands. Authentic discipleship involves a willingness to go up to Jerusalem with Jesus, where one's faith is tested by suffering and death.

In order to be sure that the reader recognizes the obvious imbalance between the payment of tithes on herbs and the practice of the law, Matthew employs one of his favorite literary devices — the hyperbole. Jesus calls those who emphasize unimportant practices at the expense of the weightier things of the law "blind guides, who strain out the gnat and swallow the camel!" (23:24).

According to Leviticus (11:41-45), the eating of any swarming creature is forbidden. In order to filter out gnats from liquids, the legalistic Pharisees would use a cloth strainer. The gnat, a minor matter, is contrasted with a camel, a major animal, whose flesh was declared unclean; that is, it could not be eaten. As Matthew sees it, people who are concerned about gnats and tithes on herbs are missing what is really important — putting the weightier matters of the law into practice. They are swallowing camels, and they don't realize it. The challenge to the community is not to fall into this ridiculous way of life. According to Matthew, God isn't interested in scrupulosity.

The fifth woe consists of a comparison between a cup and a person. Just as there is an inside and an outside to a cup, so is there an inner disposition and an outer disposition to a person.

The scribes and Pharisees are accused of observing the ritual washing of the outside of the cup but never cleansing the inside of it. In other words, their appearances are pleasing (they look good), but their inner dispositions consist of "plunder and self-indulgence" (23:25). Their hearts are ready to rob anyone: they have no self control.

According to Matthew, inner purity is not accomplished by outer washing. A person must clean up his or her inner dispositions first. Authenticity flows from the "within" to the "without" and vice versa. Inner cleansing makes the whole person clean.

As is typical of this author, the issue remains the right behavior, the conduct that God wants, righteousness. Members of the Matthean church are being warned to be authentic, to possess an inner and outer harmony. God is not interested in appearances; God is interested in the heart.

Meditation: In which ways are you more concerned about the little things than about weightier matters? In which ways does your outer appearance represent your inward disposition?

Prayer: God of justice, mercy, and fidelity, you call your people to be concerned about the weightier things of your law: justice, compassion, and faithfulness. Cleanse our hearts that we may do justice. Touch our minds that we may understand compassion and be merciful. Support our trust that we may remain faithful to Jesus, your Son, who lives and reigns with you and the Holy Spirit, one God for ever and ever. Amen.

WOE TO YOU WHO WHITEWASH

Matthew 23:27-32

Scripture: "You restore the tombs of the prophets and adorn the monuments of the righteous, and you say, 'If we had lived in the days of our ancestors, we would not have taken part with them in shedding the prophets' blood'" (Matthew 23:29-30).

Reflection: Woes six and seven (23:29-32) form the conclusion of the section from chapter 23 of Matthew's Gospel. The further denunciation of the scribes and Pharisees (23:33-36) and the lament over Jerusalem (23:37-39) are omitted in the weekday lectionary cycle, as is all (24:1-41) but a few verses (24:42-51) of chapter 24, Matthew's eschatological or apocalyptic section.

The sixth woe, a proclamation of the horror of sin and its punishment, continues the theme established in the fifth woe — the importance of outer appearance being an authentic sign of inner disposition. In this woe, the scribes and Pharisees are compared to "whitewashed tombs, which appear beautiful on the outside, but inside are full of dead men's bones and every kind of impurity" (23:27).

According to the law, contact with a dead body, even if one was unaware of it, caused ritual impurity (cf. Numbers 19:11-22). In order to protect themselves from this possibility, Jews whitewashed the tombs. Matthew compares the facade of the tomb to the appearance of the scribes and Pharisees; both nice and clean.

However, inside the tomb there is decaying flesh, stench, and filth. Likewise, inside the Pharisees there is hypocrisy, the essence of sin, and evildoing, lawlessness and impurity. Outer righteousness is not an indication of inner righteousness, according to Matthew. Inside, a person may be rebelling against God and not doing God's will; this is hypocrisy. And so, Matthew warns the members of his church to be what they appear to be. Otherwise, they are mere scribes and Pharisees in disguise.

The seventh and final woe is the most serious denunciation of the scribes and Pharisees by Jesus. It presents the scribes and Pharisees as being just like their ancestors, who murdered the prophets and the righteous. The scribes and Pharisees have restored the tombs of the prophets and adorned the monuments of the righteous and by doing so attempt to disown the murders done by their ancestors. They claim that if they had lived in the days of their ancestors, they would "not have taken part with them in shedding the prophets' blood" (23:30).

However, Jesus declares that they "are the children of those who murdered the prophets" (23:31). In other words, they are the heirs of murderers. Reflecting a Jewish notion that there is an allotted measure of suffering that has to be completed before God's final judgment takes place, Jesus orders the scribes and Pharisees to "fill up" (23:32) what their ancestors measured out. In other words, Jesus affirms the Jewish notion.

For Matthew, this points towards Jesus' own rejection, suffering, and death. It also points towards the rejection, suffering, and death of Matthew's church. In Matthew's view, those who build memorials and disdain participation in the suffering and death of the righteous are the real murderers. Outer behavior does not necessarily reveal authentic inner disposition.

Meditation: In your life, what have you whitewashed which needs to be confronted? In which ways do you propagate any kind of suffering?

Prayer: God of the prophets and the righteous, in the past your servants spoke your word to your people and called them to righteousness in your sight. Jesus, your Son, taught the way of authenticity by conversion of life. Fill our hearts with your truth that we may bear witness to your word and your love for all people. We ask this through Christ our Lord. Amen.

STAY AWAKE!

Matthew 24:42-51

Scripture: "Stay awake! For you do not know on what day your Lord will come" (Matthew 24:42).

Reflection: Chapters 24 and 25 of Matthew's Gospel form the fifth sermon of Jesus. This sermon is commonly referred to as the eschatological discourse. The daily lectionary cycle omits the first 41 verses of the sermon, which consist of the foretelling of the destruction of Jerusalem (24:1-2), the beginning of the calamities (24:3-14), the great tribulation (24:15-28), the coming of the Son of Man (24:29-31), the lesson of the fig tree (24:32-35), and the first part of the narrative dealing with the unknown day and hour of the Son of Man's return (24:36-41).

In this section of the sermon (24:42-51), Jesus exhorts the reader to vigilance. Using material from Q (cf. Luke 12:39-40), Matthew compares the coming of the Son of Man to that of a thief, who gives no warning of his sudden appearance. The members of Matthew's church are to be prepared for the coming of the Son of Man at any time.

This type of vigilance does not imply a cessation of ordinary activities with an over-balanced concentration on the future. However, it does involve a daily attentiveness both to the ordinary and to an awareness of the end. Matthew understands the end as not being near but not being that far distant either. Followers of Jesus live in the in-between time; they take care of the ordinary, but they also look to the future with hope.

In order to reemphasize this point, Matthew employs a Q parable (cf. Luke 12:41-46), the faithful and the unfaithful servant (24:45-51). The parable is addressed to the leaders in Matthew's community, who even though they are leaders, are also fellow servants. The parable, as is typical of Matthew, is more allegory than parable.

The master, Jesus, has put servants, leaders, in charge of his household until he returns. The faithful and prudent servant-leader is the one who is found doing his job when the master returns. The master will "put him in charge of all his possessions" (24:47). According to Matthew, authentic leaders in the community are those who are at once vigilant, prudent, and dependable.

However, if the servant-leader takes advantage of his "fellow servants" by beating them and by eating and drinking with drunkards, then "the servant's master will come on an unexpected day and an unknown hour and will punish him severely"(24:50-51). A servant-leader is just that — a servant-leader — in Matthew's church. Such a person cannot assume a position of superiority or the position of master. Some day the master will come; then, the servant-leader will be recalled.

The servant-leader is a guide during the delay of the Son of Man's coming. If one fails at this task, then that one will be assigned to a "place with the hypocrites" (24:51), the Jewish leaders, the scribes and the Pharisees — the unbelievers. The punishment will consist of "wailing and gnashing of teeth" (24:51), Matthew's favorite phrase for eternal damnation.

Meditation: In which ways do you live faithfully in this time in-between the first coming of Jesus and his second coming? Are you a servant-leader or have you assumed the position of the master?

Prayer: Father, you alone know the day and the hour of the second coming of the Son of Man. Keep us watchful, as for a thief in the night. Make us faithful servants to all our brothers and sisters, who wait in joyful hope for the coming of your Son, Jesus, who is Lord for ever and ever. Amen.

FOOLISH AND WISE
Matthew 25:1-13

Scripture: "The kingdom of heaven will be compared to ten virgins who took their lamps and went out to meet the bridegroom. Five of them were foolish and the other five were wise" (Matthew 25:1-2).

Reflection: The fifth sermon of Jesus in the Gospel of Matthew continues with the parable of the ten virgins (25:1-13), which is found in no other Gospel. As usual for Matthew, it is not a true parable but, rather, an allegory. It emphasizes the stance of members of Matthew's church — watching, knowing what is commanded, and doing it. The themes of the parable — delay, prudence, preparedness, and division within a group — tie it into the context of the whole eschatological discourse.

The fact that the parable divides the virgins into two equal groups of five foolish and five wise echoes the conclusion of Jesus' first sermon about the two foundations (cf. 7:24-27). The wise person is the one who builds a house on rock; the foolish person is the one who builds a house on sand. In the parable of the ten virgins, the wise are those who are prepared (bring enough oil) while the foolish are those who are unprepared (run out of oil).

One interesting detail of this parable is the fact that the oil cannot be shared. The wise cannot give some of their oil to the foolish. According to Matthew, one is either prepared for the coming of the bridegroom (Jesus) or one is not. The irresponsibility of the five foolish virgins cannot be reversed as they await the coming of the Son of Man.

However, the author also rejects an overt enthusiasm while

waiting for the coming of the Son of Man. All ten virgins "be-came drowsy and fell asleep" (25:5). Matthew is trying to guide the members of his church to a balanced view of the "in-between time" in which they were living. He is affirming the coming of the Son of Man, but he is also affirming that there is delay. The community should be prepared (have enough oil), but it should not expect the second coming to be too soon.

Another interesting detail in the story is the fact that no bride is mentioned. The bridegroom (Jesus) is mentioned.

He comes when least expected (at midnight). The virgins or bridesmaids are present. But where is the bride? The bride, of course, is the Church, all those who are ready to go "into the wedding feast" (25:10).

Once the bridegroom comes and the wise are separated from the foolish, the door is locked. Those who are righteous — hearing and doing the word of God — enter into the wedding feast, Matthew's symbol for the consummation of the kingdom. The separation of the weeds and the wheat is accomplished (cf. 13:24-30, 36-43). The division between what is useful and what is not is finished (cf. 13:47-50). Once inside the wedding feast no amount of screaming outside can prompt the "Lord" to open the door and let in those who are not prepared.

The moral at the end of the parable, "Therefore, stay awake, for you know neither the day nor the hour" (25:13) does not lit-erally mean not to sleep, since all the virgins fall asleep. "Stay awake" is a Matthean phrase meaning "be prepared" for the com-ing of the bridegroom, Jesus.

Meditation: In which ways are you prepared for the second com-ing of Jesus? In other words, how much oil do you have for your lamp?

Prayer: God of light, through the teaching and ministry of Jesus, your Servant and your Son, you have taught us the necessity of wisdom. Through the working of the Holy Spirit make us wise in your ways. By inspiring us to hear and do your word, keep us pre-pared for the second coming in glory of Jesus, who lives and reigns with you and the Holy Spirit, one God, for ever and ever. Amen.

WICKED AND LAZY

Matthew 25:14-30

Scripture: The one (servant) who had received the one talent came forward and said, "Lord, I knew you were a hard man, reaping where you did not sow and gathering where you did not scatter; so out of fear I went off and hid your talent in the ground. Here it is back." "So you knew that I reap where I did not sow and gather where I did not scatter? Would you not have done better to put my money in the bank so that I could have got it back with interest on my return?" (Matthew 25:24-27).

Reflection: The parable of the talents (25:14-30) follows the parable of the ten virgins and precedes the judgment of the nations narrative and is part of the fifth sermon of Jesus in Matthew's Gospel. The author's source for this parable is Q (cf. Luke 19: 12-27).

Although there are a number of Matthean editorial marks left on the parable with allegorical interpretations, the form is nevertheless an authentic parable. The setting of a landlord going on a journey reflects a common scene in first century Palestine. The parable, however, is about judgment and the presupposition for judgment.

Three servants are given unequal amounts of money according to each one's ability. The first two presume that the master would want them to invest his entrusted treasure.

And so they do and end up doubling their amounts. When

the master returns, they present their doubled amounts to him. They took a risk investing the money, but it paid off. The master tells each of them, "Since you were faithful over a few things, I will give you greater responsibilities" (25:21, 23).

The third servant, however, presumed that his master was "a hard man" (25:25). He attacked the master for reaping where he does not sow and gathering where he does not scatter. He admits to his fear of the master. And he tries to give back the money — something which the first two servants did not attempt. He presumes that the master wants the money returned.

The third servant has stereotyped the master, and the master lives up to the stereotype. The master declares, "So you knew that I reap where I did not sow and gather where I did not scatter? Would you not have done better to put my money in the bank so that I could have got it back with interest on my return?" (25:26-27). In other words, if the servant knew the master to be this way, then he should have done something differently than what he did; he should have acted on what he knew. The third servant presupposed the landlord to be a certain type of person, but he did not behave according to his presupposition.

The reader is forced to make a decision concerning the master as viewed through the eyes of three servants. The first two servants stereotype the master as generous. The third servant presumes the master to be harsh. Matthew is posing this question to the reader: Does one judge the master on the basis of stereotype or on the basis of action?

If stereotype is one's answer, then the appropriate response is fear. If willing to take a risk, like the first two servants, is one's answer, then the appropriate response is grace.

The reader is confronted with a choice in the parable. But the reader is also confronted with a question: What is the reader's image, presupposition, stereotype of God? Is God a master to be feared? or is God a benevolent master who entrusts his wealth to his people? What motivates action is not who God really is but what one's image of God is. The third servant took no risk based on the reports he had heard about the landlord. The first two servants disregarded the reputation of the landlord and acted accordingly.

According to Matthew, faith is not a guarantee; it is a risk. God has risked entrusting the kingdom to us. God asks that we risk trusting him. Fear is not an appropriate response. Risk is an appropriate response. Faith is a fundamental risk about who God is and that he is.

In the end, according to Matthew, a person will be judged on how well he or she risked doing God's will and not on how well he or she feared God.

Meditation: What is your image of God? How do you act according to this image?

Prayer: God of the kingdom, you entrust the treasures of your kingdom to your people according to each person's abilities. Through Jesus, your Son, you have revealed yourself to be a God of kindness and benevolence and mercy. Make of us faithful servants, who are excited about doing your will. Enable us to spread the good news of your mercy and the kingdom where you live and reign with Jesus and the Holy Spirit, one God, for ever and ever. Amen.

SO MUCH LOVE

John 3:16-18

Scripture: God so loved the world that he gave his only begotten Son, so that everyone who believes in him will not die but will have eternal life (John 3:16).

Reflection: This section of John's Gospel (3:16-18) is part of the unique Johannine dialogue between Nicodemus and Jesus.

After discussing the meaning of "being born from above" (3:3), Jesus explains that "just as Moses lifted up the serpent in the desert, so must the Son of Man be lifted up, so that everyone who believes in him may have eternal life" (3:14-15).

God's love for the world motivated God to give his only Son, "so that everyone who believes in him will not die but will have eternal life" (3:16). As usual, John's choice of words indicates a multiplicity of meanings. God's giving of his Son refers both to the incarnation and to his being "lifted up" (3:14) in death on the cross. All of Jesus' life was a gift to people from God.

God's gift of Jesus was for the purpose of eternal life, which does not so much refer to an infinitude of life as, rather, to a quality of new life. The way to share in eternal life is through faith in Jesus, who came to save, to motivate people to believe.

John makes it clear that "God did not send his Son into the world to condemn the world, but that the world might be saved through him" (3:17). In other words, God did not set up the people of the world. Jesus did not function as judge, nor did he condemn anyone. His coming into the world, however, did provoke judgment — human if not divine.

"Whoever believes in him will not be condemned, but whoever does not believe has already been condemned, because he hasn't believed in the name of the only begotten Son of God" (3:18). For John, judgment consists of not believing in Jesus as the Son of God. Those who do not believe have judged themselves. A deliberate refusal to believe in Jesus results in self-condemnation, according to John.

The focus of this section of John's Gospel is on the vastness of God's love for the world, and not on God's desire to condemn the world. Jesus manifests God's love. He offers eternal life, salvation, to those who believe. Only self-condemnation awaits those who refuse to believe.

Meditation: In which ways have you experienced the unlimited love of God?

Prayer: God of love, you so loved the world, that you gave your only Son, Jesus Christ, in the mystery of the incarnation. He manifested the limitless dimension of your love by being lifted up on the cross, and thus he demonstrated that you did not wish to condemn the world but to save it. Strengthen our faith in the name of your Son. Do not let anyone perish but bring all people to the joy of your kingdom, where you live and reign with Jesus and the Holy Spirit, one God, for ever and ever. Amen.

WITH YOU ALWAYS
Matthew 28:16-20

SOLEMNITY
of the
HOLY TRINITY
First Sunday after Pentecost

Cycle B

Scripture: "All authority in heaven and on earth has been given to me. Go, therefore, and make disciples of all nations.... I'll be with you all the days until the end of the age" (Matthew 28:18-20).

Reflection: The last scene in Matthew's Gospel is the commissioning of the disciples (28:16-20). Not only is this narrative unique to this Gospel, but it functions as the second of the two bookends, the first of which was presented in the first chapter of the Gospel.

Matthew narrates that "the eleven disciples went into Galilee, to the mountain to which Jesus had directed them" (28:16). There are only eleven disciples because Judas, according to this author, had "hanged himself" (27:5). They gather on one of Matthew's favorite places — a mountain. Throughout the Gospel, the author has been interested in portraying Jesus as a new Moses. The first sermon delivered by Jesus takes place on a mountain. Jesus delivers four more sermons to bring the total to five, the same number of volumes in the Pentateuch, the traditional books of Moses.

Furthermore, ancient peoples believed that God lived on a mountain. Moses had gone up to the mountain to get the law, the Torah. Elijah had heard the tiny whispering voice of God on the mountain. Now, Jesus gives his farewell discourse to his disciples on a mountain. When the disciples saw him,"they wor-shiped him, but some were doubtful" (28:17). Faith is never as strong as it should be, according to Matthew. People always have "little faith" (6:30).

But even with "little faith" the disciples are sent forth on mis-sion by Jesus, who, after his resurrection, possesses "all author-ity in heaven and on earth" (28:18). The mission is universal. They are to "make disciples of all nations" (28:19), a reference to both Jews and Gentiles, who have been one of Matthew's concerns since the initial story about the Magi from the East. They are to baptize "in the name of the Father, and of the Son, and of the Holy Spirit" (28:19); that is, they are to initiate people into the Church by using the baptismal formula which was already com-mon in Matthew's community. Baptism indicates a union be-tween the one being baptized, the community, and the Blessed Trinity.

Finally, the disciples are to teach people "to observe all" (28:20) that he has commanded them. Just as Matthew began the Gospel with a genealogy which demonstrates how God often re-verses things, he so ends with an interesting reversal statement. Throughout the Gospel, Jesus never commands the disciples to do anything. He simply presents a new way of life for those who wish to follow him.

Then, the final sentence of the Gospel answers a question which was asked as early as chapter one, where the author indi-cated that the child's name was to be "'Emmanuel,' which means 'God is with us'" (1:23). Finally, the meaning of "Emmanuel" becomes clear when Jesus declares, "I'll be with you all the days until the end of the age" (28:20).

There is no Ascension scene in Matthew; there is no depar-ture of Jesus into the heavens. He is Emmanuel; he is God present with his people. He will remain present until the end of the age. In this way, Matthew settles down for a long period of time be-tween the commissioning of the disciples and the second com-ing of Jesus as judge, which he believes will happen some day.

But this is not something to get excited about because God is with his people now.

Meditation: In which ways have you most recently experienced Jesus (God) being with you always?

Prayer: God of heaven and earth, you have established your presence among your people in the flesh and blood of Jesus, your Son. He has promised to remain with us, as we pilgrimage through life and make disciples of all nations. Keep us faithful to our mission. Remove our doubts. May we always worship you, Father, Son, and Holy Spirit, one God, who lives and reigns until the end of the age and for ever and ever. Amen.

SOLEMNITY
of the
HOLY TRINITY

First Sunday after Pentecost

TRUTH'S GUIDE

John 16:12-15

Cycle C

Scripture: "When he comes, the Spirit of truth, he'll lead you to the whole truth" (John 16:13).

Reflection: This section of John's Gospel (16:12-15) is taken from the author's unique discourse on Jesus' departure and the coming of the "intercessor" or "advocate" (15:26), the "Spirit of truth" (16:13) (cf. 15:26-16:15). According to John, there is much more that the disciples need to be told by Jesus, but they "cannot bear it now" (16:12). "Now" refers to the present.

The Spirit of truth is always at work guiding people "to the whole truth" (16:13). In other words, the Spirit moves people to recognize the truth about Jesus. Furthermore, "he will expose sin and righteousness and judgment to the world for what it is" (16:8).

According to John, sin is a person's refusal to believe in Jesus. Even though Jesus was condemned to death and crucified, he was righteous, that is, he behaved according to God's will. Therefore, he has triumphed over the ruler of this world — Satan — by his death and resurrection. The Spirit of truth clarifies these points.

What the Spirit reveals to the followers of Jesus, he receives from Jesus, who has a unique relationship with the Father. In John, Jesus declares, "Everything that the Father has is mine; that's why I said that he (the Spirit) will receive what is mine and proclaim it to you" (16:15).

The Spirit of truth continues to guide all of those who be-lieve in Jesus. He will proclaim "the things that are to come" (16:13) not in the sense of predicting the future, but by interpret-ing for believers what Jesus has already said and done.

Meditation: In what recent experience have you discovered the Spirit of truth guiding you to the whole truth?

Prayer: Almighty God, you revealed your face when you com-pleted the creation of the heavens and the earth and formed man and woman in your own image and likeness. You revealed your love for people when you sent your incarnate Word to show your people how to live. You revealed your truth with the gift of your Spirit. Mold us into the image of Jesus that we may follow his way of life and be guided by the Spirit of truth. We ask this of you, Father, Son, and Holy Spirit, who live and reign, one God, for ever and ever. Amen.

APPENDIX

SOLEMNITY
of the
BODY and BLOOD
of CHRIST
Second Sunday after Pentecost

Cycle A

LIVING BREAD

John 6:51-58

Scripture: "I am the living bread that came down from heaven. Anyone who eats this bread will live forever. The bread that I'll give for the life of the world is my flesh" (John 6:51).

Reflection: This section of John's Gospel (6:51-58) is part of the multiplication of the loaves and the ensuing bread of life discourse (cf. 6:1-71). It reflects the author's theological understanding of the Eucharist. He teases the reader into seeing his perspective by his use of words which are laden with multiple meanings.

In this passage, Jesus claims that he is the "living bread that came down from heaven" (6:51). "Living bread" means that Jesus, God's gift to the world, is alive after his death and resurrection, that is, now, and that "anyone who eats this bread will live forever" (6:51), that is, will share in Jesus' resurrected or eternal life. In order to share eternal life, a person must eat the "living bread," Jesus' "flesh" (6:51), which he has given on the cross "for the life of the world" (6:51).

The Jews, John's favorite word for anyone who does not understand what Jesus is talking about, ask, "How can this man give us (his) flesh to eat?" (6:52). They understand eating flesh in terms of cannibalism. John is using flesh in a sacramental way. "Unless you eat the flesh of the Son of Man and drink his blood, you

287

do not have life within you. Whoever feeds on my flesh and drinks my blood has eternal life, and I will raise him (or her) up on the last day" (6:53-54).

According to John, Jesus' "flesh is true food" (6:55), that is, that which sustains life. And his "blood, true drink." Drinking blood was as repulsive as eating human flesh to the Jews. Blood was considered to be the source of the body's life. When someone bled, he or she was losing his or her life. For Jesus to declare that "his blood is true drink" (6:55) means that Jesus is the source of eternal life.

Those who eat the flesh of Jesus and drink his blood remain in him and he in them (cf. 6:56). There is an intimate communion between them and Jesus. This union is so close that the flesh and blood of Jesus are commingled with the flesh and blood of his people.

There is another parallel. "Just as the living Father sent me, and I live because of the Father, so too, whoever feeds on me will live because of me" (6:57). The life that Jesus has received from God is now available to anyone through the Eucharist. All one has to do is to feast sacramentally on the body and blood of Jesus, "the bread that came down from heaven" (6:58).

In the desert after the great escape from Egypt, the Israelites were fed manna, bread from heaven. However, they ate this bread and they died. Jesus is bread for eternal life. "Anyone who eats this bread will live forever" (6:58).

Meditation: Make a list of all the different staples of life, kinds of human work, various fruits of the earth, and so forth, you can think of. How do these apply to Jesus?

Prayer: Father, once you fed your people with manna in the desert, but they died nonetheless. In the fullness of time, you sent your Son, Jesus, the living bread that came down from heaven. He has promised us that if we eat this bread we will live forever. Give us the true flesh and the true blood of Jesus that we may be filled with life and be raised up on the last day. We ask this through our Lord Jesus Christ, who lives and reigns with you and the Holy Spirit, one God, for ever and ever. Amen.

THE BLOOD OF
THE COVENANT

Mark 14:12-16, 22-26

SOLEMNITY
of the
BODY and BLOOD
of CHRIST
Second Sunday after Pentecost

Cycle B

Scripture: While they were eating, he (Jesus) took bread, blessed it, broke it, and gave it to them (his disciples) and said, "Take it; this is my body." And taking the cup, he blessed it and gave it to them, and they all drank from it. Then he said to them, "This is my blood of the covenant, which will be poured out for many" (Mark 14:22-24).

Reflection: The narrative about the preparations for the Passover (14:12-16) and the Lord's Supper (14:22-26) are part of Mark's passion account, which begins with the conspiracy against Jesus, the anointing at Bethany, and Judas' plot to betray Jesus (14:1-11). The narrative is divided by Jesus' prediction of Judas' betrayal (14:17-21), and it is followed by Jesus' prediction of Peter's denial (14:27-31).

The narrative about the preparations for the Passover (14:12-16) comes from the same cycle or type of oral tradition as the narrative of Jesus' entry into Jerusalem (11:1-11).

Both contain preparation by the disciples, predictions by Jesus, and fulfillments of the predictions. The placement of the narrative about the Lord's Supper (14:22-26) illustrates Mark's interest in the connection between Passover, the Eucharist, and betrayal.

Passover was the annual remembrance and celebration of

Israel's release from Egyptian slavery during the night. It began at sunset after the Passover lambs had been sacrificed in the Temple. The Feast of Unleavened Bread was joined to Passover at an early date to commemorate Israel's affliction in Egypt and the haste with which the nation left the land of slavery. By remembering the past events of salvation, the people looked forward and hoped for deliverance from their then-present domination by the Romans.

The practice of the early followers of Jesus of celebrating the Eucharist has been woven into this narrative by Mark. The words of blessing for the bread, "Take it; this is my body" (14:22), and the words of thanks for the cup, "This is my blood of the covenant, which will be poured out for many" (14:24), reflect a liturgical formula of the early Church.

The emphasis of this formula is on the absence of Jesus. "Amen, I say to you, I shall not drink again of the fruit of the vine until the day when I drink it new in the kingdom of God" (14:25). The early Church remembered Jesus by breaking bread and drinking wine; it celebrated his absence, while waiting for his coming in glory.

Also, Mark does not understand Jesus' death as beginning anything new. His blood is that "of the covenant" (14:24); only Luke makes Jesus' action a "new" covenant. Jesus' death is a continuance and perfection of the covenant which Moses sealed in blood between the Israelites and God (cf. Exodus 24:1-8).

The placement of the Lord's Supper between the prediction of the betrayal of Judas and the prediction of the denial of Peter by Mark serves to illustrate the author's theological understanding of Jesus' death. For this writer, God is found in abandonment and denial which results in suffering and death.

Not only do Judas and Peter abandon Jesus, but all the disciples "left him and fled" (14:50). He is abandoned by everyone and must face rejection, suffering, and death all alone. On the cross he voices the depth of abandonment, when he cries, "My God, my God, why have you forsaken me?" (15:34). It is at the moment of death that Jesus is most human and experiences the depths of being alone, abandoned. For Mark, this is exactly where God is found.

Therefore, every time that followers of Jesus gather together to break bread and to drink wine in his memory, they do so like the Israelites of old; that is, they remember his great deeds of the past and they look forward with hope to his coming in glory. They celebrate his death — his abandonment — as they come to realize that when they are most human, like Jesus, it is then that they have truly discovered God.

Meditation: In which experiences of abandonment or suffering have you discovered the presence of God?

Prayer: God of Jesus, once you freed your chosen people from Egyptian slavery through the blood of the lamb, which was smeared on their doorposts. With Moses you sealed your covenant with your people through blood, which was sprinkled upon them and your altar. Through the blood of Jesus, you declared your presence in the abandonment, suffering, and death of your Son on the cross. When we celebrate the Eucharist of Jesus, remind us of his lesson, as we wait for his coming in glory. He lives and reigns with you and the Holy Spirit, one God, for ever and ever. Amen.

SOLEMNITY
of the
BODY and BLOOD
of CHRIST
Second Sunday after Pentecost

TAKE, BLESS, BREAK, GIVE

Luke 9:11-17

Cycle C

Scripture: The crowds... followed him (Jesus). After greeting them he spoke to them about the kingdom of God and cured those who were in need of healing.... Then he took the five loaves and the two fish and, after looking up to heaven, he blessed them and broke them into pieces and kept giving them to the disciples to distribute to the crowd (Luke 9:11, 16).

Reflection: Luke's account of the feeding of the five thousand comes from Mark's Gospel (cf. 6:30-44); however, this author has reworked the narrative to fit his own theological perspective on the Eucharist. In Luke's community, the Eucharist is the extension of the multiplication of the loaves and the fishes and of Jesus' last meal with his disciples. It is the way that the fellowship meals of Jesus are extended to the Church. Those who gather for this meal remember Jesus' martyrdom.

Luke portrays Jesus as feeding the crowd with the word of God before he feeds them with bread and fish. Jesus "greeted them and spoke to them about the kingdom of God" (9:11). He also "healed those who needed to be cured" (9:11). Thus, Luke emphasizes the importance of hearing the word of God and acting on it.

This author is also interested in the role of the disciples. Before this scene they had been sent out on mission (cf. 9:1-6). Now, they were eager to dismiss the crowd so that they could "go to the surrounding villages and farms and find food" (9:12) but were told by Jesus to "give them something to eat" (9:13) themselves.

After blessing the loaves and the fishes, Jesus "kept giving them to the disciples to distribute to the crowd" (9:16). Throughout this narrative, Luke focuses on the role of the disciples after Jesus' death, when their mission is to continue to proclaim the word of God and to break the bread of Jesus. Luke illustrates this throughout the Acts of the Apostles, his second volume.

Jesus' acts of "taking the five loaves and the two fish," "blessing them" and "breaking them into pieces," "giving them to the disciples to distribute to the crowd" (9:16) echo the four-fold liturgical action of the Eucharist of the early Church — taking, blessing, breaking, and giving. This eucharistic formula is repeated in the Last Supper narrative (22:19) and in the narrative regarding Jesus' appearance to two of his disciples on the road to Emmaus (24:30).

For Luke, Jesus is the one who satisfies hunger. "The hungry he (the Lord) has filled with good things" (1:53), Mary proclaimed. Now, the reader begins to discover that the "good things" are the word and food of Jesus. "They all ate and were filled" (9:17), notes Luke. The author reinforces this point by locating this event in Bethsaida, which means "place of satisfaction." Also Jesus himself had proclaimed in Luke's version of the beatitudes, "Blessed are you who hunger now, for you shall have your fill" (6:21).

The author maintains Mark's numerical significance. There are "five loaves and two fish" (9:13), which add up to seven, a sign of completion. Also, when "they picked up what was left over" they had twelve baskets of fragments (9:17). Twelve refers to the twelve tribes of Israel, with which God began a chosen people. Thus, Jesus completes the old covenant and he begins a new one, with a group of twelve disciples who are commissioned to gather in the harvest of the new people of God. It is with a little that God feeds many.

Meditation: In which ways has God fed you during the past week?

Prayer: God of bread, Jesus, your Son, satisfied the hunger of the crowd by proclaiming your word and by breaking bread. He commissioned his followers to continue his action throughout the world. Give us the courage to make your name known to all people. Send us the Holy Spirit to unite us in taking, blessing, breaking, and giving the bread of Jesus to each other. Guide us to the kingdom, where you live and reign with Jesus and the Holy Spirit, one God, for ever and ever. Amen.

NAME HIM JOHN

Luke 1:5-17

SOLEMNITY
of the
BIRTH of
JOHN the BAPTIST
Vigil

June 24

Scripture: The angel said to him, "Do not be afraid, Zechariah, your petition has been heard. Your wife Elizabeth will bear you a son, and you shall name him John" (Luke 1:13).

Reflection: The announcement of the birth of John the Baptizer (Luke 1:5-17) is unique to Luke's Gospel. It follows the author's literary prologue and is itself followed by the announcement of the birth of Jesus. The announcement of John's birth by Luke serves a number of non-biographical purposes.

First, by the time Luke was writing his Gospel (80-90 A.D.), a problem concerning John had developed in the early Church. The problem was created by Mark's Gospel. "Since Jesus was baptized by John, then John must be the greater" is how the debate was going. In order to solve this problem, Luke introduces John and his role in the very beginning of the Gospel. He is "called prophet of the Most High," the one who "will go before the Lord to prepare his way"(1:76). Furthermore, before Jesus is baptized, Herod puts "John in prison" (3:20).

John's role, according to Luke, is to prepare the way for Jesus' coming. He was not greater than Jesus (cf. 3:15-16). He does not baptize Jesus. Therefore, Luke has solved the problem of who is greater. There is no doubt; Jesus is greater.

Second, Luke is the only author to tell the reader who the

parents of John were — Zechariah and Elizabeth. In the Old Testament the most famous Zechariah was the prophet. Luke states
that this Zechariah was of "the priestly division of Abijah" (1:5),
that is, the eighth of 24 divisions of Aaronic priests who served
in Jerusalem for a week at a time twice a year. The Old Testament Elizabeth is the one who married Aaron, Moses' brother,
and high priest. By portraying John's parents in this way, Luke is
declaring that the child to be born will be Aaronic, priestly.

Third, since "both were righteous in the eyes of God, observing all the commandments and ordinances of the Lord blamelessly" (1:6), why is it that they "had no child" (1:7)?

The declaration of their righteousness, correct behavior in
the eyes of God, meant that they should have been blessed. Childlessness was considered to be a curse. "Elizabeth was barren and
both were advanced in years" (1:7).

By portraying Zechariah and Elizabeth in this fashion, Luke
is able to root the reader in other Old Testament parents, who
were in similar situations. Such characters as Elkanah and
Hannah, the parents of Samuel (1 Samuel 1:1-28); Abraham and
Sarah, the parents of Isaac (Genesis 18:11-14); Isaac and Rebekah,
the parents of Esau and Jacob (Genesis 25:21-34); Jacob and
Rachel, the parents of Joseph (Genesis 29:31; 30:22-24); and
Manoah and his wife, the parents of Samson (Judges 13:2-25).
By alluding to all these people of the past, Luke is declaring that
God often does what looks impossible to people.

Fourth, Luke introduces the "angel of the Lord" (1:11), a
code name for God, for God's presence among his people.
Abraham entertained three men, who later turned out to be God.
Moses was greeted by the angel of the Lord in a burning bush.
Gideon encountered the angel of the Lord in a call to lead the
Israelites. The angel of the Lord, later named Gabriel (which
means "the strength of God"), functions as a messenger, who
brings good news to the people.

Fifth, the child to be born to Zechariah and Elizabeth will
be named "John" (1:13), which means "Yahweh has given grace"
or "Yahweh has shown favor." Furthermore, "many will rejoice

at his birth, for he will be great in the sight of (the) Lord" (1:14-15). By portraying John in this manner, Luke clearly delineates what his role will be. He does the same thing for the announcement of Jesus' birth. Thus, it becomes clear to the reader exactly who the principal character is in Luke's "orderly sequence" (1:3).

Sixth, the angel of the Lord explains the child's characteristics. "He will drink neither wine nor strong drink" (1:15). He will be a Nazirite, like Samson (cf. Judges 13:4-5) and Samuel (1 Samuel 1:11), and set apart for the Lord's service.

"He will be filled with the Holy Spirit even from his mother's womb, and he will turn many of the children of Israel to the Lord their God" (1:15-16). All of Luke's characters are "filled with the Holy Spirit." The Spirit is Jesus' gift to the Church on Pentecost, which occurs in the Acts of the Apostles, Luke's second volume. However, since Pentecost has already occurred, Luke reads the working of the Spirit backward into every event he records. The Spirit has center stage throughout Luke's Gospel and the Acts of the Apostles. In this section, he introduces the reader to the Holy Spirit for the first time.

John will go before the Lord "in the spirit and power of Elijah to bring back the hearts of fathers to their children and the rebellious to the wisdom of the upright, to make ready for the Lord a perfect people" (1:17). John looks like Elijah, the fiery-spirited reformer-prophet of the Old Testament, who was believed to return before the coming of the Messiah.

Speaking in God's name, the prophet Malachi had declared, "Lo, I will send Elijah, the prophet, before the day of the Lord comes, the great and terrible day, to turn the hearts of the fathers to their children, and the hearts of the children to their fathers" (Malachi 3:23-24). He had also said, "Lo, I am sending my messenger to prepare the way before me; and suddenly there will come to the Temple the Lord whom you seek, and the messenger of the covenant whom you desire. Yes, he is coming, says the Lord of hosts" (Malachi 3:1).

By characterizing John as Elijah, Luke both fulfills Malachi's prophecy, but he also prepares the way for the announcement of the birth of Jesus, the Messiah, whose coming was to be preceded by Elijah, alias John the Baptist.

Meditation: In which ways does John continue to prepare the way for the coming of the Messiah?

Prayer: God of Zechariah and Elizabeth, only you can declare people to be righteous in your sight. You blessed your servants with a child, who was destined to prepare the way for your only Son, Jesus. Fill us with the same spiritual fire that motivated John to fulfill your will so that we might continue to prepare the way for the coming of Jesus in glory. We ask this through our Lord Jesus Christ, who lives and reigns with you and the Holy Spirit, one God, for ever and ever. Amen.

YAHWEH HAS
GIVEN GRACE

Luke 1:57-66, 80

SOLEMNITY
of the
BIRTH of
JOHN the BAPTIST
During the Day

June 24

Scripture: The time for Elizabeth to have her child came, and she gave birth to a son. And it happened that on the eighth day they went to circumcise the child. They were going to call him by his father's name, Zechariah, but his mother said in reply, "No, he will be called John instead" (Luke 1:57, 59-60).

Reflection: The narrative of the birth of John (1:57-67) follows Mary's canticle and precedes that of Zechariah's. The narrative is set up to fulfill what was prophesied in 1:5-25.

The author declares that the "Lord had manifested his great mercy toward" Elizabeth (1:58) in giving her a child. Her barrenness was considered to be a curse, a punishment for some sin either she or her ancestors committed. By giving birth to a child, her righteousness was affirmed.

The eighth day is not only the day for the child's circumcision and naming, but it is also the day of perfection or completion. Through circumcision, the child is initiated in the old covenant, so that he had roots in the past. However, he is the last of the old prophets; what he will herald is the new day of salvation.

Because Zechariah didn't believe the angel of the Lord's message about the birth of John, he was made "speechless and unable to talk until the day" (1:20) when the angel's prediction came to pass. Now that day has arrived. Zechariah's "mouth was opened, his tongue freed, and he spoke blessing God" (1:64). Both Elizabeth and Zechariah name the child John, which means "Yahweh has given grace" or "Yahweh has shown favor."

The reader is left with the question, "In what way has God given grace or shown favor?" This is the question that Luke will attempt to answer throughout the Gospel. The author hopes that, like Zechariah's and Elizabeth's neighbors, all who hear these things will take them to heart, saying, "What, then, will this child be?" (1:66). Luke editorializes, "For surely the hand of the Lord was with him" (1:66).

Meditation: In which ways has God given grace to you or shown favor to you?

Prayer: God of John the Baptist, from before his conception you chose John to prepare the way for the coming of your Son, Jesus. On the day of his birth, many declared that you had visited and brought redemption to your people. Continue to shower us with your many gifts of grace and favor. Guide us with the Holy Spirit that we might know your will and put it into practice. We ask this through our Lord Jesus Christ, who lives and reigns with you and the Holy Spirit, one God, for ever and ever. Amen.

DO YOU LOVE ME?

John 21:15-19

Scripture: Jesus said to Simon Peter, "Simon, son of John, do you love me more than these?" He said to him, "Yes, Lord, you know that I love you." He said to him, "Feed my lambs" (John 21:15).

Reflection: The dialogue between Jesus and Peter about love and feeding sheep (21:15-19) is part of the epilogue (chapter 21) of John's Gospel. John's Gospel initially ended with verses 30-31 of chapter 20. The events described in chapter 21 were collected and added at a later time, probably before the publication of the Gospel.

The dialogue between Jesus and Peter serves as the Johannine rehabilitation scene for Peter. Historically, Peter did occupy a special place of leadership in the infant Church. However, the Johannine community wanted to know how this could be since Peter had three times denied Jesus (cf. John 18:17, 25-27). In order to paint Peter in stronger shades of leadership colors, the Johannine author portrays his rehabilitation by Jesus after the resurrection.

Just as Peter had denied Jesus three times, in this scene he must profess his love for Jesus three times. Jesus asks Peter the first time, "Simon, son of John, do you love me more than these?" (21:15). The meaning here is a love greater than the other disciples or greater than fishing.

303

Then Jesus asks Peter a second time, "Simon, son of John, do you love me?" (21:16, 17). Peter's response to both questions is the same, "Yes, Lord, you know that I love you" (21:15, 16). His third response refocuses his attention on the all-knowing qualities of the risen Jesus, "Lord, you know everything; you know that I love you" (21:17). Thus, Peter's threefold confession of love of Jesus counteracts his threefold denial of Jesus. He is restored by the risen Lord to a position of leadership in the Church. Any member of the Johannine community who questioned Peter's position has now had his or her doubts eliminated by this passage.

Not only does Peter profess love, but he is recommissioned by Jesus. Jesus tells him, "Feed my lambs," "Tend my sheep," "Feed my sheep" (21:15, 16, 17). In light of Jesus' discourse on being the good shepherd (10:1-30), Peter is entrusted with the role of the shepherd. It is not because of his worthiness that he is given this position, but because he has been reconciled in love to Jesus. Here, the Johannine author makes it clear that God works through those who are weak and through those who fail. God accomplishes his deeds in human flesh.

The author of this part of the Gospel knew that Peter had been crucified and died. So, he alludes to this in the section following Peter's restoration: "When you were younger, you used to dress yourself and go where you wanted; but when you grow old, you will stretch out your hands, and someone else will dress you and lead you where you do not want to go " (21:18). The author adds an editorial comment for the reader, "He said this signifying by what kind of death he would glorify God" (21:19).

In this way, Peter, the shepherd, would follow the good shepherd to the point of laying down his life for the sheep. He would go, like a criminal and like Jesus, to his own martyrdom. Once again, his confession of love would be tested, John is saying. However, the second time, Peter would hold fast and not deny Jesus.

The last words of this section are spoken by the risen Lord, "Follow me" (21:19). "Follow me" was used by Jesus in the Gospel of John to call his first disciples. By using it again here, the author ratifies Peter's second call and response.

Meditation: When have you most recently denied Jesus and experienced being restored to discipleship by professing your love for him?

Prayer: God of apostles, you called Peter to follow your Son, Jesus, and to make his name known among the people of Israel. You called Paul to preach the Gospel among the Gentiles. Now, you have called us to be the heralds of your good news to the ends of the earth. Deepen our love for you. Keep us faithful to our mission. Guide us with your Spirit. We ask this through our Lord Jesus Christ, who lives and reigns with you and the Holy Spirit, one God, for ever and ever. Amen.

UPON THIS ROCK

Matthew 16:13-19

Scripture: Simon Peter said in reply (to Jesus), "You are the Messiah, the Son of the living God." And in response Jesus said to him, "Blessed are you, Simon son of Jonah, for flesh and blood has not revealed this to you, but my Father in heaven. And so I say to you, you are Peter, and upon this rock I will build my Church" (Matthew 16:15-18).

Reflection: Matthew has taken the Marcan confession of Peter at Caesarea Philippi (8:27-29) and combined it with his own unique tradition concerning Peter in this section of his Gospel (16:13-19). Also, this author has made it clear that Jesus is not just the Messiah, as in Mark, but he is the "Son of the living God" (16:16).

The initial question that begins the dialogue has been significantly altered by Matthew. In Mark Jesus asks, "Who do people say that I am?" (Mark 8:27). In Matthew Jesus asks, "Who do people say that the Son of Man is?" (16:13). "Son of Man" is the title used for the rejected, suffering, dead, and risen Jesus. Matthew is employing a post-resurrectional confession of faith in Jesus. Some of this section may have originally circulated as part of a post-resurrectional appearance of Jesus.

The answers given to the initial question need to be examined. First, the answer "John the Baptist" (16:14) reflects Herod's understanding of who Jesus is (cf. 14:1-2); this answer is, of course, incorrect. Second, the answer "Elijah" (16:14) reflects an expectation of the Jews of the return of Elijah to prepare for the manifestation of the Messiah. Matthew portrays John the Baptist as being this manifestation (cf. 3:4).

Third, the answer "Jeremiah or one of the prophets" (26:14) is an addition to the Marcan source. Jeremiah was the prophet who suffered greatly during his ministry to Israel. For Matthew, Jesus is like Jeremiah; Jesus will suffer greatly in Jerusalem.

Simon Peter gives the correct answer to the question, "You are the Messiah, the Son of the living God" (16:16). "Messiah" is the Hebrew word for "the anointed one." By attaching "Son of the living God" to his Marcan source, Matthew clearly defines what the title "Messiah" means for his church. To name Jesus as Messiah is to name him the Son of God.

To have come to this knowledge is no accident for Simon Peter. Jesus tells him, "Blessed are you, Simon son of Jonah, for flesh and blood has not revealed this to you, but my Father in heaven" (16:17). Peter is blessed, that is, he has been favored by God with the revelation of who Jesus is. Such divine intervention is popular throughout Matthew's Gospel.

Just as Peter bestowed the title "Son of God" on Jesus, Jesus in turn bestows a title upon Peter. "You are Peter, and upon this rock I will build my Church, and the gates of hell shall not prevail against it" (16:18). The play on words is lost in English. It works in both Greek and Aramaic: *Petros/petra*; *Kephas/kepa*. The translation which comes closest to capturing the play on words is this: You are rock and upon this rock I will build my Church.

Matthew is the only author of a Gospel to use the word "Church." It occurs here and at 18:17; in both instances it means "assembly," or "community." Peter is here declared the rock foundation for the Church. This most likely reflects Matthew's attempt to justify the position that Peter held in the early Church in light of Peter's denial of Jesus.

The Church will be protected from "the gates of hell" (16:18). Hell or the netherworld was the abode of the dead. Death has no power over the Church. Jesus will demonstrate this through his own death and resurrection. Anyone belonging to this community will share the same fate as Jesus.

Peter is given "the keys to the kingdom of heaven" and whatever he looses "on earth shall be loosed in heaven" (16:19). Keys signify authority. In the early Church, Peter held a position of authority. By portraying Jesus giving the keys of the kingdom to Peter, Matthew justifies Peter's authority in the community. The image is drawn from Isaiah 22:15-25, where Eliakim, who succeeds Shebnah as master of the palace, is given the key to the house of David, with the authority to open and to close.

Meditation: In which ways have you experienced a need for authority in the Church?

Prayer: Living God, you have revealed yourself in the flesh and blood of Jesus, your only Son. Simon Peter recognized your revelation and declared Jesus to be the Messiah, your anointed One. Upon his confession of faith you have built a Church and given it the authority to bind and loose. Continue to guide the Church. Give her faithful leaders. Fill her with the gift of the Holy Spirit. We ask this through Christ our Lord. Amen.

SHINING LIKE THE SUN

Matthew 17:1-9

FEAST
of the
TRANSFIGURATION

August 6

Cycle A

Scripture: After six days Jesus took Peter, James, and John his brother, and led them up a high mountain by themselves. And he was transfigured before them; his face shone like the sun and his clothes became as white as light (Matthew 17:1-2).

Reflection: Matthew's account of the transfiguration of Jesus (17:1-9) finds its source in Mark's Gospel (9:2-9). However, Matthew has reworked the account to fit his own theological perspective and to enhance the apocalyptic framework of the narrative.

The narrative begins with "after six days," which refers the reader to the book of Genesis and the first story of creation. After working six days, God rests on the seventh. The transfiguration occurs on the seventh day, a day of rest in honor of the divinity. The location of the event is a "high mountain." This serves Matthew's purpose in portraying Jesus as a new Moses.

Jesus' first of five sermons, which neatly parallel the five books of Moses (Genesis, Exodus, Leviticus, Numbers, and Deuteronomy), is situated on a mountain (5:1). Also, Moses received the law on Mount Sinai (cf. Exodus 24:12-18) and Elijah heard the tiny whispering voice of God on the same mountain (1 Kings 19:8-18). Therefore, it is not by accident that they appear to Jesus and his disciples (17:3). Numbers are significant in this narrative. Jesus takes "Peter, James, and John" (17:1) with him. These make three.

"Moses and Elijah appeared to them, conversing with him (Jesus) (17:3). These make three. Peter tells Jesus, "If you wish, I will make three tents here, one for you, one for Moses, and one for Elijah" (17:4). The three sets of three proclaim the presence of the divinity; a theophany is taking place. It is similar to Abraham's three visitors (cf. Genesis 18:1-15), or the three three-year-old animals used in the covenant-making ceremony (cf. Genesis 15:1-20), or Hannah's offering of a three-year-old bull (cf. 1 Samuel 1:24-28).

The reference to the tents is meant to recall the days that Israel spent in the desert living in tents. The reference also serves to remind the reader that God once lived in a tent with his people in the desert. The manifestation of his presence was a cloud (cf. Exodus 40:34-35). Later, after the Temple was built, the sign of his presence was still a cloud (cf. 1 Kings 8:10).

Matthew incorporates imagery from the apocalyptic sections of the book of Daniel. When Jesus' face "shone like the sun and his clothes became as white as light" (17:2) the author alludes to Daniel's visions (cf. Daniel 10:6, 7:9).

The voice from the cloud proclaims, "This is my beloved Son, in whom I am well pleased; listen to him" (17:5). As in Mark, the voice repeats the words heard at Jesus' baptism (cf. 3:17). The command to "listen to him" is taken from the book of Deuteronomy (18:15), in which Moses tells the Israelites, "A prophet like me will the Lord, your God, raise up for you from among your own kinsmen: to him you shall listen."

Matthew adds a further reference to the book of Daniel, when he narrates, "When the disciples heard this (the voice), they fell prostrate and were very much afraid. But Jesus came and touched them, saying, 'Get up and do not be afraid'" (17:6-7). During his visions, Daniel acts in the same way (cf. Daniel 10:9-10, 18-19).

In order to be sure that the reader understands the transfiguration in terms of a vision, Jesus in this passage from Matthew's

Gospel tells the disciples, "Tell no one about the vision until the Son of Man has risen from the dead" (17:9). Only Matthew refers to the event as a vision, because he interprets Jesus' suffering, death, and resurrection in apocalyptic terms. Since this narrative is often considered to be a misplaced resurrection account, such a label fits Matthew's view of Jesus' ministry.

Meditation: How has your faith in Jesus transfigured (changed) you?

Prayer: God of power and might, you revealed your presence to Moses and Elijah on a mountain. Likewise, you revealed the glory of your Son on a high mountain. Through the waters of baptism we have been immersed into the brightness of his light. Keep us faithful to his word. Make us strong in faith. Raise us up to share in his new life in the kingdom, where he lives and reigns with you and the Holy Spirit, one God, for ever and ever. Amen.

THIS IS MY SON

Mark 9:2-10

FEAST
of the
TRANSFIGURATION

August 6

Cycle B

Scripture: Jesus... was transfigured before them... and his clothes became dazzlingly white.... Then Elijah appeared... along with Moses, and they were conversing with Jesus (Mark 9:1-4).

Reflection: The account of the transfiguration, which is found in Mark's Gospel (9:2-10), functions as a "re-baptism" scene, and, thus, as one of three important points of the Gospel. The identity of Jesus and who knows and who does not know who Jesus is throughout the Gospel form part of the hinge for this work.

Except for the introductory declaration of "Jesus Christ, the Son of God" (1:1), Mark reveals the identity of Jesus as "Son of God" at his baptism, his transfiguration, and after his death on the cross. At his baptism, Jesus "saw the heavens being torn open and the Spirit descending upon him like a dove. And a voice came from the heavens, 'You are my beloved Son; in you I am well pleased'" (1:10-11). After this, Jesus begins a ministry of power through exorcisms, healings, and miracles.

However, Mark reverses the Jesus-of-power in the second half of the Gospel. When Peter declares Jesus to be the Messiah (cf. 8:27) and Jesus teaches that the Messiah will be rejected, made to suffer and die, and be resurrected, Peter wants no part of such a scenario. Then the author begins to demonstrate that discipleship means powerlessness. He needs to confirm this direction in the Gospel with a type of baptismal scene. The transfiguration accomplishes this.

Just as a voice was heard from the heavens at Jesus' baptism, so at his transfiguration "from the cloud came a voice, 'This is my beloved Son. Listen to him'" (9:8). Most likely a misplaced post-resurrectional account, the transfiguration narrative serves to confirm the new direction of powerlessness in the Gospel.

The transfiguration also points beyond the suffering and death of Jesus to his resurrection, his glory. Mark is interested in a theme which is best stated in this way: real power is found in powerlessness. When Jesus hangs in powerless death on the cross, then he has attained the power of God. For as soon as he is dead, a centurion declares, "Truly this man was the Son of God!" (15:39). Thus, the way of powerlessness to power and glory is confirmed.

The transfiguration takes place "after six days" (9:2), which means on the seventh day or the day of perfection. The location is a "high mountain" (9:2), which is reminiscent of such Old Testament events as God's giving of the law to Moses on Mount Sinai and God's tiny whispering voice of prophecy given to Elijah the prophet on Mount Sinai. By raising Jesus from the dead, Mark is saying, God fulfilled the law and the prophets.

Mark uses the apocalyptic image of "dazzlingly white clothes" (9:3) here to tie this section of his Gospel to the young man who was present and "wearing nothing but a linen cloth about his body" (14:51) when Jesus was arrested and "left the cloth behind and ran off naked" (14:52) and to the empty tomb narrative in which the reader is told that the women "on entering the tomb… saw a young man sitting on the right side, clothed in a white robe" (16:5). For Mark, the transfiguration of a follower of Jesus takes place through naked baptism into his suffering, death, and resurrection.

The presence of the divinity is signaled by the use of three sets of three. "Peter, James, and John" (9:2) form the first set of three. Elijah, Moses, and Jesus form the second set of three. And Peter says, "Let us make three tents: one for you, one for Moses, and one for Elijah" (9:5). Using the Old Testament image for a theophany, such as found in Abraham's three visitors, the three-year-old animals used in the covenant-making ceremony between God and Abraham, and the offering made by Hannah, Mark declares God's presence in sign and in the voice from the cloud, which is itself another sign of God's presence in the meeting tent (cf. Exodus 40:34-35) and in the Temple in Jerusalem (cf. 1 Kings 8:10).

The new course for the Gospel is set. Jesus will begin to teach his disciples the way of powerlessness — rejection, suffering, death, and resurrection. Mark has prepared the reader for this by stating that Jesus charged Peter, James, and John "not to tell anyone what they had seen until the Son of Man had risen from the dead. So they kept the matter to themselves, arguing what it meant to rise from the dead" (9:9-10). Hopefully, the reader also questions what it means as he or she continues the new course of the Gospel, which presents authentic power as being found in powerlessness.

Meditation: In which recent experience did you discover that you were powerful because you were powerless?

Prayer: God of glory, you revealed your law on a mountain to Moses, your servant. On a mountain you filled Elijah with your Spirit. Likewise, on a high mountain you revealed the mystery of your presence in the flesh and blood of Jesus, your only Son. Open our hearts that we might listen to his word. Direct our steps that we might follow in his steps of powerlessness. Grant that we might share in the glory which belongs to you, Father, Son, and Holy Spirit, one God, for ever and ever. Amen.

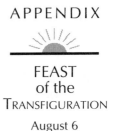

WHILE PRAYING HE WAS CHANGED

Luke 9:28-36

Scripture: (Jesus) took Peter, John, and James and went up to the mountain to pray. While he was praying his face changed in appearance and his clothes became a dazzling white. And behold, two men were conversing with him, Moses and Elijah, who were seen in glory and spoke of his exodus that he was going to accomplish in Jerusalem (Luke 9:28-31).

Reflection: Luke's source for the transfiguration narrative (9:28-26) is Mark's Gospel (9:2-10). However, the author has reworked the material to fit his own theological perspectives. The narrative follows Peter's confession about Jesus, Jesus' first prediction of the Passion, and Jesus' explanation of the conditions of discipleship (9:18-27). The healing of a boy with a demon and the second prediction of the Passion (9:37-45) immediately follow the transfiguration account.

Luke changes Mark's "after six days" (9:2) to "about eight days" (9:28). The eighth day is the day of fullness, the day of completeness, the eschatological day of the Lord. On the eighth day John the Baptist was circumcised (1:59). On the eighth day Jesus was circumcised (2:21). Now, on the eighth day, the fullness of Jesus' identity is revealed again, as it already was at his baptism (3:21-22).

With "Peter, John, and James" Jesus "went up the mountain to pray" (9:28). The motif of prayer is peculiar to Luke's account of this event. Before any major event of his life, Jesus is found at prayer: at his baptism (3:21), before the choice of the Twelve (6:12), before Peter's confession (9:18), before teaching the disciples to pray (11:1), before the last supper (22:32), on the Mount of Olives (22:41), and on the cross (23:46).

Prayer marks the stages of Jesus' spiritual process from revelation of his identity to preaching to rejection to suffering to death. Those who follow Jesus are to imitate him; that is, they are to pray as they journey through a lifetime of following Jesus. Luke demonstrates that it is through prayer that God directs the events in a person's life and in the salvation history of the world.

The appearance of Moses and Elijah represents the law and the prophets. Moses received the law from God on a mountain. Elijah was rejuvenated with the spirit of prophecy as he heard the tiny whispering sound on a mountain. Just as these two men were listened to attentively in the past, now the voice from the cloud declares, "this is my Son, my Chosen One; listen to him" (9:35). Jesus replaces Moses and Elijah with the law of the kingdom of God and a prophecy which is the result of the Holy Spirit.

Moses and Elijah speak with Jesus about "his exodus that he was going to accomplish in Jerusalem" (9:31). This motif is unique to Luke, who understands this exodus as Jesus' suffering, death, resurrection and ascension, which take place in Jerusalem. Most of Luke's Gospel is a journey to Jerusalem (9:51-18:14), where the great events of salvation take place.

However, the use of the word "exodus" also recalls the great escape of Israel from Egypt and the entrance into the promised land. Jesus will escape the throes of death, as God will raise him from the dead, and he will enter into the promised land of new life. Disciples of Jesus make this same exodus, according to Luke, if they pray and follow Jesus.

Luke is also concerned with glory, which is achieved through suffering. Moses and Elijah appear "in glory" (9:31). "Peter and his companions had been overcome by sleep, but becoming fully awake, they saw his glory and the two men standing with him" (9:32). Through his suffering and death, Jesus was glorified by the Father. "Was it not necessary that the Messiah should suffer… and thus enter into his glory?" (24:26).

The emphasis on glory reveals this narrative as a misplaced post-resurrectional story. Mark placed it after Peter's confession because he chose not to employ any post-resurrectional appearances. Luke follows Mark's lead but changes the emphasis. Jesus enters into glory through rejection, suffering, death, and resurrection; that is, by hearing the word of God and acting on it. Thus, he becomes a model for every person who claims to follow his way.

The three sets of three, signifying a theophany, a manifestation of God, are present. Peter, John, and James form one set of three. Moses, Elijah, and Jesus form another set of three. And Peter tells Jesus, "Let us make three tents, one for you, one for Moses, and one for Elijah" (9:33). Just as Abraham received three visitors, and just as Abraham used three three-year-old animals in the covenant-making ceremony with God, and just as Hannah offered a three-year-old bull when she presented Samuel — all of these experienced the presence of God — so Jesus and his disciples are privileged to a similar theophany.

Meditation: When did you last experience God's Spirit motivating you to change some aspect of your life? What was this aspect? In which way did you change?

Prayer: God of silence, you revealed your glory through the law, which you gave to Moses on your holy mountain. You shared your glory with Elijah through the Spirit, which you poured out on him in a tiny whispering sound on your holy mountain. In the midst of prayer, you shared the glory of your only Son with his disciples. Keep us faithful on our lifetime journey that we may come to the glory of the resurrection of Jesus, who lives and reigns with you and the Holy Spirit, one God, for ever and ever. Amen.

HEARING AND OBSERVING

Luke 11:27-28

Scripture: "Blessed are those who hear the word of God and keep it" (Luke 11:28).

Reflection: The short two-verse monologue of Luke's Gospel that is usually labeled as true blessedness (11:27-28) is unique to this author and is part of a unit (9:14-36) which deals with an assault on Jesus, which is followed by his double reply. In the context of casting out a demon, Jesus declares that it is not adequate to expel evil if there is no hearing of God's word and observation of it, both of which signify that a person has accepted the kingdom of God.

The beatitudinal form is used by "a woman from the crowd" who "called out and said" to Jesus, "blessed is the womb that bore you and the breasts at which you nursed" (11:27). The anonymous woman declares that Jesus' mother had finished her journey of life looking like God; that is, she was blessed.

This is in keeping with Luke's portrayal of Mary. When the angel Gabriel announces the birth of Jesus to Mary, the angel greets her as the "favored one" (1:28). When Mary visits Elizabeth, Elizabeth greets her as "Most blessed... among women" (1:42). In her own hymn of praise, Mary declares, "From now on will all ages call me blessed" (1:48). Therefore, it is not unexpected that a woman from the crowd would declare "the womb that bore" Jesus and "the breasts at which (he) nursed" (11:27) to be blessed.

However, Jesus' response alters this perspective. Jesus states, "Rather blessed are those who hear the word of God and keep it" (11:28). In this one sentence the author summarizes his basic theology that underlies not only his Gospel, but his second volume, the Acts of the Apostles. Those who truly finish their lifetime journey looking like God "are those who hear the word of God and keep it" (11:28).

People hear the word of God from Jesus, from his disciples, and from those who come after them. Observing the word of God means putting it into practice, acting on it, reforming one's life accordingly.

Luke is not portraying Jesus as rebuking his mother. Rather, he is emphasizing that listening to the word of God and acting on it is more important than blood relationships. Earlier in the Gospel, Jesus had declared, "My mother and my brothers are those who hear the word of God and act on it" (8:21). Physical relationship does not include one in the family of Jesus. Obedience to God's word and a lifestyle which reflects such obedience to the word is what designates one a member of Jesus' family. This holds true for everyone, even Jesus' mother, who continually throughout the Gospel is held up as a model of one who hears the word and acts on it. Biological relationship takes second place to Gospel obedience and lifestyle.

Meditation: In which ways have you heard the word of God and observed it?

Prayer: God of Mary, you chose the virgin of Nazareth to be the mother of your Son. Indeed, blessed was her womb that carried Jesus, and blessed were her breasts at which he nursed. However, more blessed is she because she heard your word and observed it. Through the gift of the Holy Spirit help us to be attentive to your word and to form our lives according to what we hear. Count us among those blessed in the kingdom, where you live and reign with our Lord Jesus Christ and the Holy Spirit, one God, for ever and ever. Amen.

BLESSED FRUIT OF THE WOMB

Luke 1:39-56

Scripture: Mary set out and went with solicitude into the hill country to a town of Judah, where she entered the house of Zechariah and greeted Elizabeth. When Elizabeth heard Mary's greeting, the infant leaped in her womb, and Elizabeth, filled with the Holy Spirit, cried out in a loud voice and said, "Blessed are you among women, and blessed is the fruit of your womb" (Luke 1:39-42).

Reflection: The narrative about Mary's trip to Elizabeth (1:39-45) and the canticle of Mary (1:46-55), which follows it, is unique to Luke's Gospel. The author uses this story to bring together the two women with whom he has begun the Gospel and to unite the announcements of the birth of John the Baptist and Jesus.

Once Luke has brought the two women — Elizabeth and Mary — together, he presents two canticles. In the first, presented by Elizabeth, Mary is praised as a believer. "Blessed are you who believed that what was spoken to you by the Lord would be fulfilled" (1:45). Mary is portrayed as a model of discipline from the moment of the announcement of the birth of Jesus to Pentecost; she hears the word of God and she acts on it because she believes it. Luke will use this theme of hearing and acting on the word of God throughout the rest of the Gospel, and he holds up Mary as the disciple of Jesus to be imitated.

Mary's canticle serves to clarify the link between what God does for one person and what he does for the whole world, namely overturn the structures of society. Probably a Jewish-Christian hymn which Luke found to be worth incorporating into his Gospel, Mary's canticle first focuses on what God has done for her.

"My soul proclaims the greatness of the Lord; my spirit rejoices in God my savior. For he had regard for his handmaid's lowliness; behold, from now on will all ages call me blessed. The Mighty One has done great things for me, and holy is his name" (1:46-49).

It is God's initiative that is praised. Mary focuses on her unworthiness and the grace of God which has made her worthy. God offered his grace to Mary, and she responded to it with faith. "His mercy is from age to age to those who fear him" (1:50).

In the second part of the canticle, Mary's focus is on the reversal which will take place throughout the rest of the Gospel. Throughout Luke's Gospel, the ordinary ways of society are reversed. These lines of Mary's canticle predict and prepare the reader for these events:

"He (God) has shown might with his arm, dispersed the arrogant of mind and heart. He has thrown down the rulers from their thrones but lifted up the lowly. The hungry he has filled with good things; the rich he has sent away empty" (1:51-53).

Just as in the first part of the canticle where Mary's response in faith is attributed to God's merciful grace, so the societal reversal spoken of in the second part of the canticle is attributed to God's gracious mercy: "He has helped Israel his servant, remembering his mercy, according to his promise to our fathers, to Abraham and to his descendants forever" (1:54-55).

Before these two hymns, Luke has craftily united his two unique birth announcements, which portrayed the role of John the Baptist and Jesus. When Mary greets Elizabeth, the infant in Elizabeth's womb "leaped for joy" (1:44; cf. 1:41). No doubt Luke has the movement of Esau and Jacob in Rebekah's womb (cf. Genesis 25:21-23) in mind, when writing this narrative. The movement of the child in the womb points toward the future role of the child.

Also, Elizabeth makes it clear which of the two infants is the greater. Rhetorically, she asks Mary, "How is it that the mother of my Lord should come to me?" (1:43) Even before he is born, Jesus is declared to be the Lord by the author of this Gospel. John, in Elizabeth's womb, also recognizes the Messiah.

Meditation: During the past week, in which ways have you recognized the Messiah?

Prayer: God our Savior, your mercy is from age to age to those who fear you. Once you looked upon the lowliness of Mary, your handmaid, and now all ages call her blessed. You have dispersed the arrogant of mind and heart and thrown down the rulers from their thrones. You lift up the lowly and fill the hungry with good things, while sending the rich away. Continue to do great things for us. Remember the mercy you promised to our ancestors in the faith, to Abraham and to Sarah, and to their descendants forever. May our souls always proclaim your greatness, for you are the one God, Father, Son, and Holy Spirit, who live and reign for ever and ever. Amen.